"A new American hero—William Denson—
riveting pages of *Justice at Dachau*. An Alaba
sent to Europe by the U.S. Army to prosecute ⟶ ⟶⟶chers feigning
innocence in the bloody aftermath of the Second World War. Brilliantly
written and fastidiously researched, Joshua M. Greene's narrative builds
chapter by chapter in dramatic Hollywood-like fashion. Each war
criminal Denson convicts brings a cheer to the heart. This is historical
storytelling at its finest."

—DOUGLAS BRINKLEY, FORMER DIRECTOR OF
THE EISENHOWER CENTER FOR AMERICAN
STUDIES AT THE UNIVERSITY OF NEW ORLEANS
AND COEDITOR OF *WITNESS TO AMERICA*, WITH
STEPHEN AMBROSE

"*Justice at Dachau* is a mesmerizing account of one of history's most
infamous periods. Joshua Greene takes the reader back in time by
weaving together a riveting narrative of the trial and its central figure,
Judge Advocate William Denson, a true hero and humanitarian. This
book is destined to be a classic among Holocaust histories."

—PATRICK O'DONNELL, AUTHOR OF *BEYOND VALOR*
AND *INTO THE RISING SUN*

"[This book] has immense value. First, it provides a permanent testimony
of the horror of the Hitler regime and the courage of its adversaries.
More important, it resolves a long-standing misimpression concerning
the efforts of those in the post-Holocaust period who strived to establish
a democratic foundation for human rights. *Justice at Dachau* is an
irreplaceable document."

—ARTHUR HAULOT, FOUNDER OF THE
UNDERGROUND PRISONER COMMITTEE INSIDE
CAMP DACHAU

"A remarkable account of one determined prosecutor's quest to reveal and punish the atrocities committed by German officials at the Nazi concentration accounts."

—DREXEL A. SPRECHER, FORMER NUREMBERG PROSECUTOR AND AUTHOR OF *INSIDE THE NUREMBERG TRIAL: A PROSECUTOR'S COMPREHENSIVE ACCOUNT*

"An exciting account of the course of the Dachau trial proceedings. It is not the least thanks to William Denson's sense of justice, tied to deep empathy with the victims of the accused, that the Dachau trials have become a historical lesson in dealing with crimes against humanity."

—BARBARA DISTEL, FORMER DIRECTOR OF THE DACHAU CONCENTRATION CAMP MEMORIAL SITE

Justice at Dachau

The Trials of an American Prosecutor

Justice at Dachau

JOSHUA M. GREENE

ANKERWYCKE

Cover design by Elmarie Jara/ABA Design.
Interior design by Betsy Kulak/ABA Design.

Printed in the United States of America.

20 19 18 17   5 4 3

ISBN 978-1-63425-665-0

Discounts are available for books ordered in bulk. Special consideration is given to state bars, CLE programs, and other bar-related organizations. Inquire at Book Publishing, ABA Publishing, American Bar Association, 321 N. Clark Street, Chicago, Illinois 60654-7598.

www.ShopABA.org

TO HUSCHI

God loveth a cheerful giver.

—II Corinthians 9:7

Bill Denson's death deprived the world of one of this century's great champions of human rights and human dignity. His truly remarkable career inspires awe to this day, particularly among those of us who carry on the work he began.

—*Eli Rosenbaum, Director*
Criminal Division, Office of Special Investigations
United States Department of Justice
1998

Men who take up arms against one another in public war do not cease on this account to be moral beings, responsible to one another and to God.

—*Francis Lieber*
German-American political philosopher
Columbia University
1863

Contents

Foreword

From the moment that Lieutenant Colonel William D."Bill" Denson learned that he would be prosecuting hundreds of guards, officers, and doctors who had committed horrific war crimes while working in Nazi concentration camps, Denson knew that he had both an extraordinarily important mission and an equally unenviable responsibility.

His mission was critically important because those who had *personally* tortured and murdered millions of Jews, Gypsies, and other innocent men, women, and children in the Buchenwald, Dachau, Flossenburg, Mauthausen, and other camps deserved severe punishment for their misdeeds. The victims of Nazi atrocities, whether living or dead, deserved justice—and the living certainly cried out for it. Finally, what Bill Denson was tasked to do was important because these war crimes trials were most likely to become milestones in the development of international law.

But Denson's work as the lead war crimes prosecutor at Dachau (where the trials were held from November 1945 to August 1948) also was an unenviable responsibility. That was because, while the International Military Tribunal in Nuremberg ultimately would hold the high-level military and civilian Nazi policymakers accountable for crimes against humanity and the waging of aggressive war, these Nuremberg defendants were not the "trigger-pullers"—those individuals who had actually fired the weapons or operated the gas chambers that killed millions in the Holocaust. No one in history had previously prosecuted war crimes of such magnitude, much less crimes sanctioned as official government policy.

All this meant that Bill Denson had no guideposts to follow as he began selecting his assistant prosecutors and putting together a strategy for trying these Nazi war criminals. While it was perhaps fairly straightforward for Bill Denson to decide whom he should prosecute, the more difficult issue was determining *what* crimes could be prosecuted. To clarify, the chief challenge for Denson was that linking individual concentration camp personnel with specific victims was problematic. There was no question that camp personnel had brutally mistreated and then killed literally millions of innocent human beings, but evidence that a specific guard had murdered a particular person simply did not exist, if for no other reason than the vast majority of victims had been incinerated. In a true stroke of genius, Denson decided that he would charge the defendants with "acting pursuant to a common design to commit . . . cruelties and mistreatments, including killings, beatings, starvation, abuses, and indignities." This "common design" theory was quite different from conspiracy, in that the latter requires an agreement to commit a crime and a shared intent. "Common design," on the other hand, would require only that the various defendants shared a conscious intent to violate the laws and usages of war. Using this common design theory, Lieutenant Colonel Denson prosecuted more Nazi war criminals than any other lawyer in the years following World War II: 177 guards and camp personnel. All were convicted, with ninety-seven sentenced to death and fifty-four to confinement for life.

While Bill Denson's success at trial was remarkable—and assures his place in military legal history—what makes his prosecutions at Dachau especially important is that Denson never lost sight of the importance of due process in the trial proceedings. He understood that, regardless of their guilt or the horrific nature of their misconduct, those men and women being prosecuted for war crimes must receive full and fair trials. Denson pushed back hard against those who argued that those who had carried out the Holocaust had forfeited any "right" to a trial but instead deserved only a speedy execution. Why should these Nazi killers, insisted more than a few leaders in positions of great responsibility, have a trial when their victims had not? As for due process, perhaps something was required, but the trials (and punishments) had to be swift. In fact, Denson's lawyer bosses envisaged that the Dachau war crimes trials would take no more than two months. They were greatly displeased when Denson's insistence on due process meant that the rough justice that envisaged by some resulted in nearly two years of criminal proceedings. But the greatness of Bill Denson is that he recognized that "Justice" (with a capital "J") would only be achieved at Dachau if the defendants enjoyed the due process of law in the criminal proceedings against them. As readers of *Justice at Dachau* will learn, Denson's adherence to the highest ethical and moral principles not only damaged his professional career but his personal life as well. In the end, however, Lieutenant Colonel Denson's unwavering adherence to the rule of law made these war crimes trials an unqualified success and, perhaps more important, signaled to all those Germans observing them that the rule of law and due process in all legal proceedings must be part of the re-establishment of social order in any new Germany.

I am no Bill Denson. I certainly do not have his educational pedigree (West Point '34 and Harvard Law '37) or his trial lawyer skills (Denson had tried some 300 civil cases prior to his war crimes work). But Lieutenant Colonel Denson and I do have something in common, and I can appreciate the challenges that he faced at Dachau. This is because, in early 2003, I was selected to be the first Chief Prosecutor for the military commissions created by President George W. Bush in November 2001—military courts established for the specific purpose of prosecuting al Qaeda terrorists who had planned and carried out the September 11, 2001, attacks on our nation. While separated by more than fifty years, my challenges as the Chief Prosecutor were strikingly similar to those faced by Bill Denson.

The 9/11 attacks on the World Trade Center and Pentagon were horrific crimes deserving of swift and sure punishment, and President Bush established military commissions to prosecute the offenders. But no American lawyer had tried war crimes at a military commission since Bill Denson's era—and those who had such experiences were dead and gone—which meant that my assistant prosecutors and I were very much without guideposts in deciding *how* we would prosecute al Qaeda terrorists, much less what war crimes *could* be prosecuted.

From the beginning, for example, it was not at all clear that we had an international armed conflict—a war—as a matter of law. This was an important point since, at least as traditional international lawyers saw it, one cannot prosecute an individual for committing a war crime unless a war exists—and there can only be a war between two or more nation-states. By such logic, it followed that since al Qaeda was a non-state actor, there could be no war.

Besides wrestling with this fundamental legal question, it was not at all clear what war crimes could be charged against those al Qaeda members then in custody at Guantanamo Bay, Cuba. After all, the actual perpetrators of 9/11 were dead; there would be no trials of "trigger-pullers." Those detained in Cuba arguably were part of a larger criminal agreement—a conspiracy—to attack American civilians in the United States and elsewhere, but it was not at all clear that conspiracy was a war crime. At the time, there was no court decision on whether an armed conflict between the United States and al Qaeda existed as a matter of international law and whether conspiracy was a war crime that could be prosecuted at the military commission framework created by President Bush.

But these two issues aside, my chief concern as Chief Prosecutor was that the defendants enjoy sufficient due process at every step of the criminal proceedings against them. Like Bill Denson, I believed that regardless of the guilt of the defendants, results in any trials would not be accepted unless the process was seen as full and fair. I believed this to be true not only because the individual defendants at any military tribunal deserved to receive a fair trial, but because the results of any trial proceedings would not be accepted as legitimate unless there was due process as a matter of law. As I once put it in a conversation with Deputy Defense Secretary Paul Wolfowitz, convictions were important but not something we should be too worried about, if for no other reason than I would be selecting cases that had convincing proof of guilt. Rather, the most important trial would be in the court of public opinion. Bill Denson certainly recognized this as well, and he worked tirelessly to avoid criticism that his trials were nothing more than "victor's justice," as did I. But both of us soon discovered that the due process that could or should be afforded a defendant in a military tribunal is not so easy to discern, especially when some individuals in positions in authority made it apparent that they were more interested in results than anything else.

Bill Denson's decision to use "common design" as the prosecution theory was brilliant and accounts for his successes at trial. Yet he was the model of the principled, ethical prosecutor, and no serious student of the Dachau war crimes trials legitimately questions the integrity of the process upon which Denson and his team of prosecutors insisted.

My twelve months as Chief Prosecutor were decidedly less successful, and despite my insistence that the military commissions would afford every defendant sufficient due process under the law, others did not see it that way. In 2006, some two years after my departure as Chief Prosecutor, the U.S. Supreme Court agreed and, in *Hamdan v. Rumsfeld*, declared that President Bush's military tribunal framework was unlawful since it violated both the Uniform Code of Military Justice and the Geneva Conventions of 1949.

Looking back, I can say that my experience as the Chief Prosecutor—like Lieutenant Colonel Denson's—was professionally challenging and a unique opportunity to be involved in high-profile war crimes prosecutions. I'm certain that, if Denson were here, he would see things the same way. He was proud of what he did as a prosecutor, and all those who read *Justice at Dachau* will see that he was a remarkable attorney and a model for all to emulate. The American Bar Association is to be congratulated for publishing this new edition of author Joshua M. Greene's wonderful book, which brings Bill Denson to life and shares his remarkable story with a new audience.

—Fred L. Borch III
Colonel, U.S. Army (Retired)
Chief Prosecutor, Office of Military Commissions
U.S. Department of Defense (2003–2004)

Preface

The boxes in William Denson's basement were covered with dust. A few had tipped over during a flood some years back, spilling their contents onto the gray concrete floor. Those that had escaped damage sat on sagging wooden shelves. Huschi, Denson's widow, waited a year after his death before she could bring herself to visit her late husband's basement den.

In those boxes were documents dating back half a century. Some were intact. Others crumbled as Huschi removed them. It took weeks of sorting for her to realize the scope of what she had discovered: thousands of pages of trial transcripts, miles of microfilm, stacks of photographs and newspaper clippings, death's-head insignias, bulging packets of letters from SS officers and victims of Nazi horror, handwritten notes and summations—in all, more than thirty thousand pages and artifacts from one of the most significant yet least known series of war crimes trials in history.

The folders and hand-bound scrapbooks tell the story of the Dachau trials, in which Hitler's henchmen from Dachau, Mauthausen, Flossenburg, and Buchenwald concentration camps were brought to justice. The trials, led by Denson, age thirty-two, exposed concentration camp administrators for what they were: murderers, torturers, and traffickers in human skin. More important, the trials affirmed that civilization is built on universal standards of human behavior—standards that hold a place apart from and above any nation's legal or military agenda.

By the end of the Dachau trials in August 1948, William Denson had prosecuted more Nazis than any other lawyer in the entire postwar period: 177 guards and officers. All were found guilty. Ninety-seven were sentenced to death, fifty-four to life imprisonment, and the rest to terms of hard labor. The proceedings also nearly ended the life and career of chief prosecutor William Denson.

We lived more or less in the same neighborhood—his office was only ten minutes from my home—but I never had the pleasure of knowing this remarkable man. In interviews videotaped by the Shoah Foundation, the Washington Holocaust Memorial Museum, and other organizations, Denson comes across the way family and friends describe him: keenly intelligent, mannerly, amicable. He stood almost six feet tall, lean, boyish features never quite disappearing in old age. When he spoke his drawl flowed smooth and slow, like the streams he fished as a boy in Alabama. What makes his story so striking is the contrast between the humanity of the man and the inhumanity of the world he took on. The U.S. Army sent Denson to Germany to prosecute abominations so cruel and vast that no law had ever been created to cover them. No vocabulary existed to describe what Nazi officers and men awaiting trial at Dachau had done to their victims. Denson was a country lawyer assigned to prosecute war crimes that the courts of civilized nations had never before confronted.

For twenty-one months, Denson labored in the shadow of headline-making trials taking place sixty-five miles to the north in Nuremberg, where the International Military Tribunal was prosecuting a handful of top Nazi officials. The venue for that trial was the majestic Palace of Justice, with two hundred members of the international press in attendance. Denson's work, meanwhile, unfolded in almost complete obscurity in a small courtroom cobbled together from workshop tables and folding chairs. Yet something more important than notoriety or grandeur separated the Dachau trials from the Nuremberg trials. At Nuremberg the accused were Nazi policymakers: chieftains who drafted and supported Hitler's battle plans as well as his "Final Solution," the systematic annihilation of European Jewry. Hitler's chieftains, however, never lifted a gun. It was at Dachau, sixty-five miles south, on the grounds of the former concentration camp, that men stood trial for personally aiding, abetting, and performing torture and murder compelled not by government policies but by their own disregard for human life.

Denson's assignment was to demonstrate that the accused at Dachau were personally responsible for atrocities committed against other human beings. He had to disprove arguments by Buchenwald commandant Hermann Pister that executions of Russian prisoners of war were carried out under legally justifiable "superior orders." He had to counter excuses by Dr. Klaus Carl Schilling that lethal experiments in Mauthausen to find a cure for malaria were conducted "in the interests of humanity." He had to reveal Ilse Koch for what she was: not the obedient wife of a camp commandant, but a sexual sadist who collected human skins and had prisoners killed for daring to look at her. The U.S. Army put Denson in the middle of these horrors and told him to win convictions—and to do it quickly.

The young lawyer, away from America for the first time, confronted formidable obstacles. Of great concern was the accusation that any convictions he might win would amount to nothing more than "victor's justice." The term denoted executions handed down by courts that were guided more by vengeance than due process, and it hovered darkly over the Dachau trials, threatening to destroy not only the validity of guilty verdicts but the credibility of those who, like himself, sought to defend the integrity and effectiveness of international law. In war, the accusation implied, victors will always be in the right, the defeated always culpable of crimes for which they must pay. Many who understood the depth of the Holocaust tragedy felt that executing Hitler's henchmen without trial was a perfectly legitimate punishment. Why dignify Nazi killers by providing them with trials? The murder of six million Jews and millions of other victims merited a swifter, more effective kind of response. To insist on proving in a courtroom what had so obviously been done was not to serve justice but to make a mockery of it. Allowing Nazis to stand trial, these voices argued, also meant risking that many might go free.

Denson disagreed and went to great lengths preparing his cases according to recognized rules of law, winning as many enemies as admirers. Trials meant to end quickly dragged on as he and his team of investigators interrogated hundreds of potential defendants and witnesses. What the Judge Advocate's Office hoped would take two months took nearly two years. The work was further complicated by defense accusations that many of the accused had been coerced into signing their confessions—a charge that plagued the trials from start to finish and led to an investigation that only partially exonerated the American interrogators.

Denson's dedication to his task took a personal as well as professional toll. His first wife, a New York socialite who had never adjusted to the life of a stay-at-home bride, left him halfway through the trials. His health deteriorated as constant exposure to descriptions of Nazi atrocities robbed him of his appetite and wore away at his body. By the end of his third trial he had lost nearly fifty pounds, his hands trembled, and he suffered a collapse. After less than two weeks' recovery time, Denson rallied enough strength to lead a fourth and final trial: guards and officers from Buchenwald concentration camp.

Denson achieved 100 percent convictions, but the glory and success that might have been his reward never came. With the rise of the Cold War, U.S. priorities shifted from punishing Germans to winning Germany's support in the fight against the Soviet Union, and one by one the sentences of Nazis found guilty at Dachau were either commuted or completely reversed. Among those who received this clemency was Ilse Koch, a beautiful, sadistic woman known as the "Bitch of Buchenwald." The clandestine reduction of her sentence to a mere four years was discovered by the press and publicly condemned as a scandalous betrayal of justice.

At first Denson vehemently fought the commutation and spoke openly of his objection to how army review boards had assessed his work. When even a Senate subcommittee supporting his cause failed to get the decision reversed, he stopped, put it all behind him, and did not speak again of Dachau for nearly half a century.

Genocide, however, did not stop, and Denson's silence over the Dachau trials preyed on his conscience. Reluctantly at first, with encouragement from friends and with a growing sense of purpose, he began speaking of his experiences. Over the next fifty years, he resurrected documents from attics and archives around the country—an exercise that led to the basement cache that Huschi Denson showed me a year after her husband's death.

Denson died in 1998 at the age of eighty-six. His last wish was that the story of the Dachau trials be told, not for his own aggrandizement but to educate future generations that no one is genetically exempt from inhuman behavior, and that the sacrifice for avoiding such tragedy again is a vigilant defense of human rights.

PART ONE

War's End

He that is slow to anger
Is better than the mighty;
And he that ruleth his spirit
Better than he that taketh a city.

—Proverbs 16:32

1

The Liberation of Dachau

By mid-March 1945, in the final days of World War II, the U.S. Army's 42nd Infantry Division, known as Rainbow, had suffered heavy losses. In a recent offensive the Germans had cut down nearly half of Rainbow's men, then retreated back into the wooded Harz Mountains. Undeterred, Rainbow followed, and in the town of Dahn their chaplain held Passover services, the first public Jewish ceremony in Germany in recent memory. On April 1, Easter Sunday, they crossed the Rhine. As they passed through towns and villages severely damaged by bombing raids, Rainbow's arrival provoked mixed reactions from local residents, some of whom remained indifferent and sullen while others declared their unqualified love for Americans. All, however, denied any connection with the Nazis. "That Hitler must have been quite a guy," a Rainbow corporal said. "All by himself he governed the country, commanded an army—and without a soul to help him!" Rainbow pushed on toward Munich in pursuit of what was left of Germany's armed forces.

———

Alvin "Doc" Weinstein, a sergeant with Rainbow, was formerly an intern at Queens General Hospital in New York City. Back in 1943 one of his patients began ranting and raving in German. When the episode passed, Doc asked the man about his condition. The patient explained that in 1933 he had openly opposed the Nazis, which had landed him in a place called Dachau. Five years later he and two others bribed the camp commandant and managed to escape. The horrors he described left Doc skeptical.

On April 28, 1945, Rainbow came upon a sign: 5 KM NACH DACHAU, and Doc told his superior, Maj. Gen. Harry J. Collins, what he had heard about the camp. Collins sent a reconnaissance party under Assistant Division Commander Brig. Gen. Henning Linden to investigate.

Two weeks earlier, anticipating the arrival of U.S. troops, Heinrich Himmler, head of Hitler's SS security forces, had sent a telegram to Dachau commandant Wilhelm Weiter: "Surrender of the camp to the enemy is unthinkable. The whole camp is to be immediately evacuated. No prisoner is to fall alive into the hands of the enemy." Himmler confirmed the order with a second telegram instructing that, if necessary, Weiter was authorized to massacre the entire camp population with gas bombs. Wary of Allied retribution, Weiter ignored the order, assembled the camp administrators in his office, and announced that Dachau would be handed over intact to the Americans with the Red Cross acting as delivery agent. The announcement sent SS officers scurrying to the clothing depot, where they exchanged their uniforms for civilian and prisoner clothes. During the night of April 28, hundreds of officers in disguise melted into the surrounding countryside. By the time General Linden and his task force arrived at the gates to Dachau, only 130 armed men remained inside the camp.

Linden and his men pulled up. The gates opened, and Dr. Victor Maurer of the Swiss Red Cross emerged with an SS officer. Maurer had tied a white cloth to a broomstick, which he waved in front of him as they approached. Linden's jeeps surrounded the men. Maurer announced that the Germans had agreed to turn over the camp, and Linden's men entered Dachau. Their first impression was smell, "a combination of burning garbage and singed chicken feathers," as one soldier described it. Then they heard voices from wooden barracks two hundred yards away.

"Are you Americans?" the voices cried out in a dozen languages.

The soldiers nodded, and there followed an eerie wailing that grew to a roar, and out from the barracks staggered the remnants of Dachau's victims, the healthier running in front, others limping, crawling behind. They mobbed the Americans, grabbing at their hands and feet, desperate to touch their liberators. A few of the stronger prisoners grabbed whichever American was closest and tossed him into the air, screaming at the top of their lungs. To disperse the frenzied crowds, Rainbow GIs fired over their heads.

Meanwhile, outside the gates, Lt. Col. Donald E. Downard had come upon something that made him doubt his eyes. A line of open boxcars stood silently on railroad tracks leading to the camp, overflowing with corpses. Downard counted thirty-nine cars, maybe two thousand bodies. Many showed signs of cannibalism and other horrors that challenged his sanity.

"Hey, colonel," shouted Lt. Tony Cardinale, "here's a live one!"

Downard ran back. Sticking up from under a mass of dead bodies, a hand waved feebly. Downard and Capt. Roy Welbourne climbed into the car and pulled out a man six feet tall, weighing less than one hundred pounds. His eyes peered out at them from holes sunk deep in his emaciated cheeks, and his jawbone seemed to cut through his skin.

"*Frei . . . ? Frei . . . ?*" he asked, bewildered.

"We are American soldiers," Welbourne said. "You are *frei*."

Downard lifted the man in his arms, carried him to his jeep, and his driver started off toward an aid station. Gunfire erupted. Downard's driver lost control of the jeep and Downard was thrown to the ground. When he awoke, he found himself lying on a litter in the aid station with contusions and a concussion. To his left was the six-foot man, wounded but alive.

While prisoners and GIs began hunting for anyone in SS uniform, a prisoner committee escorted their liberators on a tour of Dachau. They showed the Americans a crematorium lined with meat hooks from which SS hanged their victims. Skeletal corpses filled a room next to a brick furnace. One wall displayed a bizarre portrait of a headless man in SS uniform riding a huge inflated pig and digging his spurs into the animal's haunches. A bewildering inscription beneath the image read: "Wash your hands, cleanliness is your duty." The concrete floor was slanted, blood still draining from the pile of bodies. Retreating SS had booby-trapped the entire building. As they moved from room to room the American soldiers defused wires that would have set off the charges.

They moved on to a ditch holding two thousand bodies, hastily collected by guards too busy with their own escape to burn them. The Americans were shown barracks overflowing with corpses and with half-dead victims unable to rise from their bunks. In a nearby woods the committee of prisoners showed their liberators a two-room torture chamber with twelve hundred contorted bodies piled up, and execution grounds where prisoners had knelt to be shot in the back of the neck. The Rainbow soldiers met women inmates of the Dachau system who told of being repeatedly raped by SS guards. Stories of torture, humiliation, starvation, and death came pouring forth.

Rainbow's arrival from the east was followed by arrival from the northwest of the 45th Infantry Division, known as Thunderbird. Lt. Col. Felix Sparks, the division's twenty-seven-year-old commander, had been given orders to detour from his push toward Munich and to proceed instead to a place called Dachau. No further explanation was given. Thunderbird, named for a Native American god of war and terror, boasted one real Native American, 1st Lt. Jack Bushyhead, known back home in Tulsa, Oklahoma, as Chief Glorious Eagle. In 1943 the division had taken part in the invasion of Sicily, then moved on to secure beachheads at Salerno and Anzio. Italian children danced with glee when Bushyhead confided to them that the entire division was made up of real Indians.

"Where are your feathers?" the wide-eyed children asked.

Now, two years and countless battles later, Thunderbird arrived in the village of Dachau and found railroad tracks heading in the general direction of the camp. Sparks turned to 1st Lt. William P. Walsh. "I want you to take the company and go up these tracks. Don't let anybody out." Walsh and his men headed up the tracks and encountered the same thirty-nine boxcars Rainbow had discovered. Seeing so many skeletal corpses, some of the Thunderbird soldiers screamed, others cursed. The rest were stunned into silence.

"Now I know what we're fighting for," said Bushyhead. "We can't live in the same world with them. They're nothing but animals. They must be destroyed."

The men entered the camp. Four Germans approached with their hands on their heads. Walsh, weeping in anger, pushed them into one of the boxcars, opened fire with his pistol, then returned to the camp to grab more Germans. Others in Thunderbird, caught up in the wave of raw emotion, grabbed any Germans wearing SS insignia and lined them up against a brick wall outside a coal yard. Walsh ordered his men to shoot them if they moved. A young private, following orders, set up a machine gun. The SS prisoners, aware of their captors' intentions, began moving toward the Americans. "Let them have it!" someone shouted. Someone else yelled, "Fire!" Salvos erupted from Browning automatic rifles. The machine gun strafed left to right, right to left.

Sparks, who had gone deeper into the camp, heard the shots, raced back to the brick wall, and fired his pistol into the air, signaling furiously for the men to stop shooting. He rushed over to the machine gun, grabbed the young private by his collar, and dragged him away from the gun. "They were trying to get away!" the private cried. Germans lay crumpled at the base of the wall.

By the gates a jeep driver watched a dozen inmates staggering out. Cloth patches on their uniforms revealed that they were Polish. "Where are you going?" he asked in Polish.

"We are walking home," one said.

"Where's home?"

"Warsaw."

"Stay here," the driver urged. "You'll be taken care of."

"No, no. We walk home to Warsaw."

A few steps later they collapsed to the ground.

The Americans moved through the camp and arrived at a neatly kept one-story building, a porcelain factory. Tables and shelves displayed dainty figurines, busts of Hitler, miniature soldiers holding Nazi flags, medieval knights, drummer boys, peasants in regional German costumes, horses, bears, eighteenth-century courtiers wearing silk stockings and playing flutes. The soldiers moved on, lost in their own disbelief.

Outside, camp inmates begged the Americans for guns and knives with which to shoot and decapitate the Germans. The Americans obliged. A young Rainbow corporal stood agape, watching an inmate stomp an SS trooper's face until he ceased to move.

"You have a lot of hate," the young soldier said. The prisoner looked at him and nodded. "I don't blame you," the soldier said and moved on.

Inside bunkers and offices the Americans discovered large framed photographs of SS chief Himmler. One such photo dominated a kitchen in the SS mess hall where a storm trooper sat eating alone at a table.

"What are you?" a Rainbow soldier asked.

"SS."

"How could you do these things?" someone whispered.

The SS man shrugs. "These human swine . . ." He was holding a spoonful of beans when they shot him.

Twenty-one-year-old Cpl. Harold Collum, 392nd Field Artillery, was driving a four-man team to Dachau. He slowed their jeep to a halt as skeletal prisoners who had wandered out of camp approached with outstretched hands. Dumbfounded, Collum handed them Red Cross doughnuts left over from breakfast. The sticklike forms sunk to their knees in thanks. The team departed. Farther on they came across a woman inmate staggering down the road, on the verge of collapse. She wore a veil. They stopped, lifted her veil, and shrank away from the battered remnants of a face.

Inside the camp an American chaplain with a silver cross on his helmet climbed atop his jeep. "We must thank the Lord," he said to the growing crowd of prisoners, then continued on in Latin. Everyone was silent. Some knelt, some wept, some made the sign of the cross. Another soldier climbed up next to the chaplain. "Last night Mussolini lynched!" he said in broken German. "Munich taken! You are all free! I salute you in the name of the United Nations!" Each phrase was interrupted by wild acclaim.

Nobody slept that night. The camp was alive with bonfires. Former prisoners sang, cooked over makeshift fires, while on all sides hundreds more continued to expire, having lived through the unbelievable just long enough to be free.

2

A Call for Trials

The unbelievable had revealed itself earlier that month to soldiers of the 4th Armored Division in a small subcamp of Buchenwald called Ohrdruf. The young Americans found thousands of skeletal corpses strewn across the parade ground, stacks of bodies burned by lye, and pyres of human flesh smoldering in open pits. The GIs, most of them away from home for the first time, wept openly, not understanding what they were confronting. They had already killed and seen buddies shot and thought for certain that the worst was behind them. And now: bodies turned inside out with intentional accuracy, limbs at impossibly odd angles, headless cadavers, and a stench so odious it muddled the brain. Someone managed to pick up a radiophone and urgently request that a senior officer come to explain what it was they had found. Generals Dwight D. Eisenhower, Omar N. Bradley, and George S. Patton arrived later that day.

"The smell of death overwhelmed us even before we passed through the stockade," Bradley wrote in his diary. Patton fell ill, then got up on his jeep and started screaming, "See what these sons of bitches did? See what these bastards did? I don't want you to take a prisoner!" Eisenhower raged, then telephoned Winston Churchill to describe what he had seen. One week later, units of the 4th and 6th Armored Divisions discovered Buchenwald. Then the British entered Bergen-Belsen, and before the month was out Allied troops liberated Landsberg, Flossenburg, Mauthausen, and dozens of subcamps. Eventually liberation forces discovered nearly fifteen hundred concentration and labor camps throughout Nazi-occupied territory. As reports of the numbers of people interned in these camps climbed, army headquarters staff would occasionally look at one another in disbelief. The total was rising above six million.

Rumors of death camps had been in circulation for some time among army units in Europe, but no stretch of the imagination had come anywhere near the extent of suffering and death they discovered when the camps were liberated. Eisenhower sent a telegraph to the War Department in Washington: reporters and government officials were to come immediately to Germany, inspect the camps, and report their findings to the world.

They came by the dozens: senators, governors, journalists, joined by heads of state from England and across Europe. Prior to these visits there had been a good deal of skepticism about concentration camps. In the May 19, 1945, issue of *The Nation*, critic James Agee dismissed footage shot by producer George Stevens in Dachau as misleading and warned of exaggerating the crimes in the camps and of the danger in allowing vengeance to take precedence over justice. That same month, Milton Mayer, writing in *The Progressive*, went further, declaring that "vengeance will not raise the tortured dead" and that the evidence found in the camps "would not under ordinary American judicial practice be held sufficient for conviction in a capital crime."

A committee of journalists under the leadership of Joseph Pulitzer arrived to make up their own minds. Pulitzer, son of the man who established the Pulitzer Prize, had also harbored doubts about the accuracy of the reports. After one day in Ohrdruf he wrote to *The New York Times* that the reports "have been understatements."

———

War crimes trials had been in discussion since 1942, when President Franklin D. Roosevelt announced "that just and sure punishment shall be meted out to the ringleaders responsible for the organized murder of thousands of innocent persons and the commission of atrocities." FDR's announcement sent a clear warning to the Germans: there would be no repeat of the failed trials that had taken place at the end of the First World War. In 1921, three years after war's end, the Allied powers had turned over to the German Supreme Court a list of 896 persons charged with specific crimes against the Geneva Convention and other laws of land warfare. The Allies assumed that defeat had transformed Germany into a law-abiding nation capable of conducting fair trials and meting out appropriate sentences. Instead, the German court brought only forty-five men to trial and acquitted all but nine. The nine were given minimal sentences, ranging from six months to four years. Not one served his full term.

Wanting no repeat of that fiasco, on October 30, 1943, the Allies signed the Moscow Declaration, a stern confirmation that they would hold the Nazis responsible for their war crimes and bring them to justice. Just how these trials should be conducted was not clearly addressed, and the U.S. spent most of 1944 debating whether to punish Germans or ensure their nation's economic and political revival, and creating what historian Bradley F. Smith called "The Great German War on the Potomac."

Finally, on August 8, 1945, the Allies signed the London Agreement and Charter, announcing that each of the four major powers, the United States, Great Britain, Russia, and France, would independently try those Germans captured in their respective zones of occupation. In addition, one court, to be called the International Military Tribunal, or IMT, would be created to jointly prosecute the top Nazi officials. Russia, France, and Britain quickly launched their war crimes programs. The United States announced that it would establish its court sixty-five miles south of Nuremberg, on the site of the former concentration camp at Dachau. Congress, anxious to show the depth of its outrage over the concentration camps, allocated several million dollars in funding for the war crimes program, which was under the direction of the Judge Advocate Generals Department of the U.S. Army.

Judge Advocates had served as attorneys and legal advisers to the army since 1775, when Col. William Tudor, a twenty-five-year-old Harvard graduate, was appointed first Judge Advocate by the Second Continental Congress. In 1862, Congress authorized creation of a corps of Judge Advocate Generals, commonly called JAGs, to serve the army's legal needs. During the Civil War, thirty-three JAGs were appointed, and their responsibilities gradually increased to include service on courts of inquiry and courts-martial. During World War I, the JAG Department—known today as the JAG Corps—expanded to 426 officers. In World War II the JAG Corps mounted war crimes trials in Germany and Japan, trying a total of 1,672 individuals for violations of the laws of war in 189 proceedings from 1945–49.

JAG Headquarters for the war crimes program was under the command of Col. Lucien Truscott, who reported directly to General Patton. Truscott's immediate staff included Col. Clio "Mickey" E. Straight, chief of the JAG's War Crimes Branch, and Gen. Lucius D. Clay, whom President Roosevelt had appointed deputy governor in Germany. Clay would later be credited as the person who contributed most to creating a stable, democratic postwar Germany. He supervised the denazification program, directed the Berlin Airlift, instituted currency reform, and helped establish constitutional law and self-government. His duties also included reviewing verdicts and sentences in war crimes trials. With such a crowded agenda, Clay provided a perfunctory signature to most matters relating to the trials, relying heavily on recommendations by the JAG War Crimes chief. Mickey Straight was, for all intents and purposes, the decision-maker with regard to trial review.

And like the entire JAG legal staff, Straight was in over his head. The crimes of the Nazis were too extreme to have ever been described in law books, and prosecuting them would challenge even seasoned legal experts. A dedicated soldier, Straight was nonetheless a reserve officer who had had no prior experience with war crimes. He was adrift in vast legal waters for which charts had never been drawn, pulled by unpredictable currents toward the single largest legal action in recorded history.

In that uncertain environment, with no maps, no precedent, no idea what charges to bring or how to properly conduct the trials, JAG HQ urgently needed a chief prosecutor for the Dachau trials—someone who could win convictions quickly, effectively, and by the book.

3

An Appointment in Court

William Denson could fix almost anything. The small pocketknife he carried on his key chain was all he needed to repair a lawnmower, tighten a door hinge, or fashion a fishing rod. He started driving at age twelve, changing his own tires, replacing faulty connections, and generally demonstrating that the best tool for solving problems was a sharp mind. By the time he graduated Harvard Law School and began teaching law at West Point, Denson had evolved from solving simple problems with a pocketknife to solving complex problems with the laws of civilized nations. "He had more legal thoughts per minute than anybody I'd ever met," said Marion H. Smoak, one of seven men who taught law with Denson at West Point in the early forties. "Bill was a role model, a little older and much more experienced legally. He was also an awfully good guy to work for—smiled a lot, always laughing, always saying something funny."

Denson believed that the laws of man mirrored the laws of God, and that conviction had inspired unshakable dedication to his craft. Prior to

West Point he had successfully tried three hundred civil cases, more than most lawyers did in their entire career. Men in Denson's family had all known that love of the law. His great-grandfather had been a colonel in the Confederate Army. His maternal grandfather had been an Alabama Supreme Court judge. His father was a respected Birmingham lawyer and politician. For Denson, whose childhood buddies in Alabama included black children, all men stood as equals before God and the courts. There was no compromising this point. William Denson at age thirty-two felt deep pride in the Constitution, and putting that pride to work in service to others was a passion he fully enjoyed.

It was a passion, however, that his first wife, Robina, did not share. Born into an influential New York family and educated in Paris, Robina Denson tolerated her husband's legal and religious zeal as the price she had to pay for marriage to an Alabama blue blood with good prospects. Their relationship reached a turning point in January 1945, when Denson learned that Edward O'Connell, a West Point buddy stationed in Europe, had recommended him to Judge Advocate Col. Charles E. Cheever. Denson's job as law professor at West Point had its advantages, but becoming a judge advocate general—called JAG—could be his payoff for years of legal practice, a prestigious appointment that might even lead to a judgeship like other men in his family.

Robina was devastated. She had seen Movietone news reports: Germany was in shambles. Spending months in such poverty and despair might be fine for a lawyer pursuing his own glorious destiny, but not for a vivacious young woman like herself. The confrontation forced Denson to take stock of their life together. There was little to keep him there: no children, few common interests, a fundamental incompatibility that surfaced only now, when a vital task disrupted selfish plans for a life among the Alabama elite.

The following week he departed for Europe with the blessings of his superiors at West Point. "Best wishes for a pleasant and victorious tour in your new assignment," wrote his superior, Col. Charles W. West, achieving with words such as "pleasant" and "victorious" an irony that he could not possibly have anticipated.

———

Denson was stationed in Freising when he learned of Dachau's liberation from the army newspaper *Stars and Stripes*. Liberation forces were occupying hundreds of camps in their sweep across Germany, and the article differed little from others he had read that week. While the description of Dachau was particularly grim, Denson agreed with his fellow JAGs that the astonishing numbers of dead and nightmarish reports had to be, overall, exaggerated. And whatever truth they did contain was at that moment of little practical consequence to him. Denson's job was to comment on points of order and other routine matters in trials against Germans who had killed American pilots shot down in action. "Flier murders," as they were known, constituted a large part of the JAG court calendar. No judges or juries took part in these military trials, only a seven-man tribunal and a law member, usually a senior ranking officer with a substantial background in military law. Denson had already served as a law member in more than ninety cases since his arrival in January, earning him a promotion to lieutenant colonel and the unqualified respect of superior officers at JAG HQ.

———

Membership in the privileged world of JAGs and degrees from West Point and Harvard Law School may have set Denson apart from the rest of the legal staff in Freising, but he was still considered one of the guys, joining in occasional baseball games, bus trips to the lake at Bad Wiessee, and late-night poker sessions. The Freising community accepted and respected him. He was one of the team, wiser perhaps, but never aloof and always willing to help younger officers in their assignments. And if outrage over Nazi crimes led some young American interrogators to excess, they protected Denson from knowing about it and never faulted him for holding to a different scale of justice.

Debate raged in Freising the week Dachau was liberated: was it necessary to try Nazi camp officials? Those opposed, mostly younger members of the interrogation team who followed the logic of General Patton and Treasury Secretary Henry Morgenthau, argued that trials were superfluous. The Nazis were clearly guilty of crimes for which death could be the only penalty. Those in favor of trials, mostly older-generation JAG staff, cited arguments by General Eisenhower and Secretary of War Henry Stimson: "victor's justice" contradicted the democratic principles for which the

Allies had fought so hard. Denson and his fellow JAGs held the position that trials would do more than just punish Nazis. They would also create a record of what the Nazis did, which could act as a deterrent to future Hitlers. Killing them without due process, on the other hand, would create Nazi martyrs and give revisionists a chance to claim that the charges were all fabricated.

The notion that a courtroom could also serve as a classroom figured prominently in Denson's thoughts. Germans, from his perspective, were not so different from everyone else; and a critical function of the trials would be to send a message out to the world: be vigilant. Even the most decent human being, subjected to the right pressures, is capable of doing things he could never imagine himself doing. Denson's position sprang from childhood experience. In the Jim Crow South of the twenties, anti-Semitism was as palpable as discrimination against Negroes. It formed invisible walls in restaurants and clubs, permeated public discourse, and nestled innocently between the lines of popular classroom literature. Money-crazed Isaac of York in Sir Walter Scott's *Ivanhoe*; thieving Fagin in Dickens's *Oliver Twist*; cruel, murderous Shylock in Shakespeare's *Merchant of Venice*—typical depictions of Jews that reflected typical attitudes cemented in place over centuries. That he had not succumbed to such biases he credited to a humanism dating back generations in the Denson family: his grandfather, a Supreme Court justice of Alabama, had defended Negroes at a time when to do so was tantamount to sedition.

———

The Nuremberg court was accorded every imaginable resource. Money and manpower poured in from the Allied nations to restore the Palace of Justice and install padded seats for press and spectators. IBM audio technology that permitted simultaneous translation in five languages was flown in from the League of Nations headquarters in Geneva. Sophisticated camera equipment would record the entire proceedings. Meanwhile at Dachau, no funds were allocated for audio equipment: translations would be one-by-one, time-consuming, and laborious. There was only enough money to hire American court reporters: trial transcripts would be kept in only one language, English. No cameras were purchased: if any of the Dachau trials were to be filmed, it would happen because a press office somewhere sent its own crew.

The position of chief prosecutor at Nuremberg was awarded to Robert Jackson, friend of the late FDR, former special counsel to the Treasury, and for two years attorney general before his appointment to the U.S. Supreme Court. Jackson was a celebrity chosen by President Harry Truman to serve as guiding spirit and practical planner for the conference. His orders were to evaluate the evidence and formulate the charges against "the leaders of the European Axis powers and their principal agents and accessories." The press was lavish in its praise of Jackson's appointment, but Denson read with concern the four charges Jackson announced:

1. A common plan or conspiracy to seize power and establish a totalitarian regime to prepare and wage a war of aggression.
2. Waging a war of aggression.
3. Violation of the rules of war.
4. Crimes against humanity, persecution, and extermination.

The first charge, Denson surmised, would not apply to any but the top leaders of the Nazi Party. The second made little sense to him. What war is not waged aggressively? The third charge made better sense. "Violations of the laws and customs of war" was a recognized offense. The fourth charge, however, "crimes against humanity," had dubious precedent before the Nuremberg trials, and it struck him as unjust to invent a charge after the fact—*ex post facto.*

Notwithstanding his concerns about the charges, prosecuting Nazis was the kind of righteous duty Denson appreciated, the kind of work you dreamed of if you were born into a military family and your father and his father and his father before him had all fought for family and country. As a result, when a messenger from JAG HQ knocked on his office door and announced that Colonel Straight wanted to see him, Denson might have sensed providence at work, a confirmation of something already in motion rather than an unexpected honor. "Amazing grace!" was his usual response at such moments.

Dachau trials stenographer Barbara Ann Murphy remembered Straight as a sober-faced, driven soul whose task was to act as the army's talent-

spotter for the war crimes program, one of the no-nonsense professionals who were supposed to introduce a breath of Washington realism into
postwar Europe. History has not recorded what was said when Straight
told Denson that he had been appointed chief prosecutor at Dachau. But
articles from August 1945 describe an American public outraged by reports
of the camps, a Congress anxious for results, and an army with nothing
to show—no trials and no convictions despite millions of dollars in funding. One can imagine the handshake coming with orders that Denson
get started quickly and make sure the press was informed that trials were
imminent.

————

Denson drove to JAG rear headquarters in Munich—known affection-
ately as "Lucky Rear"—where the Dachau trials were being prepared. He
arrived at the Munich inn that would be his new home, unpacked quickly,
and set out in his jeep for Dachau. Munich had been heavily bombed in
the final weeks of war, and roads were strewn with rubble from toppled
buildings. He drove out of the ruined city and into fields and hills in the
bloom of summer. Six miles west he crossed a stone bridge, traversed a long
road flanked by poplars and a row of look-alike houses, and drove through
the gates of the camp.

The bodies were gone, but everything else was as it had been at liberation. The crematorium chimney rose from its brick foundations near
the *Schiesstand*, or execution wall. The ground beneath the wall was still
stained rust red and the smell of blood was still strong. He walked around
the periphery of mass graves, beneath the limbs of hanging trees, across
the roll call yard. A large area inside the camp was enclosed with barbed
wire. Inside the holding cage were barracks. German prisoners moved in
and out of the buildings. Some of them watched him as he made his way
around the camp.

He entered the Records Room, a twenty-by-thirty-foot office. Wooden
shelves and metal cabinets lined the walls. He took folders from a shelf
and read reports of men, women, and children crowded together like cat-
tle, suffocating in sealed boxcars. He read of typhus epidemics that went
unchecked, killing more than three thousand inmates per month. He read
statements by liberation soldiers who had discovered emaciated prisoners

lying on bunks saturated with blood and excrement. He read interviews with victims who spoke of medical tortures, beatings, grossly inadequate food, scant clothing in subzero winters, nonexistent sanitation, and numbers of people killed—numbers so large they made him dizzy.

Denson exited the Records Room, lit a Lucky Strike, and wondered what in heaven's name he had walked into. Years later he confessed to simply not believing what the evidence told him. Lynchings and torture had always been exceptions to human behavior, not the rule; and Germany was the home of classical music and philosophy, not the barbarism these reports described. He did not believe because his religious training rejected the notion of absolute evil, yet biblical descriptions of the Apocalypse did not come close to the nightmares of Nazi camps. He did not believe because Harvard Law School had taught him to distrust circumstantial evidence, illogical reports, and anything his innate intelligence found suspicious. Like most Americans, he had read a few articles and knew prisoners had been killed in the camps. But mass murder on this scale was unfathomable.

Denson did not believe because believing would mean that the world was not the neat and tidy place he had always thought it to be. A man is born, be it in Birmingham, Alabama, or Warsaw, Poland. He grows up, studies hard, works sincerely, serves God, leads a good life, and is entitled to expect that such sacrifice and decent behavior will bear fruit. But from these reports, leading a virtuous life had proved useless against Nazi terror. Even worse, virtue proved to be a deficit in the camps. Gestures of kindness were rewarded with floggings and death. Goodness and mercy were luxuries from a privileged world: they had no place in Dachau. When Germany's first concentration camp opened its gates, a crack had appeared in the structure of things, and now the army was saying he was responsible for sealing the fissure. He did not believe because believing would mean giving up the provincial, mannerly approach to law that had been his style until now and turning ruthless in pursuit of convictions. Bill Denson had never been a ruthless man.

To overcome his disbelief, he spent the next several days speaking with JAG senior officers. Army personnel who had preceded him to Dachau, who had studied the evidence, told him it was all true. Surviving victims of the camp, people from different countries, speaking different languages, corroborated what other victims had seen. One such story concerned a place called the arrest bunker. In the arrest bunker were standing cells: wooden boxes too small for a prisoner to sit, stand, or lie down. A prisoner forced to half-crouch in a standing cell received no food or water and no chance to change his position for three to seven days. At the end of that time, SS took him out. If the prisoner was still alive, he was given a pitcher of water. Racked by thirst and half-mad from days in an impossible physical position, the prisoner would guzzle water, causing his emaciated stomach to protrude. The SS would throw him to the ground and stomp on him, rupturing his stomach walls and causing a slow, agonizing death.

These former victims had had no opportunity to fabricate such stories among themselves, and Denson's skeptcism began to crumble. Spending time with witnesses to what would soon be called the Holocaust, Denson realized the extent of his naïveté. Like so many Americans, he had believed that camps were the brainchild of Hitler and a handful of uneducated madmen. Those first days in Dachau revealed a more sinister picture. The "handful" had included thousands of camp administrators supported by the complicity of countless Europeans. While many camp administrators had indeed been uneducated, many others held college degrees. The torture, beatings, starvation, and exterminations had been orchestrated by one of Europe's most enlightened people. "I finally reached a point," he recalled in later years, "where I was ready to believe most anything."

The more Denson accepted the reality of what had happened in the camps, the more prosecuting camp administrators assumed the status of a mission: to bring to justice everyone who had been involved irrespective of title or authority. Whatever his job may have been, no one working inside a concentration camp could have avoided knowing what was taking place. And because they knew and chose to remain, the thirty-five hundred Germans now in the Dachau holding cage had supported a diabolical, inhuman enterprise for which they must pay with their lives. The evidence to convict was irrefutable, and for Denson the moral imperative was clear.

Within days he had warmed to the task, and his consumption of Lucky Strikes was up to a pack a day. Nuremberg may have had the celebrity Nazis, but here at Dachau were the brutes who held the whips, the "doctors" who had injected benzine into the hearts of their victims. Here were the guards who had shot thousands of helpless prisoners "while trying to escape," the camp administrators who were only "following orders" and consequently did nothing to stop the tortures and abuse. If he could prove that these individuals were personally responsible for war crimes, then the Dachau trials would be a defining moment in the development of international law.

The trials would also be defining for him personally. The army had entrusted him with a historic assignment based on his reputation for efficiency and professionalism. But until now he had operated on familiar ground: flier murder prosecutions were fairly routine from a legal perspective. Back home the cases he had pursued in his father's firm were small-time affairs—a railroad injury, a stolen car—that afforded ample opportunity to exercise the virtues of old-time religion: clemency, mercy, forgiveness. Before Dachau he had dealt with familiar transgressions of civilized human behavior. This was an uncivilized world he was about to enter, a world outside the scope of normal behavior. Maybe the army needed someone with thicker skin. Furthermore, what would stand trial at Dachau was not just Nazis whose guilt was obvious, but the ability of a victorious government to provide a defeated enemy with due process of law. That would take massive preparation and an ability to withstand strong opposition, possibly from within his own ranks. Did he have that kind of fire in his belly?

Denson felt outrage at what he had discovered in Dachau. He also felt profound concern, for what had been done would happen again unless legal convictions created a deterrent for future Hitlers. But was he the man to do that? He had prosecuted only one murderer in his entire career, and the experience had so shaken him he vowed never to do so again. What was he getting himself into?

––––––––

Preparing for trial would require sifting through hundreds of thousands of documents and interviewing thousands of potential witnesses and defendants. He needed an assistant he could trust, someone who worked quickly and effectively. Phone connections were one of the few services one could depend on in postwar Germany, and the call to Freising went through instantly. Denson left word that Paul Guth was to join him at the inn as soon as possible.

———

Across the hall from Denson's old office in Freising, twenty-two-year-old Paul Guth rang a small brass bell on his wooden desk in the Investigation Section of the War Crimes Group, and armed MPs brought in the mayor of a town in northern Germany. Guth began his interrogation with polite questions about the mayor's family and education. He gradually built to more sober inquiries about an American pilot who had parachuted out of his burning plane and landed near the mayor's village. Any ideas, Guth asked, who might have killed him after he hit ground? Maybe the mayor knew townspeople who should be questioned, a few names in exchange for some consideration in his own case when the time came for trials. Cooperation was tempting for Germans summoned to Freising: most flier murder trials resulted in hangings.

Guth was surprisingly young for the job of interrogator. Thick, dark hair and a strong jaw compensated for a boyish face. The slightly formal way in which he addressed others, in intellectually crafted sentences, left hearers uncertain whether he was speaking to them or the universe. This cultured demeanor had been nurtured by parents who owned a success-ful linoleum factory in Vienna and sent him to school in England. After finishing, Guth settled in the U.S. and, at age nineteen, received army intelligence training at Camp Ritchie in Pennsylvania, graduating first in a class that included European officers twice his age. From Ritchie he was assigned to the 21st Army Group Intelligence Center in Devizes, England, an hour south of Bath.

Guth's mentor in Devizes had been a police officer in Austria before Hitler's rise to power. "Forget everything they taught you at Camp Ritchie," Count Atmansdorf instructed his young countryman. "If you want to get confessions from Germans, imitate a Prussian officer. Behave like Herr *Doktor* Guth and watch what happens. There will be no need to shout." Guth followed the count's advice, displayed the self-confidence of a professional, and secured more confessions than any other interrogator in Freising.

Denson placed his call to Guth early in the morning. Munich was only fifteen kilometers away. Guth jumped into his beat-up army jeep and arrived in time for breakfast. They met in the downstairs dining room, shook hands, and ordered the one meal on the menu: eggs, thick country bread with margarine and jam, sausages, wedges of cheese, an apple, and lots of coffee. During the war, coffee was scarce and expensive. Most of Europe drank hot water filtered through cloth packed with burnt grains. Along with the Americans at liberation came the real stuff in tins and burlap sacks, providing hotel guests with a modicum of peacetime comfort. Looking around him, Denson could not have helped wondering how much these people had known. The camp was in their backyard. Had anyone raised a voice in protest?

"Paul, I'd like you to join me at Dachau."

Guth listened, then admitted that his real ambition was to finish his studies at Columbia Law School. "But that's not about to happen," he said. "I lack the points." Army personnel earned their discharge by racking up points: so many per month, so many per special duty. At one hundred they could go home. Denson made Guth an offer. If he agreed to join the prosecution team at Dachau, he would receive a commission—lieutenant's bars—and extra points toward his discharge. Then Denson added a stipulation.

"Third Army wants the trial to start quickly, no later than Thanksgiving, and end before Christmas. They want headlines in time for the holidays. We have four weeks—and that's it. Are you in?"

Guth extended his hand. They finished breakfast and pushed back the bentwood chairs. Denson retrieved his notebooks from beneath the table and the two men walked out into a bright, brisk morning that had emerged from behind the mountains.

4

Preparing for Trial

On the approach to Dachau from Munich, a stone road spanned the sinister peat bog known as the Dachauer Moor. When Himmler announced in 1933 that an old munitions factory on the far side of the moor, unused since the last war, would be converted into a camp, the city of Dachau expressed its appreciation with offers to help in the construction. The city's finances were in a pitiful state, and the prospect of a camp with its need for municipal services and goods infused the citizenry with a self-interested spirit of cooperation. Their model in constructing a road across the swamp was Mussolini's successful reclamation of the Pontine Marches between Rome and Naples. Whether or not the citizens of Dachau knew what kind of camp this would be, they agreed to make one modification to Mussolini's model. Instead of calling for volunteers, they used slaves supplied by Himmler, mostly political prisoners, who laid the foundation with stones, gravel, and sand dragged for miles in wheelbarrows sunk axle-deep in mud. In 1945, Allied troops renamed it Tennessee Road, and at the time of the Dachau trials it meandered past tall pine trees and green buildings, formerly armament factories and now residences for trial witnesses convened from all corners of Europe. At the end of Tennessee

Road was the south entrance to camp, and just inside, a right fork leading to the courthouse. Over the courthouse's main door a large wooden
sign read DACHAU DETACHMENT WAR CRIMES GROUP, then, in smaller
letters, JUDGE ADVOCATE DIVISION, UNITED STATES FORCES EUROPEAN
THEATER.

The JAGs had two reasons for choosing Dachau, the Nazis' first concentration camp, as the place to conduct war crimes trials. First, the Moscow Declaration signed by Roosevelt, Churchill, and Stalin in 1943 had
pledged that those who had committed the atrocities would be "brought
back to the scene of their crimes" to be judged. Second, Dachau contained
spacious buildings with operable plumbing and heating. The U-shaped
courthouse was a two-hundred-meter-long main building with east and
west wings extending seventy meters. During the years of camp operation,
the long middle corridor had housed a boiler room, kitchen, and laundry.
The east wing had been storage for belongings taken from prisoners on
their arrival. The west wing had been a factory for clothing and shoes.
American army personnel removed machinery and workbenches to make
room for three courtrooms: "A" for the bigger trials, in particular the "parent" concentration camp trials; "B" and "C" for smaller cases, such as
flier murders and "subsequent trials": those of lesser functionaries in the
concentration camps.

Denson worked with a four-man team. Apart from Paul Guth, there
were Capt. Phillip Heller and Dalwin J. Niles, both from New York; Capt.
William D. Lines of Florida; and Capt. Richard G. McCuskey, a tall,
thin Ohioan who had recently succeeded his father as general counsel to
the Hoover vacuum cleaner company. All were competent lawyers. None
had had the least experience with war crimes. Their day started at 7 A.M.
with breakfast served up American-style in the officers' mess, fifty men
and women eating together at any given moment. Then Denson's group
assembled in his office to review their strategy for the day. McCuskey and
Denson did most of the rehearsing, with Guth and the others serving as
audience to provide feedback.

"You'll never be allowed to elicit that," one would say. "That's going to
be ruled hearsay." Another might comment, "First tell the court you will
lay the predicate for that with the next witness," or "The witness will never
tell you the answer to that question."

Each day Denson and the prosecution team analyzed the information they had gathered on crimes committed in Dachau, the officers responsible, and the whereabouts of surviving victims. Often they met in the Records Room, which resembled a large office library. Industrial-grade metal shelving lined three walls of the room. Recently compiled confessions, testimonies, and reports filled filing cabinets across the fourth wall. A wide wooden table occupied the center space.

A dozen young staff members were responsible for organizing the mountains of material. Exhibits earmarked for trial were labeled with the name of the assistant who had found them. "Lanner 1" listed the number of priests in Dachau from 1940 to 1945. "Slawski 1" listed Russian officers shot on a particular day in 1944. The documents included purchase orders for drums of deadly chemicals, worksheets describing daily assignments for slave laborers, punishment forms stamped "Approved" in Berlin, and correspondence between camp administrators and SS headquarters. The quantity of documents was staggering. From the German Foreign Office alone, U.S. officials had confiscated nearly five hundred tons of paper. Exhibits piled up as Denson's team developed their strategies. Coffee and cigarettes were their constant companions. The younger staff would take stacks of evidence back to their desks and label the exhibits before storing them in large envelopes. Packages for transfer to other posts were inspected by Leo Goodman, a New York lawyer whose duties included assigning translators and stenographers to each day's proceedings. Goodman initialed the envelope, verifying that everything was in order. Days were long. Guth had a girlfriend, but they could never make plans before Sunday.

Denson's staff examined a death book retrieved after the liberation of Dachau. Tiny, obsessive script filled columns labeled Prisoner Number, Date, and Cause of Death. The explanation for this miniature handwriting had to do, like all actions in the camp, with survival. Prisoner scribes knew the entries they were told to make were grossly inaccurate. They also knew that, as potential witnesses to such deceptions, they would be shot as soon as their book was filled. Scribes who wrote smaller lived longer.

Denson penciled his notes on lined sheets in three-ring binders. As evidence mounted, so did the number of binders until they formed a Maginot Line of blue cloth-covered notebooks across his desk.

The prosecution team did not work alone. In the early forties the U.S. Army had begun recruiting people from around the United States to help with interrogation of German prisoners of war. After two weeks' training, recruits were sent to prisoner of war camps across the country. Places such as Brady, Texas; Lansdowne, Pennsylvania; Camp Carson, Colorado; Houlton, Maine; Camp Gruber, Oklahoma; Camp Wheeler, Georgia; Dexter, New Mexico—all hosted interrogation centers. In Europe, three hundred more U.S. intelligence staff conducted interviews and gathered evidence for the war crimes trials. Stacks of documents from these many centers filled the Dachau Records Room, neatly typed and numbered, some on plain sheets of paper, others on preprinted government forms stamped variously "Confidential," "Secret," "Recorded and Indexed," or "Classification Canceled."

A report from Camp Butler, North Carolina, described 1st Lt. Burton Spear's interrogation of Karl Hirschmann. The former Dachau guard had been captured by the Americans in southern France in late 1944. Spear quoted Hirschmann as saying, "In Dachau, it was SS officer Jarolin's special pleasure to extort confessions by hanging people on a pole and whipping them with a cat-of-nine-tails. It was Commandant Weiss who created a bordello of women prisoners. The women were promised that if they submitted for intercourse they would gain their freedom. In this way Weiss got for himself considerable financial gain." That document had particular relevance: both Jarolin and Weiss were under arrest in the Dachau holding cage. Denson's team became familiar with these reports, selecting those that referenced arrestees in custody or that substantiated crimes reported by surviving victims of the camp. Like Denson, the other prosecution lawyers became gradually acclimated to the degree of horror that had taken place. Convincing the tribunal that incredible abominations had indeed occurred would be a large part of their assignment.

————

In July 1945, the War Department had issued a gray manual listing Germans to be considered "mandatory arrestees": army officers, members of the Nazi Party, government officials, concentration camp personnel—all those who might eventually stand trial for the crimes of Nazi Germany. Within three months, planes and trucks had disgorged more than 30,000 arrestees into the holding cage. At one point the number of arrestees grew so great, the army placed a DC-3 at Denson's disposal to help bring them to Dachau from "displaced persons" camps across Europe. After an initial triage, 3,500 remained, those fitting the general description of war criminals. The prosecution's job was to identify, from among these, individuals who would stand trial in the Dachau parent case. Men who had played main roles in the camp, such as Commandant Martin Weiss, were obvious candidates, as was Dr. Klaus Carl Schilling, about whom most former inmates had something horrible to say. Try these department heads, JAG HQ instructed Denson, and the army will assign other lawyers to prosecute the rest later on.

One week before start of trial, Denson accompanied Guth on an excursion through yet one more DP camp, looking for witnesses. At that time, in November 1945, nearly a million refugees, many of them former concentration camp prisoners, filled hundreds of such DP camps in the British, American, and French zones. In these camps—some housing as many as seven thousand residents—doctors, lawyers, scientists, students, bricklayers, homemakers, thieves, gymnasts, artists, poets, and other former "enemies of the Reich" crowded together. Many refused to go home: some, such as the Poles, were fearful of the Soviet presence in their homeland. Others simply did not wish to return to places devastated by nearly six years of war.

Guth implemented the same system in this DP camp as he had in dozens of others. His translator and reporter set up their portable table and typewriter. Guth instructed the camp supervisor to escort residents in one by one, and he began his questions, looking for details that would tie suspects to the crimes of the camps.

An older man approached Denson and introduced himself. "I am Ruppert Kohl," he said. "I am a former prisoner in Mauthausen. I am from Vienna and wish to offer my services as a translator." Kohl's tattered sweater and trousers were worn to near transparent thinness, but his antique leather shoes gleamed like polished stones. His bright eyes and pointed ears and chin gave him a pixielike quality. Denson shook his hand, and Kohl burst into a smile, revealing a picket fence of gold teeth.

"Mr. Kohl," Denson marveled, "prisoners died for one-tenth as much gold as you have on display there. How in heaven's name did you survive?"

"Colonel," Kohl replied with a chuckle, "never once I smiled during all those years. And when I ate," he said mashing his lips, "my mouth, always closed."

Denson extended a hand and welcomed him to the team.

———

Guth made good on a promise to instruct his fellow prosecution teammates in the art of interrogation. He was quartered in the house of a former senior SS officer on the outskirts of camp, and one morning at seven o'clock he rose from bed, sprinted to breakfast at the officers' dining room, then jogged two minutes to Denson's office in the courthouse. Ernst Leiss greeted him at the door with black coffee as he had every morning since the first day of Guth's appointment. As a former district judge in the Munich public prosecutor's office, Leiss had met the description of an automatic arrestee and found serving as Guth's assistant a desirable alternative to standing trial. Lines, McCuskey, and Heller arrived and took seats. Guth began by reviewing sample questionnaires from hundreds filled out by German arrestees in the Dachau holding cage. The questionnaire had been his idea, an effective way of conserving precious time during interrogations and a useful indicator of which arrestees were most likely to stand trial. The form included questions about their background, education, location of assignments, and duties in the camp. Guth gambled that the Nazis would prefer to reveal something of what they had done rather than defend themselves against snitchers. The gamble paid off: the questionnaire induced many concentration camp personnel to confess crimes for which no evidence, other than their own voluntary admission, existed.

"The process of interrogation," Guth said, "starts by looking for a lead. If a prisoner writes in the questionnaire that he was a *Blockältester,* or block leader in the camp, you might casually mention that some other prisoner has already admitted seeing him kill a prisoner or turn someone over for 'processing.' Most block leaders killed somebody, so your intimation about eyewitnesses should provoke a degree of cooperation. 'Actually,' he will say, 'I was like a father to my prisoners. It was Sergeant so-and-so who was the beast.' Then, of course, you summon Sergeant so-and-so who will predictably deny everything. 'Not me,' he will say. 'It was *the other* so-and-so. Ask that one over there. He'll tell you it wasn't me. He saw it happen.' Now you have another lead.

"Another item you should remember," Guth added. "Give the prisoner the impression you are trying to help him, that he has your sympathy. Take the most officious-looking NCO in the group, tell him to stand at attention, then to stand at ease. Tell him how you have heard about his great organizational skills and other abilities, and tell him that you plan to put him in charge of the whole interview process, and that he won't have to do anything except sign papers. The prospect of clemency is a powerful inducement. Watch what happens."

Guth followed his own advice. Having already interrogated several high-ranking Germans in Freising, upon arriving in Dachau he studied the list of internees. He identified those whom he had known previously, then walked over to the holding cage and greeted them like old friends.

"How good to see you, *Mein Herr*," he effused. "You know, I hope I can rely on you again for your help."

Some of the Germans felt comfortable with Guth: he spoke their language, had done minor favors for them in Freising, such as getting letters to their families. Others were more circumspect, watched him warily, avoided him when possible.

————

Music poured out from offices across the Dachau camp. Most radios were tuned to DJ Sally's *Luncheon from Munchen,* which featured American jazz and pop tunes. Denson preferred classical, but from twelve to one, when sharing working lunches with his staff, he went along with the Andrews Sisters or Frank Sinatra or whatever the group wanted. Weeks ran seven working days long, yet however hard he pushed them his staff obliged because he set a good example. They responded enthusiastically to his escalating requests for more reports, more evidence, because he was as industrious as they and generous with instruction and with appreciation, letting them know that their work was "outstanding," "first-rate." Like most 3rd Army recruits, Denson's aides were young idealists who had not seen action. They entered the war after it was over, nurtured on reports of heroism and glory, with no prior warning about what they would find at Dachau. During the day they traded jokes, news from home, gossip, and favors. But at night, when the easy banter of busy offices was over, their surroundings haunted them. The air carried a stench that Barbara Ann Murphy called "the Dachau aroma," and it troubled their sleep. Rain intensified the smell, and at such moments the recent horrors of the camp were palpable. Denson's encouragement and friendly arm around the shoulder went a long way toward keeping their spirits high. He saw them as younger siblings, and they saw him as a gallant mentor, a soldier as praiseworthy as any veteran of battle. "He was our hero," Murphy recalled. They discussed his techniques, repeated his comments, admired his Southern manners. Colonel Denson was a gentleman JAG, defending the democracy for which so many had died.

Denson, too, suffered from nightmares. He was not inured to the haunting; he merely jumped clear of it with greater dexterity.

———

JAG HQ maintained pressure to begin quickly. The Brits had already conducted their own trials—twenty-eight guards and officers from the Bergen-Belsen concentration camp—and a competition was heating up to see who could convict arrestees faster. "You're sitting on maybe ten thousand murderers," Mickey Straight chided. "Pick out thirty or so and get started with the parent case. One more week should be sufficient." Some JAG higher-ups were proving to be tedious bureaucrats who made demands from a safe distance, and Denson found them irksome. Had there been more time and less preoccupation with rushing to press with stories of victory against Nazis in the courtroom, his team could have identified hundreds more to stand trial. Nazi Germany had yielded more than a million arrestees. Most were "denazified," made to pay a fine, and sent home. From a million, 30,000 were interned at Dachau. Most of these were dismissed for lack of evidence. From the remaining 3,500, time permitted the prosecution team to identify forty who would stand trial for the crimes at Dachau and its subcamps—forty, to be held accountable for the torture, starvation, dehumanization, and murder of tens of thousands.

By the end of October, less than two months after being told to prepare one of the largest legal initiatives in history, the prosecution's pretrial work was done. Denson submitted his paperwork to JAG HQ. In addition to the names of 40 accused, the documents listed 170 witnesses and almost

2,000 trial exhibits. It took JAG HQ only two days to approve the lengthy outline.

On November 2, 1945, Paul Guth walked into the Dachau holding cage under armed guard. The Germans lined up inside the barbed-wire enclosure—Hitler's executioners interned in the same barracks that once housed their victims—and Guth read out forty names and told them they were going to trial. Of the forty named, nine had been camp commandants or deputy commandants, three *Rapportführers* (office clerks), four labor officers or their deputies, five medical officers, two medical orderlies, three administrative staff, four *Blockführers* (SS men accountable for prisoner barracks or "blocks"), one head of a political department, one adjutant, one officer of the guards, one officer in charge of supplies, three guards from prisoner transports, and three prisoner functionaries. All had held some position in the hierarchy that ran Dachau and its many subcamps. Half wore their Nazi uniforms and caps. The rest, those who had attempted to escape in disguise, wore civilian clothes. When Guth informed them they were going to trial, it came as a complete and stunning surprise. Given their own experience, the Germans had fully expected to be summarily executed. Some laughed, others stood with their mouths open not knowing what to say. Even more incredible were the rights Guth then described. If they wished, they could summon anyone of their choosing to defend them. If they did choose to bring in their own lawyers, Uncle Sam would pay the legal fees. None of the accused would be obliged to testify. If they did testify, they could refuse to take an oath. And perhaps most surprising of all, the prosecution would limit itself, voluntarily, to a maximum of ten witnesses against any one accused.

The Germans could hardly believe their ears.

PART TWO

Dachau

———

Therefore, all things whatsoever
Ye would that men should do to you,
Do ye even so to them:
For this is the law and the prophets.

—Matthew 7:12

5

Common Design

The Nuremberg trial would not start for another week—there had been problems restoring the expensive parquet floor—and reporters, top brass, and military elite came south in the interim to attend the Dachau opening. Admission to the three-hundred-seat room was by ticket only; more than four hundred spectators crowded into the courtroom on November 13, 1945.

In the front rows sat every recognizable army officer known to Denson since his arrival in Germany, including Gen. Walter Bedell Smith, chief of staff to General Eisenhower, and Lt. Col. Lucien B. Truscott Jr., 3rd Army commanding general. Denson's buddy from West Point, Lt. Col. Edward O'Connell, sat next to Sen. Claude Pepper, who had come over from his home state of Florida to attend. Packed behind the army seniors, cameramen adjusted lenses, checked film packs, and signaled to aides to refocus lights or tape a wayward cable to the wooden floor. Behind the press sat officers and observers from across Europe, friends and relatives of the accused, and former concentration camp prisoners. A standing-room-only crowd of civilians from the Munich area filled the back of the courtroom. Conversations spooled out in a dozen languages.

Spectators faced a stadium-sized American flag that dominated the far wall of the two-hundred-foot-long room. On a raised platform beneath the Stars and Stripes, a fifteen-foot-long table with eight chairs awaited arrival of the American tribunal. In front of the long table sat court reporters, half of whom used small typing machines. The rest wrote in shorthand using the Gregg or Pittman system. The reporters' job was to keep pace with the proceedings and hand in a finished transcript by the following day.

To the right of the spectators sat the defense team. The five men responsible for defending the accused had also been appointed by Mickey Straight and his 3rd Army JAG staff. Like Paul Guth, the defense attorneys lacked enough points to return home and had little say in the matter. In the chair nearest the tribunal sat chief defense counsel Lt. Col. Douglas T. Bates, whose background bore an uncanny resemblance to Denson's. Born and raised in Centerville, Tennessee, Bates too was carrying on his family's legal and military tradition. Like Denson, he wore his flag as proudly as his faith. Both men were tall, articulate, and uncompromising in their work. Bates was in combat from June 1944 until VE Day in May 1945, when he was assigned as an investigator for war crimes. Reputed to be a fine lawyer and a decent man who never said a nasty word about anyone, Bates regularly defied an order prohibiting Allied soldiers from saluting captured enemy officers. Serving with him for the defense was defense counsel Maj. Maurice J. McKeown of Maplewood, New Jersey, who impressed Paul Guth as the one who most resembled lawyers in movies, passionate and prepared to defend his clients "like Joan of Arc." Capt. John A. May of Houston, Texas, and Capt. Dalwin J. Niles of Schenectady, New York, were the other American lawyers on the team. A German lawyer named Hans Karl von Posern was the final member at the defense table. Guth had interrogated him as a possible defendant—"a borderline case," he reported. Von Posern had joined the Nazi Party in the 1930s. His public critique of certain party policies had landed him in Dachau. The Nazis on trial appointed him co-counsel, giving him a second chance to prove his loyalty after failing so miserably the first time.

"Between us prosecutors the relation was very friendly," Guth recalled, "but not particularly so with the defense team. We were on opposite sides, and there were completely strict lines of separation between the prosecution and the defense. We were busy—there wasn't much time to fraternize."

At ten o'clock sharp the room fell silent, and armed guards escorted the accused to their seats. Forty men ranging in age from eighteen to seventy-four took their places behind the defense table. The six rows of chairs sloped up, stadium style. It was a warm fall day and noise from the crowd gathered outside poured in through open windows. Guth hurried out and ordered guards to keep people quiet.

A young American MP wearing white gloves and helmet announced the court, and everyone stood. Eight men entered, ribbons and medals glistening against their starched green uniforms. The tribunal, composed of senior field-grade officers with the rank of full colonel, included George E. Brunner, G. R. Scithers, Laird A. Richards, Wendell Blanchard, John R. Jeter, Lester J. Abele, Peter O. Ward, and president of the court, Brig. Gen. John M. Lentz, former commanding general of the 3rd Army's 87th Infantry Division. They sat and Lentz began the proceedings with formal statements for the record, identifying the time, place, and circumstances of the trial. Then he announced that because there were so many accused, numbered cards had been prepared to make identification easier. As he read their names, a guard passed out white cards suspended from loops of string, each numbered in thick black ink. Lentz indicated that the accused were to hang the cards from their necks. Footage of that moment, stored in the National Archives, shows the Germans bristling as they draped the cards from their necks, shaking their heads as though saying, "We are officers, not schoolchildren."

Lentz then read two charges. The first charge alleged that the Dachau accused, "acting in pursuance of a common design to commit the acts hereinafter alleged . . . did at or in the vicinity of Dachau and Landsberg, Germany, between about 1 January 1942 and about 29 April 1945, willfully, deliberately, and wrongfully encourage, aid, abet, and participate in the subjection of civilian nationals of nations then at war with the then German Reich to cruelties and mistreatment, including killings, beatings, tortures, starvation, abuses and indignities, the exact names and numbers of such persons being unknown but aggregating many thousands. . . ." The second charge was worded exactly the same, except that in place of civilians it specified "members of the armed forces."

Lentz turned to the defendants and asked each to stand as his name was called and respond to the question, "How do you plead?"

Defense counsel May rose. "If it please the court, at this time I wish to address a motion to quash the charges. The charges are vague and uncertain. 'Acting in pursuance of a common design' does not apprise the accused of any offense."

———

From the outset the Nazis' defense lawyers attempted to discredit the charges against their clients. Other conditions of the trial had been determined without much difficulty. For example, both sides agreed that only crimes committed after 1941, when America entered the war, would be prosecuted. Both sides also agreed that only crimes alleged against Allied nationals—such as American, French, British, or Belgian citizens—would be prosecuted, while crimes committed by the Germans against their own citizens would be left to German courts. There was agreement as well concerning the definition of war crimes, in particular those addressed in international conventions. The Geneva Convention of 1929 provided, among other things, that belligerents shall see that the dead "are honorably buried and that the graves are treated with respect and may always be found again." The Hague Convention of 1907 prohibited resorting to certain methods of waging war, including inhumane treatment of prisoners, employment of poison weapons, improper use of flags of truce, and similar matters. The defense attorneys raised no argument over charging the men on trial with alleged violation of these established laws. They insisted, however, that the prosecution specify exactly which laws their clients were alleged to have violated. Had defendant number seven murdered someone? If so, then the charges should make that clear. Had defendant number twenty beaten someone to death? If so, that too should be made clear, along with an alleged time and place of the crime. Saying they had taken part in a "common design," they argued, was "vague and uncertain."

Denson had come across the concept of common design in the writings of Lord Wright of Durley, lord chancellor of England and first chairman of the United Nations War Crimes Commission. Wright (who was present in the courtroom on opening day) had analyzed the charge of "conspiracy" to commit a crime and found it limited. Conspiracy required a conscious collaboration among individuals gathered for the purpose of committing an illegal act. Wright asked, what if individuals involved in a crime never met at the same time or place? What if the crime transpired over the course of years—was "of a continuing nature"—involving parties who consciously aided or took part in that crime but never knew one another? Their crime would not meet the definition of conspiracy, yet their guilt would be no less. Such conscious intent among disparate participants he described as a common design, and his conclusions had since been incorporated into several standard legal texts.

Common design appealed to Denson as an effective tool for establishing that camp personnel were guilty of violating the laws and usages of war. He rejected the Nuremberg charge of crimes against humanity, which applied only if the offense charged could be connected to a broad pattern of such crimes for reasons of political, ethnic, or religious persecution. The defendants at Dachau had not themselves created policy and could not be snared in the Nuremberg net. In common design, Denson discovered an alternative wide enough to catch everyone who had worked in a concentration camp while avoiding the restrictions attached to the charge of conspiracy.

———

"May it please the court," Denson said, responding to defense's objections, "we submit that the offense was one of a continuing nature. This design was in operation in January 1942 and also in April 1945. Participation by these individuals is sufficient to apprise them of what they are called on to defend."

"I don't know whether the prosecution intentionally passes over the most important feature of the motion," May said, "but stating that this was 'a continuing offense' does not explain what each man is charged with. Is Martin Weiss being charged with murder? Torture? Beating? Is Boettger? Eisele? It is necessary to know that before we can intelligently present a defense."

Court president John Lentz intervened. "The court rules that good cause has not been shown why the charges and particulars should be quashed. The motion is denied." Lentz then again asked each of the defendants to stand and respond to the question, "How do you plead?"

Martin Weiss, wearing a card that read "1," was former commandant of Dachau. He stood, snapped smartly to attention, spit out his name, age, and other particulars, then announced *"Nicht schuldig!"* in crisp German. One after another the other thirty-nine defendants rose and repeated *"Nicht schuldig!"* in a loud voice. AP reporter Don Doane was present at that moment and wrote, "Weiss stared antagonistically at the judges and held his head high. With few exceptions, the others imitated his demeanor." Members of the audience, many of whom were former prisoners in Dachau, laughed at the continual pleas of not guilty. Defense counsel Bates finally addressed the tribunal.

"May it please the court, it doesn't seem to occur to the audience that there are forty individuals on trial for their lives, and it isn't a light matter from their point of view."

"The audience will maintain complete and absolute silence," Lentz admonished. After the last defendant had spoken, Lentz turned to Denson.

"Does the prosecution desire to make an opening statement?"

Denson rose and addressed the tribunal. A former inmate of Dachau who was present at the time noted, "He speaks slowly with an agreeable voice and shows the free smile so characteristic for him."

"May it please the court, we expect the evidence to show that during the time alleged a scheme of extermination was in process here at Dachau. We expect the evidence to show that the victims of this planned extermination were civilians and prisoners of war, individuals unwilling to submit themselves to the yoke of Nazism. We expect to show that these people were subjected to experiments like guinea pigs, starved to death, and at the same time worked as hard as their physical bodies permitted; that the conditions under which these people were housed were such that disease and death were inevitable. Further, we expect to show that during the time that Germany overran Europe these people were subjected to utterly inhuman treatment, and that each one of these accused constituted a cog in this machine of extermination. Prosecution calls Lawrence Ball."

———

Medical Corps Col. Lawrence C. Ball had come to Dachau on May 1, 1945, two days after liberation, to bring an evacuation hospital to the camp.

"Will you tell the court what you found when you went over the camp?" Denson asked.

Douglas Bates stood at the defense table. "I object. The witness's observations were later than the scope of time described in the charges. Also, this line of testimony has no connection with any of the defendants."

"We expect to later connect up these conditions with the accused," Denson replied. "These men participated in a common design to commit these acts, and the testimony will bring this fact out."

"It is evident," Bates said, "that the prosecution intends to bring whatever it can lay its hands on into court and cover up with this allegation of common design." From the outset, Bates was signaling defense's intention to challenge Denson's main charge. "Liberation was April twenty-nine," he continued. "That's the date in the charge. May second is another date entirely. The prosecution introduces testimony of a questionable nature and tells the court that later he will tie it up. I say he should connect the accused with the testimony first and then introduce it."

"The motion is denied," Lentz ruled. "The question will be answered."

"First we saw a train of thirty-eight cars," Ball continued. "The cars had in them ten to twenty corpses, thinly clad. Many had their pants down as if they had had dysentery. They had used other corpses as pillows. Inside the camp, the crematorium had large piles of corpses piled about it. We also visited the hospital in the company of Dr. Blaha. He was a prisoner doctor from Czechoslovakia."

May moved quickly on cross-examination to discredit Ball's testimony. "Do you know whether that train of boxcars was coming into Dachau or going out of Dachau?"

"No, sir."

"Do you know the nationality of any of the bodies you found?"

"No, sir."

"So as far as you are concerned, they may have all been German?"

"That is possible."

"To go back to the bodies you found in the crematorium, can you tell the court what was the nationality of those bodies?"

"No, sir."

The American tribunal was limited to prosecuting crimes committed by Germans against citizens of nations then at war with Germany. Offenses committed against German citizens—German Jews and other

German "enemies of the Reich"—were technically outside the jurisdiction of the court.

"No further questions." The opening salvo had gone to the defense.

————

"Prosecution calls Dr. Franz Blaha."

Franz Blaha was a fifty-year-old surgeon who became head of a district hospital in Prague after the war. He arrived at Dachau in 1941, having survived two years of imprisonment in twenty-three different jails, several months of solitary confinement, and numerous interrogations by the Gestapo. In a 1946 article on medical abuses in the camps, he wrote, "Even the most vivid description is unable to present the whole terrible truth" of what he discovered at Dachau. On arrival he was marched to sick bay with other prisoners. Only one of the staff was a certified doctor. The others were laymen "who excelled in brutality and roughness and showed no human relation to their suffering comrades. X-ray examinations were done by a carpenter, operations by a waiter and engine-driver, examinations were performed by anybody who thought himself impressive looking in a white overall or rubber gloves. These people amputated and operated . . ."

Blaha caught pneumonia shortly after arrival, for which the "cure" was time in the "thermotherapeutic box," a metal oven kept at extremely high temperatures. After two days in the box Blaha's weight dropped to seventy pounds and he was transferred to the surgery ward as a "cretin," where he was scheduled for an experimental and lethal resection of the stomach. Instead of submitting himself to such a deadly procedure, he took the risk of admitting he was a surgeon, which landed him a job in the camp's chemical laboratory.

In summer 1942 he was told to report to the hospital, the first prisoner-doctor in camp history. He was never allowed to see a patient nor know his case history before meeting him on the operating table, but was simply given a diagnosis and told to operate. If the diagnosis was wrong, Blaha closed the incision. If correct, he addressed the problem as far as the primitive hospital facilities would allow. Many of his operations were a success, to the disgust of the SS staff. When confronted with an order to take part in useless operations on living patients without anesthetic, he refused. As punishment he was transferred to the death chamber as the lowest-ranking assistant and ordered to remove skin from the backs and chests of dead prisoners.

The largest experimental station at Dachau was under the management of Dr. Klaus Carl Schilling. Blaha performed the autopsies of Schilling's victims and saw the results of Schilling's research. "Schilling proved to be a very rough and inconsiderate experimentalist," Blaha wrote, "and an unscrupulous chief to his prisoner-assistants."

Blaha also served under Dr. Sigmund Rascher, a friend of SS chief Himmler, who had committed horrible perversions in the name of medical research. Rascher never stood trial: at the end of the war his friend Himmler ordered him killed.

Blaha's deep-set eyes and high forehead suggested intellect and sophistication. At the trial, however, his eyes were sad, his forehead creased. Testifying later at Nuremberg, he was described by one writer as "presenting a wretched physical appearance."

––––––––

"What was the invalid block, doctor?" Denson asked.

"People who were not capable of working were sent there, or the ones suffering from chronic diseases. Also healthy ones were sent there as a punishment."

"Why was it a punishment?"

"Because the invalid blocks received less food, and everyone there was in danger of being sent out in an invalid transport. In 1943 there were big transports prepared and sent to Auschwitz, Lublin, Linz—often two hundred people at a time."

"Do you know," Denson asked, "whether it was a matter of common knowledge that these people were destroyed?"

"Objection," Bates said, "for obvious reasons." Bates was pointing out the clearly speculative nature of Denson's question. "Common knowledge" was nothing more than a polite way of asking the witness to provide hearsay testimony. Lentz, however, allowed the question to stand.

"It is considered that this evidence contains matters of probative value. The objection is overruled."

Probative value would play a central role in the Dachau trials. Under normal Anglo-Saxon law, hearsay evidence was not usually admissible. Under rules established for the war crimes trials, however, such testimony was permitted if it seemed "relevant to a reasonable man." The concession was intended to compensate for the fact that most eyewitnesses had been killed.

"This was known all over camp," Blaha said. "We called invalid transports the Heaven Detail."

"Can you tell us what were the forms of punishment between 1942 and 1945?"

"The mildest was taking away special rations. Then hanging up—for example, on a tree—beating, standing bunker, then death penalty."

"You said hanging up on a tree. Will you describe that, please?"

"In my case, for not working properly I was hung up on a post by chains in the shower room with my hands tied behind my back for an hour, like this."

Blaha stood up from his seat, turned around, locked his fingers behind his back, and stretched up as high as he could. Then he resumed his place.

"Who was present?" Denson asked.

"Several superior officers including *Rapportführer* Jarolin." Eyes went to Jarolin, seated in the defendants' dock.

"Will you go over to that group of persons and point him out to the court?"

Blaha rose, walked to the box, and placed a hand on the shoulder of the man who had tortured him. Then he returned to the witness chair.

"Do you have any scars from this hanging?" Denson asked.

"Not from the hanging, but from beatings by the Gestapo. There was a whipping bench and one had to bend over it, and from both sides the *Blockführers* beat with sticks." Anyone who had toured Dachau in recent months knew about the whipping bench. Earlier that year, ex-prisoners working in the army's International Information Office had set up an exhibit in the crematorium–gas chamber building. The exhibit used life-sized mannequins to depict an SS officer, raised hand holding a stick, beating a prisoner bent over the bench.

Blaha described other tortures he had undergone. He told of a French transport that arrived in the summer of 1944, and how defendant SS doctor Witteler ordered him to dissect some of the hundreds who died from thirst in the blazing summer sun. He described special subcamps built for Jews, such as Kaufering and Mühldorf. He reported how Russians received the worst treatment, the most beatings and executions, and how for weeks he and his fellow prisoners heard machine gun fire coming from an execution spot northwest of the camp near the railroad tracks. He spoke of the time defendant Mahl—"sitting there in the dock, number thirty-three"—put a rope around the neck of a young Russian and how defendant Boettger—"second man in the last row, number eighteen"—kicked away the stool on which he stood, and how the boy's body remained hanging during the noon hour when all the work details marched by.

"You mentioned that Rascher was in charge of experiments. What was the nature of these experiments?"

"There were two groups of experiments, air pressure and cold water. Twenty or so prisoners were locked up in a bell-like thing. Then by means of machines the air pressure was raised and lowered suddenly. All the dead ones were dissected. Some had hemorrhages of the brain, stomach, lungs. More than a hundred prisoners died of these experiments."

"You described another type, the cold water, is that correct?"

"Yes," Blaha said. "Prisoners were put into a big basin without clothing and kept there for up to thirty-eight hours. Their temperature was measured with a thermometer in the rectum. Every time the prisoner's temperature dropped ten degrees, blood was taken from an artery at the throat and examined in the laboratory. At twenty-five degrees the people usually died. With some of them, the experiments were interrupted and they were warmed up again."

"How?"

"Either with a heating apparatus, or there were two women in a bed and they put the frozen person in between them and they had to warm him up. All the dead bodies were dissected and the organs taken out, sometimes while they were still in the living condition—brains, thyroid, stomach, spleen, testicles—and dispatched to Munich to the Pathological Institute."

"Doctor, who was camp commandant when these experiments were being conducted?"

"Commandant Weiss. Number one."

"What other experiments were performed?"

"Liver puncture experiments without anesthesia, malaria experiments, phlegmon experiments. Healthy people received injections of pus from phlegmon-diseased people into their rectum muscles. At first it caused inflammation, then, if untreated, general blood poisoning. Many people died. Others were turned into invalids."

"Who were the chief doctors at the time these experiments were being performed?"

"Walter and Brachtel."

Bates finally saw an opening. "I move to have this testimony stricken. Neither of these men is a defendant in this case."

Denson had anticipated objection to introducing crimes purportedly committed by persons other than the defendants. "Every one of these men," he responded, "is charged with participating in a common design to perform the mistreatments here alleged. Simply because these two doctors happen not to be sitting there with them is no reason why this should be stricken. If the defendants were present at that time in Dachau, it is sufficient."

Lentz agreed. "Motion is denied."

"Doctor," Denson continued, "what did you do after the hospital?"

"Because I didn't want to do the operations, as punishment I was sent to the death chamber where autopsies were performed. I did six to seven thousand autopsies."

"Did you ever have to remove skin from the bodies of dead prisoners?"

"That was done when Bruno was in charge of autopsies, and then Willy Mirkle. We took the skin from the chest and back, then used chemicals to treat the skin. Then the skins were placed outside in the sun and parts were cut out according to drawings given to us by the SS men. These were used for saddles, riding breeches, gloves, house slippers, ladies' handbags."

"Can you tell the court what disposition was made of some of the heads of the prisoners?"

"They were prepared and sent either to SS schools or given to some of the SS men. Whole skeletons were also treated sometimes."

"When you say the heads were prepared, what do you mean?"

"They were cut off and boiled, then the soft parts were removed, the skulls bleached in concentrated peroxide, dried, and put together again."

"You mentioned another kind of experiment, namely malaria. Who was in charge of the malaria experiments?"

"Dr. Schilling. He infected prisoners of all nations, also priests, then treated them in different ways."

"Do you know whether any of these human guinea pigs died as a result of these experiments?" Denson asked.

"Yes. I performed the autopsies."

"Did you ascertain causes of death other than those directly attributed to the malaria?"

"Yes, severe intoxication by neosalvarsan and pyramidon. People could not tolerate such big doses, which acted as poisons on them."

"Would you recognize Dr. Schilling if you were to see him?"

"Yes. The old gentleman, number fifteen."

"Do you know a man by the name of Becher?"

"Yes. I saw him when the priests' block had to go for punishment. He pushed them and beat them with a piece of wood."

"Would you recognize this man?"

"Number twenty-seven."

Denson went down the list of accused: did he also recognize Redwitz? Lippmann? Knoll? Eisele? Then, having elicited Blaha's eyewitness identification of a dozen of the defendants, he stopped. "No further questions."

———

Chief defense counsel Douglas Bates rose for cross-examination. "When you first arrived here, things were not so bad considering it was a concentration camp, were they?"

"It was very bad even then."

"You testified there was not so much overcrowding, and sanitary conditions were fairly normal, weren't they?"

"Better than afterward," Blaha conceded.

"There was more medicine at the beginning, wasn't there? The shortage became acute toward the end, is that correct?"

"Yes."

"And food was better in the early part of 1942 and became progressively worse as time went by, is that correct?"

"Yes."

"Dr. Blaha, what were the normal accommodations of Dachau? I mean, how many people could Dachau comfortably accommodate as prisoners?"

"When the camp was filled, normally there were eight thousand prisoners."

"And during the latter part of 1944, how many people were sent into this camp?"

"More than fifty thousand."

Bates sought to shift responsibility away from the Germans on trial and onto officials from other camps, Nazis who sent their victims to Dachau without considering how adversely the additional population would affect conditions.

"You testified to the execution of Russians. Can you tell us who was present at those executions?"

"I did not see that. I only saw the bodies being taken to the crematorium."

"So you don't know what part Ruppert or Boettger played, if any, do you?"

"No."

"You said this man Jarolin was present when you were hung by your wrists. Did he hang you up by your wrists?"

"No."

"Then he was merely a spectator."

"Yes."

"Did Jarolin give the order to hang you up?"

"No, that was done from the headquarters," Blaha admitted.

"In other words, Jarolin was only following orders from someone else, is that correct?"

"Yes."

"Doctor, you have a large hospital in Prague?"

"Yes."

"And in your hospital's pathological laboratory do you have organs of human beings?"

"Yes, for study purposes."

"Do you have skeletons?"

"Yes. Two."

"No further questions."

Denson wasn't sure how many points Bates had scored, but one detail had to be made clear before the day ended. He rose for redirect. "You stated that Jarolin was present at your hanging by the wrists. Did Jarolin give any orders?"

"Several of us were hanging slightly low, and our shoes touched the floor. Jarolin gave the order that we should be hung up higher."

"No further questions."

The Dachau trial opened to a packed house, then died. By day five the crowds had disappeared and the press had returned to cover the Nuremberg opening. They also left to escape the boredom of the Dachau trial's endless translations. Many of the translators were refugees, called "thirty-niners," referring to the year they left Germany. Few had lived long enough with the English language to speak it well, and each sentence took painfully long to go from English to German, or Polish to English. In that opening week, American journalist Walter Lippmann, co-founder of the weekly the *New Republic*, came to listen in. His secretary had wired ahead that he planned to stay three days. Paul Guth spent hours arranging quarters, organizing meals, scheduling interviews. Lippman arrived at nine o'clock the first day. By ten-thirty he was gone. Then Margaret Higgins arrived. Her reports of liberation of the camps, filed as she followed Allied forces across Europe, had made her one of America's most popular war correspondents. Her assistant had written to say she might stay as long as a week. Within two hours, she, too, had left the courtroom.

The lack of press attention weighed on Denson. From Movietone news reports, radio broadcasts, and articles in the army paper *Stars and Stripes*, he knew that Nuremberg chief justice Robert Jackson was suffering setbacks from a similar kind of courtroom ennui. Jackson's dilemma, however, arose from a preponderance of written documentation. Testimony alone, Jackson calculated, would not sway the Nuremberg tribunal: witnesses might be seen as unreliable or prone to vengeful exaggeration. To avoid such skepticism, Jackson was relying on massive quantities of paper documents to prove his case. The choice had a predictable impact on the media. Journalist Rebecca West, reporting in the *New Yorker*, described the Nuremberg courtroom as "a citadel of boredom . . . boredom on a huge, historic scale." Thinking back on the empty courtroom he had left moments before, Denson could not have helped making a comparison: if a Supreme Court justice of the United States, with all the facilities that the Nuremberg court provided, could not excite the press—if even Robert Jackson failed to stir passions—what hope did a skinny country lawyer have here at Dachau? What the world needed was a memorable end to the Nazi catastrophe, not tedious homework. Denson would continue to stress the experience of living victims over the mute data of paper documents.

6

Credibility

Going into the trial, Denson knew his most difficult challenge would be convincing the tribunal that testimony by victims of the camps was true. He had confronted his own skepticism when he first arrived: their stories were simply unbelievable. Why should the judges feel any different?

Denson's team had interviewed more than five hundred potential witnesses, looking for those who exuded credibility. They listened to how a witness spoke, watched for nervous tics, discussed what sort of impression he would make on the court. The credible ones were recalled, terms of their participation discussed—room, board, daily stipend—then billeted in houses along Tennessee Road. The rest were sent home.

Credibility included the way a witness sat in a chair, his facial expressions and gestures, the tone of his voice. The eight men on the tribunal considered these indicators of reliability as readily as the details of their testimony. An educated witness who quoted statistics might add weight, but a sincere witness who spoke with feeling often made a deeper impression. Ten days into the trial the court had an opportunity to see what sincerity could do. Denson called Arthur Haulot, a thirty-two-year-old journalist, former lieutenant in the Belgian army, and for three years a prisoner in Dachau. Haulot, who would later become a minister in the Brussels government, was extremely credible. He had no malice, no bitterness, and projected careful reflection and sincerity. He began by recalling how the SS responded to news of approaching American forces by ordering all Jewish prisoners to assemble on the parade ground. There they were beaten and made to stand at attention throughout the cold, windy night. The next day Haulot and two comrades counted sixty dead bodies.

"Was there any condition," Denson asked, "which was worse than the beatings? Was there anything harder on the prisoners?"

Haulot answered thoughtfully, "I think, for a normal person, it was much harder to live in the camp than any other place, not only because of the beatings, but from a moral standpoint. I wish to call myself an example, and what I can say may be true for thousands of others. When I was brought here from Mauthausen, I was so thin, so finished from a physical standpoint, that I had to use all my strength just to stay alive.

"But the worst that I had to go through while in block twenty-five in Dachau for three years was not that I was beaten, but that I was forced to respect people who were criminals—that I had to live, day and night, with hundreds of men who were professional criminals and had a better position in this dirty camp only because they were criminals and German. It became so bad for me that one day I actually stole bread from another comrade." Haulot choked up and tears came. "I didn't eat that bread. I put it back in my comrade's pocket. But that I, who had a decent upbringing, should fall so low in those three years—that was the worst for me. I know of many people, and at least six of my Belgian comrades, who died in block twenty-five, not only because they were beaten or starved, but because they had had enough. Up to the neck, if you want to use that expression."

Years later Denson recalled that moment in court. "You could hear a pin drop," he said.

Arthur Haulot may have been one of the prosecution's most credible witnesses, but he took a beating on the stand. Douglas Bates was waging a vigorous defense of the German accused, and attempts to discredit prosecution witnesses played a vital role in his strategy. Bates leaned heavily on the fact that, as a socialist in the 1940s, Haulot had been a criminal according to German law. How believable, Bates argued, was the word of a criminal? As head of the underground inmate organization inside camp

Dachau, Haulot also spoke for all those who had been tortured and killed. Was he not seeking revenge any way he could get it? The barrage was more than Haulot could bear, and one evening after court had adjourned he approached tribunal president Lentz.

"Colonel," he said, "my friends and I came here voluntarily to testify against these Nazi scum. Why must we take such verbal abuse from the Americans?"

Lentz patiently explained that the defense attorneys were simply doing their duty. They had the right, under American legal practice, to exercise wide latitude in cross-examinations in order to gain favorable verdicts for the accused.

"Then this trial will continue without us," Haulot said. "For years we supported beatings and insults from these German bastards. We will not tolerate such indignities from those who represent freedom and democracy," and he strode off to the officers' mess for a last meal before returning to Belgium. An hour later Douglas Bates and the other defense lawyers entered the mess. The chief counsel approached Haulot and put a friendly arm around his shoulder.

"We just wanted to thank you," Bates said. "By speaking up, you got us properly scolded. We were doing what we had to do, and frankly it disgusted us. You won't be bothered like that again."

Such a change of tactics would not likely have occurred had the trial been taking place in an American civil court. At Dachau, however, the defense lawyers were soldiers who took seriously any reprimand from superior officers. They were also men with no illusions concerning the crimes of the accused and deep respect for a man like Haulot who had withstood them.

———

That evening after a perfunctory dinner at the inn, Denson worked his way dutifully through another stack of sworn statements and other documents, adding meticulous notes to his three-ring binders. A handwritten diary drew his attention. A coversheet described that the waterlogged pages had been discovered by 7th Army investigators in their search for documentary evidence to be used in the trials. The diary's author was an internee identified only as E. K. He addressed his thoughts to an unseen lover, real or perhaps imagined.

20 November 1942

These pages that I now begin to write would lead to certain death if ever they were found. But what is death? How few of those I knew here are still alive today? How close to death we all stand. I really thought I would record all this for you, so that when we will meet again some time later, I would have nothing more to say. I would give you the pages and be silent, for I am tired of speaking. My friends think I am secretly writing a poem, most likely a love poem, or one about flowers and stars. If they knew what I was doing, they would burn these pages out of fear. In fact, they would be right, because I endanger their lives as well as my own. . . .

21 November 1942

Something happened yesterday that excited even the most hardened of us, and that means something, for we have lost all feeling. Nothing more can astonish us in any way. Five hundred invalids came yesterday from a camp near Danzig. To be an invalid among us prisoners means to be at death's door. Fifty-one of these "invalids" came in dead, but their bodies had already been partly eaten by the others. The remains and bones were thrown out of a chink in the cattle-truck door during the journey. Only a few unrecognizable parts of bodies remained. The whole side was missing from one body, from others the nose or cheek or genital organs. The prisoners, during the six days that their journey lasted, received only one piece of bread, six hundred grams I believe. Hunger delirium broke out among them. Forty-nine of the survivors died yesterday, the day of their arrival. Soon there will be more, and every day the number will increase. That they brought them here can only be explained by the fact that manpower is needed.

Will you ever read these pages? Each page is a source of danger. It is so hard to hide these pages. May a good power protect them and keep them safely, so that one day I can give them to you—together with a heart of stone. I have grown older. My temples are turning gray, and age is changing my features. I sometimes notice it when I look at myself in the small mirror of the washroom. I am only 36 years old.

22 November 1942

I must tell you something that shocked me so much today. It is Sunday. We are standing on the roll call court and are waiting for the order to march out. Beside us a few hundred Ukrainians are led up. The two first lines are children, their small bodies clad in garments far too large for them, their pale faces with childish, half joyful eyes. Their voices sound like the lark's song in a churchyard. Someone led past me a dying, whimpering infant. I had to turn my face away. Hearts must grow hard here, otherwise one would cry from morn till evening.

8 December 1942

At night in bed I drew the blanket over my head, but I heard what somebody was saying. His friend is a litter bearer. The job doesn't move him any longer. Yesterday as he was piling up the corpses, his attention was accidentally drawn to one face. It was his brother. Someone came and pulled the blanket from my head. It was a Polish friend of mine. He told me about a priest, a schoolmate of his. Here in Dachau they met again. The priest was suddenly taken into the Revier—that is the name they give to the hospital here—to be experimented on. The priest secretly sent a short note to his friend. The last sentence was not legible, for, as he himself said, he had forty degrees temperature. He did not ask for help because he knew all was lost. Many hundreds will still die in this way and we must look on, helpless. Day before yesterday another 300 invalids came in, merely living corpses.

Another friend made me very sad today. His wife, whom he loves and who loved him, left his parents and her child and went to another country. He doesn't know why. He is weak and sensitive. I am surprised that he is still alive, and now this happens to him. The wives outside get tired of waiting and claim divorce. Now the men's wives and children are lost to them, and with that all ideals, all hold on life. What do those outside think we are, we here inside the camp? In fact, I know it has been spread about that only the most dangerous subjects, traitors and the like, remain locked up here and in other camps. If only they saw us here! If only they knew!

10 December 1942

Yesterday, I saw again thin men creeping out of the front room of our barracks. They had stolen potato peelings out of the dustbin and filled their pockets with them. They were old and young men. Hunger hurts, and the majority haven't the willpower to master the gnawing of the stomach. But, as compared to other camps, this is heaven. One of our prisoners coming from Mauthausen told me today that there they had daily from 40 to 50 casualties out of a total of 4,000 to 6,000 men. On a certain winter day, the number went up to 180. Only those who have lived and seen can believe that.

22 December 1942

One of the former block leaders is said to be hospitalized in the Revier. It isn't such a long time since he left for the front. We called him "The Hamburger," a giant, brutal face, only 20 years old, paws like those of a rhinoceros. Only a year ago or maybe it was this year, he beat a man to death because this man had eaten potato peelings. But he did not kill him slowly, as is customary. No, he killed him with one blow of his fist. He is also one of those who took pleasure in horse-whippings. Many have already been killed by him or have been hastened to death at the whipping place. They say he lost one hand and one leg. Fate has caught up with him, if it is true. Now he cannot either beat or kick anymore. I wonder if his heart has changed, too.

23 December 1942

I was talking to a friend today. Some years ago he left with a transport to Mauthausen. There were 1,600 of them. Now after nine months, he too returned, as in another world, more dead than alive, he and 19 men. That means that 20 men remained out of 1,600. Yes, Dachau is, in spite of everything, the golden camp.

Here was someone credible. Denson would have preferred that journalists writing about the trials take their language warm from the hearts of feeling human beings like this E. K. instead of from the official papers of army bureaucrats. He had read enough magazines and seen enough newsreels to know that victims of the camps were again being sacrificed, this time to shallow reporting and selective hindsight. People like E. K. deserved more than passing mention by columnists with deadlines—and more than one country lawyer's effort at justice. The weight of that realization imposed a heavy burden.

On the bedside table lay a King James Version of the Bible that his father had given him for his seventeenth birthday. The leather cover was supple from years of daily use. Denson read from it every night before saying his prayers, and tonight was no exception. Nor were the nightmares that followed, keeping him once again from a good night's sleep.

———————

The next day in court, a thin boy hobbled forward on crutches. He mounted the wooden platform to the witness chair and sat.

"What is your name?" Denson asked.

"Schmul Kuczinsky."

"How old are you?"

"Eighteen." Denson had no children, but he had a younger brother, Render, whom he loved dearly. As kids, Denson had fought Render's battles for him and knew what it felt like to protect someone you love who is younger and weaker.

"Where do you reside at the present time?"

"At Saint Ottilien Hospital."

"Before the war, what were you doing?"

"In school."

"Were you a prisoner at one of the Kaufering camps?"

"Number four."

"And where had you come from?"

"Auschwitz."

"Did any other members of your family come with you?"

"My father and three uncles."

"What happened to your father in camp number four?"

"In the evening four men brought my father. I saw that his right eye was blue and swollen. I almost didn't recognize him. My father started to cry, and two of the people that brought him said Tempel had beat him. The next morning when I felt his pulse, he was dead."

"Would you know Tempel if you saw him?"

"Yes. Unfortunately, I know him very well."

"Mr. Kuczinsky," Denson said, offering whatever comfort a respectful form of address could provide a broken eighteen-year-old, "how do you happen to know him?"

"Because he beat me, too."

"Will you look over there among the defendants and tell us which one you recognize as Tempel? What is his number?"

"Twenty-five."

"Nothing further." Denson sat.

McKeown rose, but there was nothing to say. "The defense has no questions."

––––––––

Nuremberg had opened one week before, the spectacle of Nazi trials providing a jolt of sensationalism to newspapers and radio worldwide. Such coverage of military affairs could have far-reaching consequences. During the Civil War more than five hundred correspondents descended on the battlefields of the South, and it was their reports that prompted President Lincoln to authorize articles of military conduct in 1863. The following year, twelve European governments signed the first international agreement, now known as the Geneva Convention. Laws of war dated back to the ancient Persians and Greeks, but it was nineteenth-century journalists who had precipitated their recognition and acceptance internationally.

It must have bothered Denson to see the press focused so much on the accused at Nuremberg—men who had never fired a gun—and so little on the criminals on trial at Dachau. Here were the men who had personally caused so much suffering and death, and, if properly reported, the Dachau trials might contribute as much to international law as the Nuremberg trials. But what could he do? As attention-grabbers, the former locksmiths and auto mechanics in his court were no match for the top honchos at Nuremberg.

"We were the basement," Paul Guth said comparing the two trials, "not even pebbles in their shoes."

————

Witnesses for the prosecution appeared and gave testimony one after another until more than one hundred had testified, often as many as fifteen in a single day. Always sensitive to how incredible many of their accounts must seem to the tribunal, Denson called upon former "privileged prisoners" to reinforce his case. Among them was Prince Frederick Leopold of Prussia, a trim sixty-year-old who had been in Dachau for seven months. He spoke of seeing formations arrive, of train doors opening and dead bodies falling out, of new arrivals forced to undress outdoors in freezing weather while SS men boxed their ears and kicked them in the stomach. Other "privileged prisoners" in Dachau had included Kurt von Schuschnigg, ex-chancellor of Austria and the first European government leader to openly oppose Hitler; Leon Blum, former premier of France and architect of France's Popular Front; Prince Xavier of Holland; Winston Churchill's nephew; the mayor of Vienna; and the nephew of Germany's former kaiser, along with his secretary, valet, and chauffeur.

While pedigree might enhance a witness's credibility, Denson knew that fancy titles alone would not make incredible reports more credible. Who would accept that respected physicians had practiced resectioning stomachs of live victims without anesthesia, or that one human being had taken other human beings by their legs and torn them in two, or that an officer had thrown infants into buckets of water to drown before heading home for the day to his own wife and children? The men of the tribunal knew war was hell, but could their imaginations encompass the surreal history of Dachau?

Denson followed a pattern. He first introduced evidence of minor abuses one might expect to occur in a penal environment: slapping around and other small displays of force. Then he introduced witnesses who described harsher beatings and by degrees conditioned the court to the more bizarre events that had transpired. The slow process of translations interfered with effective pacing of these witnesses, and Denson timed their testimony on his wristwatch to be sure attention never flagged. After each session he gathered his team to discuss to what extent they thought the tribunal was ready to hear some of the more incredible stories. The pattern seemed to work.

To establish some minor abuses, Denson introduced a twenty-one-year-old Lithuanian student who testified he had seen defendant Kirsch beat prisoners. Denson called to the stand a forty-one-year-old German construction engineer who observed defendant Degelow at executions. He questioned a woman doctor from Vilna who had watched as defendant Kramer shot her husband. Denson then called a Polish office worker who described how defendant Lippmann had picked out a fifteen-year-old boy for a work detail. The boy clung to his father's leg, the worker described. He begged not to be taken from his father, until blows from Lippmann's stick rendered him unconscious. The witness described how the father stood weeping as guards carried his son away. Having set the stage, Denson asked the witness to describe what happened toward the end of March 1945, when the camp was being dissolved. Prisoners were assembled on the formation place in preparation for the last transport, the witness said. They stood near a large pit used for garbage, and some of the prisoners saw potato peelings in the pit and jumped in to retrieve them. Lippmann spotted them, took out his pistol, and shot four times. Denson then had another witness, Ali Kuci, pick up the storyline. Kuci was a thirty-two-year-old Albanian and former student at London University.

"There were twenty-four hundred people on the last transport," he told the court. "Only six hundred survived."

"How were these people brought together?" Denson asked.

"The commandant issued an order that all Jews should report to the formation place. They were dressed in rags and remained standing there all night. It was raining, and a cold wind was blowing. The next morning they were marched out of the main gate to the railroad station and forced into the wagons. That train never left Dachau. They remained in those closed wagons from the twenty-first of April until the liberation on the twenty-ninth. The SS strictly forbade us to go near the wagons. We called it the Morgue Express."

Denson allowed the image of two thousand people imprisoned in closed cars for nine days to sink in. "No further questions," he said.

7

The Prosecution on Trial

T wo weeks into the trial the prosecution prepared to rest its case. Prosecution witnesses had identified the accused as men who ran camp Dachau, had provided testimony of atrocities committed in the camp, and had linked specific defendants to specific crimes. But many of these prosecution witnesses had not seen the crimes about which they testified. Their reports were hearsay, things inmates had talked about, and not necessarily sufficient to convict. If the Nazis who ran Dachau were to hang, some other tangible evidence would be needed to confirm their guilt. That other evidence was their signed confessions. But how had those confessions been obtained? Why would the Germans have voluntarily signed statements that could get them hanged? Lawyers for the accused knew that discrediting those confessions might be their only chance for acquittal. At the very least, proving that the confessions had been coerced might win their clients reduced sentences.

Denson acknowledged to himself that his assistant, Paul Guth, was young, headstrong, and aware of how fear could sometimes uncover truths that did not exist. But Guth had no appetite for coercion, of that Denson was certain. Denson knew little, however, of how other interrogators had conducted themselves, and accusations of coercion threatened to compromise the prosecution's entire case. Denson began the prosecution's final day determined to put any doubts concerning his team's behavior to rest and called his young assistant to the stand.

"Lieutenant Guth, on or about the twenty-ninth October 1945, did you have occasion to examine one Franz Xavier Trenkle?"

"I did, sir."

"And before he made his statement, did you threaten him in any manner?"

"No, sir."

"Did you promise him any hope of reward if he made a statement?"

"No, sir."

"I hand you Trenkle's statement. Did he read that over before signing it?"

"Yes, sir, and he also made several changes."

Denson asked the same questions about a dozen other statements made by the defendants. Guth denied any misdoings.

————

"Lieutenant Guth, what was your assignment prior to VE Day in the army?" Bates asked on cross-examination.

"I was attached to various interrogation units."

"And for what length of time did you do interrogation work?"

"Approximately a year. That was at the Army Interrogation Center in Freising. Before we moved to Freising we were in Bamberg. I also did evaluation work."

"But your primary work was interrogation, was it not?"

"Yes, sir."

"On how many different occasions did you interrogate the defendants—Dr. Hintermeyer, for instance. How many times did you interrogate him?"

"I believe twice."

"For how long?"

"Well, sir, I couldn't recall that. It was several hours in each case."

"Regarding this statement," Bates said, holding up Hintermeyer's signed confession, "I ask you whether or not you composed the thing."

"No, sir. I think if you look at the last few lines, you will find that it was written by some clerk or secretary and read by Dr. Hintermeyer. He made what changes he considered necessary and signed it afterward. So neither he nor myself physically wrote it."

"Who constructed the sentences and phrases and clauses that appear in that statement?"

"Hintermeyer made the original statement verbally. I and another officer made notes. Some of the words—I think most of the words—are Dr. Hintermeyer's. Some of the organization, that is, setting of the manuscript into paragraphs for instance, is mine."

"How many times did you interrogate Trenkle?"

"Once, sir."

"And for what length of time?"

"Sir, I am afraid I don't know that. I haven't got a watch and wouldn't look at a watch while interrogating if I had one. I really don't know."

"An approximation?"

"Several hours. I'm not quite sure."

"Who read those statements to the typist?"

"Inasmuch as they were my notes, I did. I should like to add, however, that whenever any one of the accused gave a reason for his actions . . ."

". . . that whenever an accused gave a reason for his actions you generously permitted that reason to be added to the statement. Is that right?"

"Well, I don't know whether your words are chosen very happily, but if you want to put it that way, I did permit it to be put in the statement, yes."

"No further questions."

———

Denson stood for redirect and asked, "After the statements were prepared, was any force used to require any one of the deponents to sign his statement?"

"No, sir, not at all. I would like to add that as soon as a man came in I would swear him in. I then told him that I was an investigator-examiner, that you were the prosecutor, and that you would make any use you considered fit of any statement that he chose to make."

"No further questions."

Bates stood for re-cross. "You will recall taking the statement of Dr. Witteler. Did you know that Dr. Witteler had just come from the hospital the day you saw him?"

"No, sir. I heard that afterward."

"At what time of day did you begin the interrogation?"

"About six-thirty in the evening."

"Do you recall what time it concluded?"

"Some time that evening."

"Would you say it was two o'clock in the morning?"

"No, sir. It was earlier."

"Was he required to stand during the entire interrogation?"

"Only after he accused me of being a liar."

"Then you did make him stand?" Bates repeated.

"Until he requested to sit down—it wasn't more than half an hour."

"That is all."

———

When asked years later why the Germans had signed confessions if they had not been coerced into doing so, Denson commented, "I think basically they felt they could hide behind a defense of superior orders. Then, too, there were some people who had a certain amount of morality who were willing to sign in order to clear their conscience with their God and tell the truth." Still, to avoid the stigma that the only evidence was questionable confessions, he "made damn sure there was independent evidence corroborating what the defendant had done."

After his questioning of Paul Guth, Denson called half a dozen other American interrogators to the stand. One after the other, each testified that he had made no threats, offered no inducements, and that the defendants had voluntarily signed their statements. With those assurances to the court, the prosecution rested its case.

———

On December 10, 1945, the defense began by calling the Dachau camp commandant to the stand. Martin Gottfried Weiss was a graduate of the SS training camp at Dachau and had previously been commandant at the Neuengamme and Majdanek camps. He did so well as commandant of Majdanek that he was promoted to inspector of the camps, a prestigious position first held by Theodor Eicke, known as "father of the concentration camp system." Weiss was commandant of Dachau from March 1942 to November 1943, replacing the previous commandant, Alex Piorkowski. Dachau's last commandant, Wilhelm Weiter, committed suicide at Itter castle in Austria (a Dachau subsidiary camp) on May 6, 1945. Weiss had been promoted on January 1, 1944, to Chief of Amtsgruppe D, *SS-Wirtschaftsverwaltungshauptamt* Berlin—the SS's highest rank. In April 1945, when Weiss learned that the American 7th Army was approaching, he fled along with most of the regular guards but was later captured.

"I was born in 1905," Weiss began. "My civilian occupation was electrical engineer. I have been in the German army from 1933 until my arrest on second May 1945."

"Will you tell the court what conditions you found here at Dachau?" asked defense counsel Douglas T. Bates.

"I determined that people were being bound to posts here, that prisoners had to stand for days at a time without food. I found that the camp elders and their assistants had vast powers. Some I relieved immediately, others I had transferred."

"When you arrived, did you find any experiment stations in progress?"

"I had received orders from superior authorities not to concern myself with these experiments, as they were under the personal supervision of *Reichsführer* Himmler. At that time, the malaria station was under the direction of Dr. Schilling and the experimental station was under Dr. Rascher."

"Did Himmler come to Dachau?"

"In November 1942. He went directly to the experiment station. I only learned he had arrived some time after, when his adjutant came to fetch me in my office. An experiment was already underway when I entered the station. Himmler was very angry. Rascher had complained that I didn't follow all of his wishes, and the *Reichsführer* said, 'Well, here is the man Weiss,' then immediately told me I was to give no orders to Dr. Rascher, that Rascher was under his personal protection. I was to comply with his every wish—if he demanded cognac or coffee, no matter what."

"What about the malaria station? Did you have any control over Dr. Schilling while he was conducting malaria experiments?"

"No."

"Were there any executions in Dachau while you were commandant?"

"Not of camp prisoners. Only of people who were brought in from outside by officers of the State Police."

"Did you have authority to change such orders of execution?" Bates asked.

"No."

"While you were here, were there deaths as a result of general sickness?"

"Yes. TB, heart weakness, typhoid of the stomach, other weaknesses, which can be traced to the fact that we received patients from other concentration camps. These people weighed no more than eighty or ninety pounds when they arrived. I made a report to Berlin asking that physicians of other camps only send people who were fit to outlast a transport. Many were arriving dead. I had pictures taken and sent to my authorities in Oranienburg. It did no good. Transports continued to arrive in bad condition."

"Did you have anything to do with the transports of invalids that left Dachau?"

"No. As a matter of fact, I pointed out to Berlin that it made no sense for such transports to be sent from Dachau when we were expected to receive other invalid transports coming in. After my message, no more invalid transports took place.

"There seems to be a mistaken idea," Weiss said, addressing the tribunal, "among the prisoners who have appeared before this court that any transports which left for other work camps were so-called liquidation transports. The fact is that small and big transports left Dachau all the time for Augsburg, Haunstetten, Kempten, Kotteren, different bycamps—delivering workers. And these were supplemented with invalid prisoners only after those prisoners had been nursed back to health."

"Weiss, did you inaugurate the standing bunker?"

"This phrase I heard for the first time during this trial."

"You testified that upon your arrival you discovered that prisoners were tied to poles."

"Yes, by both hands behind their back, and the tips of their toes did not touch the floor."

"After you became commandant, did you continue this practice?" Bates asked.

"No."

"Prisoners standing from morning till night without food—did that practice continue?"

"No."

"During your tour of duty at Dachau, will you tell the court whether or not you were aware of or participated in a common design or conspiracy to murder, beat, mistreat, or otherwise perform indignities upon any of the prisoners in concentration camp Dachau or its subsidiaries?"

"No."

"That is all."

————

Denson cross-examined. "Weiss, as commandant of camp Dachau, is it not a fact that you were in charge of all the by-camps and had in your custody and care the prisoners of Dachau and its by-camps?"

"Yes."

"During your time here, Weiss, how many prisoners did you ship out of Dachau?"

"By order of the Reich Security Main Office, several thousand were transferred to other camps and armament industries." The Security Office in Berlin would be referenced innumerable times throughout the trial. This was the Reich authority that appointed commandants and other camp senior officers and issued orders concerning camp administration. Defense argued that their clients' actions with respect to rations, clothing, medical and other supplies, disciplinary actions, and executions—all were in accordance with standards prescribed by the Security Office in Berlin. Denson's research, however, had unearthed evidence that, notwithstanding orders from Berlin, camp officials wielded powers of their own.

"Is it not a fact, Weiss, that requisitions for prisoners had to be approved by you before those prisoners were made available to Dr. Schilling?"

"It was an order from Berlin that the prisoners were to be given to him. . . ."

"Just answer my question, Weiss. Did you have to approve the requisitions?"

"Yes."

"The same was true for Rascher's experiments, was it not?"

"Yes."

"Weiss, you knew how these experiments were being conducted by Dr. Schilling, did you not?"

"No."

"You mean you had no idea—no knowledge at all that these prisoners were being inoculated with malaria by Dr. Schilling?"

"No."

"How many prisoners died during your time as a result of shooting?"

"None were shot during my time. There were only hangings."

"Are you telling this court that from March 1942 until November first, 1943, no prisoners were shot in concentration camp Dachau?"

"Only during attempts at escape. I estimate there were four or five such cases."

No one expected Nazi officers to admit their sins and beg for mercy, but the brazenness of their denials was stunning. "No further questions," Denson said, allowing Weiss's audacity to be his best concluding note.

———

To establish a common design, the prosecution had to show that Dachau was, in its entirety, a criminal operation. To that end Denson had named as defendants representatives from each of the camp's functional divisions. These included the political department, the commandant's office, protective custody, labor allocation, medical, crematory, and administration. In response, the defense's strategy was to show that these various departments had indeed functioned cooperatively—not as conspirators in a sadistic common design, but as soldiers responsibly and legally fulfilling the duties of their office.

Johann Kick, forty-four years old, had been a traffic cop in Munich from 1925 to 1933. From then until the end of the war he was an official of the Gestapo, arriving in Dachau in May 1937 as chief of the political department. He was also one of the most brutal defendants in the dock.

Defense attorney Bates began by asking Kick to explain the source of his authority at Dachau.

"I got my orders exclusively from the camp commandant," he said. "I was responsible for registering prisoners, keeping files and death certificates, notification of relatives, and so on."

"Did you know that in Dachau executions took place?"

"Yes, by order of the Reich Security Main Office, or else the Reich Leader himself. I saw to it that these orders were fulfilled, and after the execution had taken place my department notified the Security Office."

"Did you ever take part?"

"During all my time as political chief, I was never present at an execution. I could not even request such an execution. Only the commandant could do that."

"Kick, a witness for the prosecution testified that he saw prisoners come into the political department for interrogation and return to work with their fingernails and toenails pulled out. What do you have to say about that?"

"Anybody who knows me at all has to laugh about this accusation."

"Another witness, Krajewski, stated he was beaten by you with an ashtray and then taken and hung up in the shower room. What do you say to that?"

"I value my own conscience. Never in my life did I beat a person. I never made any punishment during interrogations. I would swear to that."

"Prosecution witness Wolf testified that prisoners were sent from political interrogation to the standing bunker. What do you say to that?"

"As long as I was chief of the political department, I never knew such a thing existed. I found out about it only here."

―――――――

"I have a few questions," Denson said, modulating his words with remarkable self-control. During weeks of trial preparation he had learned of Kick's outrageous and frequent abuse of prisoners. Now he had sat patiently listening while this petty degenerate pontificated over the value of his conscience. Denson cast his line, trawling carefully.

"Between January 1942 and August 1944, is it not a fact that approximately three hundred orders for execution of camp inmates passed over your desk?"

"I found out about these only after the executions, when we received the death reports for our files."

Denson referred to an exhibit and asked, "On the fifth of November, 1945, did you not make this statement to Lieutenant Guth: 'Under camp regulations, it was impossible to execute an inmate unless the order passed through my department'?"

Kick shook his head. "I never made such a statement. To the contrary, I protested to Lieutenant Guth about this, that he was giving an importance to this purely administrative procedure. There are very few words in that statement that spring from me. Lieutenant Guth asked me . . ."

Lentz interrupted, looking at the translator. "Instruct the witness to answer the question and not ramble on about extraneous matters." Denson pushed forward. If he noticed the court's favoritism, he said nothing about it.

"Kick, is it not a fact that on the fifth of November 1945 you also made this statement to Lieutenant Guth: 'I did not protest in any of the ten cases I can recall during Commandant Weiss's tenure, as I did not see any reason to prevent these executions'?"

"I can't believe I said that."

Denson approached the witness chair and offered the document. "Is it written here?"

"Yes."

"You understand the question. Did you make that statement to Lieutenant Guth?"

Kick turned from Denson to Lentz. "The attitude of the chief prosecutor . . ."

"Just a minute," Lentz interrupted again, and once more spoke to the translator. "I want you to instruct the witness—you tell him that to a question of this nature he will answer yes or no."

This was more than the defense lawyers could bear. "May it please the court," McKeown said, "I just simply want to remind the court that defendants in this proceeding are not required to answer any questions. Now, we don't want to curtail how much information the court receives, but if this argumentative cross-examination continues, I will ask permission to remind the defendant of his right not to answer."

Lentz repeated his instruction to the translator. "You will advise the witness that he is to answer the question as clearly and as shortly as he can. A question such as the last one can be answered yes or no." Then he added, "He is to understand that he is not required to answer a question that he feels will incriminate or degrade him."

The concession, for McKeown, fell short. "Sir, I think that statement by the court is too limited. The rights defined by the *Manual for Military Government Courts* do not require him to answer *any* question, whether it would incriminate him or not. He is not under oath. Our position is that he can answer any question in any way he sees fit."

Denson disagreed. "Not any way he sees fit. This man took the stand at his own election, and the reasoning of the defense counsel as to the interrogation . . ."

McKeown pointed his rejoinder at Denson. "The court's instructions at the outset of this trial included this: 'You will not be held in contempt for your refusal to answer,' or substantially those words."

Lentz refereed. "We will proceed with the trial," he said, in effect ruling for the prosecution without answering McKeown's objection.

"Kick, I will ask you," Denson continued, "if on November fifth 1945 you made this statement before Lieutenant Guth, that sick people would be brought in small groups to another installation where they would be gassed."

"No, I did not make that statement," Kick replied.

"And is it not a fact," Denson pushed on, "that on November fifth you made this statement before Lieutenant Guth: 'In the summer of 1943 Commandant Weiss handed me another roster containing the names of six hundred so-called invalids'?"

"It is not correct."

"Is it not a fact that Weiss explained to you that these so-called invalids would be brought to another installation to be gassed?"

"No. This addition also was made by Lieutenant Guth."

Turning to the last page of Kick's confession, Denson extended the document and pointed to a signature and various edit marks. "Whose handwriting is this?"

"I wrote that upon dictation of Lieutenant Guth."

"Did you make these handwritten corrections under his dictation as well, or did you make them of your own accord?"

"I made them myself."

Kick was cornered and, no doubt to the dismay of his lawyers, shifted gear in an attempt to improve his case. "I want to emphasize that I sometimes succeeded in saving men, priests for example, who were on the list—six or seven hundred men, by telling Commandant Piorkowski they did not appear fit for transport. . . ."

By implication, Kick was admitting not only that he knew about the transports but knew as well that they were illegal. Denson had made his point. "No further questions."

McKeown rose for redirect, determined to protect the accused from his own admission of guilt by bringing the conversation back to methods used by the Americans to obtain confessions.

"When were you arrested, Kick?"

"Sixth May 1945."

"And where were you imprisoned?"

"First for ten days in Dachau, then I was brought to Augsburg, then to Zuffenhausen camp, and from there on second November back here."

"Will you in your own words describe to the court the treatment you received prior to your first interrogation?"

Denson stood, seeking to stop McKeown from landing punches on an open wound. "I object to that, may it please the court, as not relevant to the issues in this case—unless it is shown at what point of time before the interrogation he received this alleged treatment." Denson may have realized too late that the phrasing of his objection opened Pandora's box. Instead of objecting to defense's introduction of a rumor, he had validated the rumor by demanding that defense show when it happened. McKeown saw the opening and took it.

"This bit of evidence," he said, "is submitted for the purpose of showing the defendant's psychological condition when he made these statements. The treatment he received in the hands of interrogators will certainly be relevant to his state of mind during interrogations."

Denson had no choice but to pursue the line of his own objection. "He should limit his question to when this alleged mistreatment occurred, so that the court may determine if it is relevant." Then he added a surprising coda. "If the time is established, it could be material."

That olive branch to the defense must have raised concern, for Lentz ruled even before McKeown could respond. "The court," he said, "naturally desires any testimony that will reveal the witness's condition at the time he made this statement. The court feels, however," making a quick calculation, "that a six-month period prior to the signing of the statement in question here is an excessive period of time."

"May I ask the witness just one question," McKeown said, "which may clear the matter up in the court's mind? Kick, did the treatment you received immediately following your arrest in May have any influence whatsoever on the statements you made on the fifth of November?"

"I object to that question," Denson said, "on the same grounds assigned to the previous question."

Despite their leanings, there was no way the tribunal could forbid defense from asking a question that had arisen logically from the course this issue had taken. "The objection is overruled," Lentz said. "The witness will answer the question."

"I ask to refuse to answer this question here in public," Kick said, intimating that reprisals would follow if he revealed details of what had been done to him.

"The court desires to have the question answered," Lentz said.

"I was under arrest here in Dachau from sixth to fifteenth of May," Kick said. "During this time I was beaten all day and night. I had to stand at attention for hours. I had to kneel down on pointed objects. I had to stand under a lamp for hours and look into the light, at which time I was also beaten and kicked. As a result of this treatment my arm was paralyzed for about ten weeks."

"What were you beaten with?" McKeown asked.

"With whips, rifle butts, pistol butts, hands, fists."

"Would you describe the people who administered these beatings to you?"

"I can only say that they were persons wearing the United States uniform."

"And as a result of those beatings, when Lieutenant Guth called you in, what was your frame of mind?"

"I had to presume that if I were to refuse to sign I would be subjected to similar treatment."

"That is all."

———

Futility was not an emotion Denson often experienced, but a trial meant to reveal factual crimes by Germans had detoured into alleged crimes by Americans. Rather than see his case derailed, he swung attention away from May 1945 and back to the confession obtained by Paul Guth six months later. "Kick, did Lieutenant Guth beat you at any time?"

"No."

"Did he threaten you in any way, at any time?"

"No."

Then Denson made a logistical leap that demonstrated masterful courtroom agility. "As a matter of fact, at the time you made that statement you did not know you were going to be an accused in this case, did you?"

Kick must have weighed the question, wondering where this unexpected turn would lead. "No, I did not know that."

"No, you did not. And consequently, when you gave this statement, you were fully cooperative. There was no need for Lieutenant Guth to behave improperly, was there? He treated you like a gentleman at all times, did he not?"

"Yes," Kick admitted.

To finish this off, Denson needed to establish that the propriety of the interrogation would not be merely Guth's word against Kick's. "Was anyone else present at the time you made this statement?"

"Lieutenant Guth's assistant, Dr. Leiss."

"No further questions."

8

Manna from Heaven

Once in a while, when the day's battles were over, Paul Guth would don his best uniform and arrange an evening for himself and his boss, Colonel Denson. Guth's family connections kept him in contact with a wealthy crowd, and it was about this time, partway into the first trial, that Denson accepted Guth's invitation to join him for dinner at the home of Nudi von der Lippe. The party was an elegant pre-Christmas affair and Denson, who excelled at gentle conversation, welcomed occasional distractions from the pressures of the courtroom. It was, as well, his kind of company. Nudi descended from German aristocracy, had recently separated from her successful architect husband, and was celebrating her independence with friends from Munich's artistic and business elite. The gathering included barons, counts, and a princess or two. Members of the Bernheimer antiques family were there. Other guests may have included the curator from the House of German Art, one of Hitler's first building projects, or the owner of the Vierjahreszeiten Hotel, where the annual Fasching masquerade ball took place. Munich's most glamorous hotel had been a favorite watering hole of the Gestapo. Now it catered to visiting army brass and American dignitaries. Just the other day Denson had been there to receive Sen. Claude Pepper of Florida. Pepper, a distant relative of his, strode across the hotel lobby, waved a fist in his face, and bellowed, "Fight!" Ambiguous, but firm.

Nudi's friends were a boisterous and fun-loving group, and, outside of Guth, Bill Denson was the only American allowed entrance into their private circle. Not only did he pay his way—always arriving with liquor, cigarettes, and other luxury goods—but his education and breeding made him good company.

Nudi favored American jazz, and Louis Armstrong's raspy voice sprayed from a record player in the corner of the crowded living room. Guth had a favorite story that merited repeating that evening. "Now I ask you," he began, engaging the crowd with a description of the accused at Dachau, "what protection can a plea of superior order provide that crowd of roughnecks? There's an old joke in Vienna. A lawyer is prosecuting a professional thief in a case of breaking and entering. 'Your honor,' he says, 'the absolute gall of this man—to break a store window in broad daylight!' Well, the defense is outraged. 'I really must object,' he says. 'My client was tried two years ago for the same offense. At that time the prosecutor said, "The absolute gall of this man—to break a store window in the middle of the night!" Now I ask Your Honor: When exactly is my client supposed to burglarize?'"

Denson admired his young aide's talent for shuttling effortlessly between the many worlds they shared. One glimpse at Dachau's history was enough to create nightmares in seasoned murder lawyers. Yet Guth, for all his exposure to it, seemed untouched.

In the course of the evening, having already established chemistry between themselves, Nudi turned to Denson and said, "I know! We'll all go visit my friend Huschi for a winter picnic. You are going to *love* her."

––––––

Upper Silesia, bordered on one side by Poland and Czechoslovakia on the other, was one of Germany's key industrial provinces. In January 1945, the Soviets launched a series of powerful offensives aimed at capturing the region, with Berlin their final destination. The Red Army in its push west committed widespread atrocities, driving hundreds of thousands of Silesians from their homes. Countess Constance von Francken-Sierstorpff, known to her friends as Huschi, sat huddled in a horse-drawn cart and hugged her six-month-old daughter, Yvonne, to her body. Her friend Dorothy sat next to her, protecting her two toddlers from the freezing wind. It was bitter cold, colder than anyone on that exodus could remember. Huschi wore a Hungarian shepherd's coat, several sweaters, two pairs of socks, and a scarf wrapped tightly around her neck. She took a small silver bowl from a pocket of her coat and from another pocket she withdrew a small pouch, poured some of its powdery contents into the bowl, scooped snow from the side of the cart, and mixed them together. She held the batter in her hands to warm it, then fed it to her child finger by finger. The Russians were no more than six days behind them.

She was twenty-two years old and as lost as the thousands of others around her, almost all women and children. Prior to fleeing Silesia, boys under sixteen and men over seventy were considered unfit for battle. But in these final weeks of war the Nazi regime was drafting any male capable of holding a gun to fend off the Russians, which even Huschi, who had no interest at all in military strategy, found insane. She looked behind the cart. The columns of people extended farther than she could see. Huschi's mother, Princess Lily zu Hohenlohe-Oehringen, trailed several miles back in an overcrowded Red Cross truck. Huschi had promised Dorothy she would not leave her alone with two children, and they had set out on their own, two women and three children on a horse-drawn cart, fleeing Russians in the middle of the coldest winter on record.

Noise from behind, a loud Klaxon, and as if by magic the Red Cross truck appeared through the sea of refugees. Huschi yelled out, "Here! Over here!" The truck pulled up and Huschi's mother reached out her arms. Huschi knew her baby would not survive the harsh trek in an open wagon. She felt bound as well by her promise to stay with Dorothy and her two infants. Left with no option, she quickly placed Yvonne in her mother's arms and handed over the powdered milk and cloth diapers.

"Listen to me," Lily yelled, the pandemonium around them drowning out her voice. "Your father-in-law has arranged for your lodging in Dresden. His adjutant is named Fritz Kreutzkamm. You are to go to his mother's home." She thrust a slip of paper with the address into her daughter's hand.

"Go to the Irl family in Bavaria," Huschi yelled back. "I'll meet you there."

Princess Lily withdrew into the truck, and the driver set out, working his way through the throngs. Huschi watched the truck fade into the horizon and wondered with dread whether her aristocratic mother remembered how to feed or diaper a baby.

———

For ten days the caravan of women and children pushed west, knowing only that to be overtaken by the Russians would mean a horrible fate. Along the route, rich and poor opened their doors and shared whatever provisions they had. They, too, were preparing to join the exodus and sensed instinctively that survival would be a cooperative achievement. The temperature continued to spiral down, splitting lips, freezing hands and feet, dropping so low that some gave up hope and sat down on the side of the road to die. Huschi felt strangely free. What was left for her to be attached to? Her husband had returned from the eastern front wounded and bitter. Her brother had disappeared fighting the French. The Russians were no doubt already living in her family's forty-room castle. She would miss the gramophone and her twenty-six record albums, but those could be replaced. She reached into the lining of her coat, reassuring herself that a hidden packet of jewels was still there. The feel of those diamonds and rubies between her fingers helped stave off visions of becoming like the White Russians who fled the Bolsheviks in World War I. They ended up in Paris driving taxis.

By the eleventh day of their trek the snow had abated. Huschi, Dorothy, and the two infants disembarked on the road to Dresden, and the wagon moved on. Dorothy's parents lived not far. She can manage alone from here, Huschi thought. The friends embraced. Huschi flagged a truck and continued on.

A day later, she arrived in Dresden. Following directions her mother had hastily scribbled out, Huschi made her way down streets and lanes until passersby pointed out the gates to Villa Kreutzkamm, home to the founders of Dresden's century-old bakery. Frau Kreutzkamm ushered Huschi quickly indoors and restored her with hot breads, Sacher tortes, and spiced tea. The exhausted girl bathed, then slept for two days. On the night of February 13, bright lights filtered in through the living room window. Huschi, Frau Kreutzkamm, and three neighbors watched in amazement as glowing balls of fire suspended from parachutes slowly fell from the sky, illuminating the ground for miles, tails of luminescent gas trailing behind like twine hung from the heavens. Angry bees droned in the blackness.

"My God, they're bombing," the mother whispered, shooing everyone away from the windows. Two couples out for a stroll and caught in the air raid banged at the door. Frau Kreutzkamm let them in and everyone headed for the cellar. The blitz began with a deafening drumbeat of explosions.

"They say the one you don't hear is that one that kills you," one of the strangers quipped. A bomb struck the house next door with the impact of an avalanche, forcing everyone to the floor. As discreetly as she could, from an inner pocket of her coat Huschi withdrew a pistol carried from home and clutched it to her chest. "If this house is hit and I'm trapped beneath rubble," she told herself, "I have my own way out."

The strangers panicked, scrambled up from the cellar and out the front door. Huschi followed and watched from a hole in the wall where a window had been. The city blazed, flames shooting up into the night sky. Then the bombing stopped, and people emerged slowly from their homes. Within the hour a second salvo struck—incendiaries that swallowed oxygen from the air and left thousands of people choking on the ground. Huschi ran back down the steps of the cellar. By early morning, when at last the raids ended, she climbed up the stairs and stared out at a solid wall of flame.

Nothing was left standing. The British Royal Air Force had launched more than eight hundred bombers in the two attacks, incinerating the inner city and killing in excess of thirty-five thousand civilians. She let herself out and picked her way cautiously through the ruins. The strangers from the night before lay dead on the road along with thousands of others. Huschi sidestepped the bodies and simply guessed at the route she should take. Several hours later she emerged on a rise outside Dresden and sat down under a tree, thinking back on another lifetime: horseback riding, ice-skating, house parties. Motherhood and bombs and dead bodies had made scant impact on her assessment of the world. She was young and immortal, and life was to be taken one day at a time. Morning sun had not yet burned away the nighttime haze when bombs again fell on the city—

dropped this time by four hundred bombers of the U.S. 8th Air Force—startling the crows and creating gray mushrooms of smoke on the horizon. She turned from the smoke and walked away.

———

The Sunday after Nudi's party, Denson placed a bag of Florida oranges on the passenger seat of his jeep, picked up Guth and Nudi, and the three headed out to the Bavarian village of Velden an der Vils. They drove past an open market. Workers in blue overalls rolled wooden beer barrels off a flatbed truck. Merchants stacked cabbages and potatoes in waist-high pyramids. Children roasted chestnuts in tin cans by the side of the road. Wood smoke permeated the air. It was on rare occasions such as today that Denson felt reconciled to living in Germany. He was country stock and needed only to cross the border into God's country for the animus that encompassed him at Dachau to fall away. They drove for more than an hour, surrounded by austere birch forests and purling streams reminiscent of those that flowed by his family's plantation in Lafayette. Some men drank to relax. Bill Denson fished.

The cottage where Huschi and her daughter lived was small. In the one downstairs room a cast-iron stove burned wood and served for heating and cooking. A narrow stairway led to three tiny upstairs rooms and a miniature attic accessed by ladder. As they squeezed into the cottage, Denson bowed politely and offered the oranges.

"Manna from heaven!" Huschi said in perfect English. She emptied the bag onto the table and sectioned off a slice for Yvonne, now one year old. Guth and Nudi excused themselves, leaving Denson and Huschi staring at one another in surprise. In the ensuing conversation, perhaps due to the brilliance of the day or the aroma of apple wood emanating from the stove, Denson felt at liberty to listen without distraction. There were no camps, no nightmares, only Huschi and the thousand details that had brought her to that place at that time. When satisfying her curiosity about his life in America, he permitted himself to mention university honors and aristocratic roots, but in other respects he was modest and self-mocking.

His father was the finest lawyer he had ever known, Denson told her. He made no mention of his father's strictness or how sparing he was with affection toward his children. Denson men defended one another as diligently as they did the law, and whatever loneliness they knew was no one's business but their own. When it was Huschi's turn, she told him about growing up on a big country estate, helping nearby village children with their chores so they would have time to play together, and shooting her first pheasant at age eight. Bill suggested they go for a walk.

Outside, they did not see Guth and Nudi. So they sat on a stone bench under a tree and Huschi told him about the blitz, how she had walked for days afterward, the fear of not knowing if her daughter and mother were still alive, and the relief of finally rejoining them two months later at the Irls' home in Bavaria. He listened, not speaking, remembering the lost humanity they had once known in their separate corners of the world, and hoped this would not be the last time he could visit with this remarkable young woman.

9

In the Name of Humanity

"Will you state your full name?"

"Karl Claus Schilling."

"And how old are you?" defense counsel Bates asked.

"Seventy-four years old." Schilling's white hair, goatee, and thick spectacles gave him a scholarly appearance. He punctuated his responses by pointing a thin finger in the manner of a classroom teacher.

"I am a physician and have specialized in tropical diseases since 1898, conducting research in first line malaria from 1899 to 1900 in East Africa and Tanganyika. Also in sleeping sickness and tsetse disease."

"Were you acquainted with anybody in the Rockefeller Foundation?"

"Yes, a Dr. Hackett. I worked for the Rockefeller Foundation in Berlin after receiving a grant of 20,000 marks from them in 1911 for my study of tsetse diseases. I received a second Rockefeller grant of 3,000 marks in 1932 for a studying trip to Rome for my assistant."

"Do you recall being in Italy and meeting a Dr. Conti?" Bates asked. Conti had been Reich chief of public health.

"Yes, in 1941. It was at a conference at the Institute of Infectious Diseases. Dr. Conti stepped up to me and asked how my experiments of malaria were doing. I was of the conviction that immunization with a vaccination against malaria was possible. Dr. Conti said it was proper to continue these experiments in Germany. Then in December I received an invitation from him to make a trip to see Himmler. Himmler himself gave me the order to continue my studies in Dachau."

"Did he tell you that you would be able to use the prisoner patients here for your experiments?"

"I talked with Dr. Conti about voluntary use of prisoners, but as far as I can remember there was no talk about that with Himmler himself."

"How many prisoners here in Dachau did you inoculate with malaria?"

"It must be thousands."

"And what kind of malaria did you infect them with?"

"With benign tertian."

"Ordinarily, professor, is benign tertian fatal?"

"No. It is the most harmless form of malaria."

"What was the purpose you had in mind when you infected those thousands of patients with malaria?"

"The sole purpose was to find a vaccination against malaria—nothing else."

"Will you explain your methods of injection of malaria parasites?"

"The most natural way is to have the human being stung by affected anopheles mosquitoes. The mosquitoes were put into a cage ten centimeters wide and long and just as high. The cage was covered by mosquito gauze. Such a cage was then put in between the legs, or an arm was put on top of the cage. Then the mosquitoes bit through the gauze. The second way is to transmit blood from a person suffering from malaria to a healthy person by means of a syringe. To be entirely correct, I have to state that patients also came to me who were infected with malaria before I ever saw them—some Italians, Spanish, and maybe one Russian."

"After these patients were infected, what was your course of procedure?"

"The body temperature was examined every three hours and the blood every two or three days. After a mosquito bite, incubation took about fourteen days. If I injected the patient into the vein, incubation was only one day. The parasites were to be seen in the blood usually one or several days later."

"Was the patient treated by you immediately after the infection?"

"It depended on the purpose of the injection. One group of my patients was only used to keep up the strains. In order to produce the infection from human being to human being, or from human being to mosquito to human being again, I used several strains of malaria. The second group—that was the more important group—was the cases where I tried to achieve immunization. Most of these were injected repeatedly in order to step up their immunity."

"What drugs did you use for treatment?"

"Mainly quinine, atabrine, and neosalvarsan."

"Did you build up any immunity in any of your patients?"

"I believed some patients had been immunized. In order to prove immunity, I had to infect these persons again. These tests for proof had to be carried out very energetically—again, in several ways: through mosquitoes or through injections. Only this way could I determine whether these people had achieved resistance. I have been asked hundreds of times why I do not work with animals. The simple answer is that malaria of the human being cannot be transmitted to animals. Even highly developed apes and chimpanzees are not receivers of malaria. That is a recognized principle of malaria experiments."

"Were the patients that you used here in Dachau voluntary or involuntary?"

"There were only four or five patients who refused to be immunized. I explained to them that the vaccination would not be dangerous and that these experiments were of great importance and could lead to a great scientific discovery. These patients did not offer any resistance anymore. Maybe I can explain how the selection of the patients took place."

"I wish you would, doctor."

"The highest offices in Berlin determined that thirty patients per month would be made available to me. After the number kept in reserve decreased, I wrote an application for new prisoners. This letter went through the camp physician's office to the commandant, and from there to the camp labor leader. He selected healthy prisoners, and I ordered my assistants to examine these people. I want to state that I never selected patients for these malaria experiments. I let my assistants select these patients—that is, the SS doctors. Of course, the patients were given a thorough physical check. I told my assistants that they should only give me patients that did not suffer from hidden diseases."

Bates had Schilling describe drugs used to lower a temperature and other precautions he had taken to guard against unwanted complications. "Did you instruct your patients to return to you if there was a relapse after they left the hospital?"

"When people were released, I instructed them to come back if they felt sick in any way at all. All patients released were told to come back after two weeks, and if they were having a cold spell or any reappearance of malaria, then they were sent immediately to the laboratory and a blood test was made. If parasites were found, he was admitted again into the sickroom. I told the patient, 'In your own interest, tell us if you have been ill. If you don't tell me or don't report yourself, then how can I treat you?' If patients were afraid of my treatment or if they obtained medicine from outside the camp, that I never knew. For such stupid patients I could do nothing."

"How many cases, doctor, would you say died in Dachau of the one thousand that you infected with malaria?"

"According to my knowledge, not a single one died of uncomplicated malaria. Not a single case was reported to me by Dr. Blaha, who performed the autopsies."

"Did you ever transfer infected patients who were about to die from the malaria station to another station, so they would die in another ward?"

"It would have been a crime against my duty as a doctor," Schilling bridled. "It would have been against my scientific interest not to say the real cause of death. A man who acts in such a way has no idea what scientists consider their highest principles."

"Doctor, if Himmler were to ask you today to conduct these experiments that you conducted at Dachau, what would you answer him?"

"On volunteers, yes. On people who do not volunteer, no. I believe that the burden on the soul of a person who has to do such things without consent is too heavy. But because of the tremendous importance of such a protective inoculation, I would have continued the experiments. In 1932 the Malaria Commission of the League of Nations determined that in that year about seventeen million cases of malaria occurred in the world. You can see what importance such a prophylactic inoculation would have."

"Tell the court just why you accepted this commission to come here to Dachau and perform these experiments on prisoners."

"I stood, you might say, in front of a scale. On the one side there were the thoughts and considerations that each doctor must have if he desires to perform experiments on human beings. On the other side there was the great importance of these experiments. The millions of cases of malarial sickness and death constituted the heavy weight that tipped the scale. I knew of the responsibility, and I took it upon myself in the name of science and, above all, in the name of humanity."

————

"You say you did this in the name of humanity," Denson said on cross-examination. "Then why didn't you experiment on yourself?"

"I myself had malaria in 1933. I was infected at least three times in Africa. If a man has even once malaria, his state of immunity is changed. If you had injected it into me, you wouldn't have proved anything."

"Malaria is a recurring disease, is it not?" Preparing to prosecute Dr. Schilling had required late nights exploring a vast field of knowledge. Discovering such new universes was for Denson, under ordinary circumstances, a great joy. But this excursion was intended to bring down murderers in white coats, and the all-night vigils had succeeded only in exacerbating his sleeplessness.

"Yes."

"Will you tell the court how malaria affects the heart?"

"That might be best answered if I explain how the human body reacts in the early years of childhood."

"Doctor, if you can't answer the question, you have the right to say so. All I want to know is how malaria affects the heart."

"I am going to answer, but in the course of the picture I wish to give you . . ."

Denson turned to the tribunal and said, "I would like to have the witness instructed that later he can elaborate, but now he should just answer those questions that I ask him."

"I don't claim to be scientifically informed," McKeown said rising, "but I do know that scientific questions require more than a yes or no, and I request the court to let Dr. Schilling answer as he sees fit."

"Doctor," Lentz said, turning to the witness, "we do not want to limit your defense, but we do feel it is reasonable to expect you to answer the prosecution's questions as briefly and concisely as possible."

"Acute malaria will take a very small part in a simple heart attack," Schilling said to Denson. "It is different with chronic malaria, in which the heart muscles suffer from the malaria poison. If the patient should die, you will find several muscles shrunken, the heart flabby, possibly diminished in size."

"And what is the effect of malaria on the blood of an average human being?"

"Decrease in blood cells, anemia, and the so-called monolytes—the watery substance of the blood—will increase at the cost of red corpuscles."

"Red corpuscles feed the nervous system of the brain, do they not?"

"The most important changes will be in the brain," Schilling acknowledged. "The smallest capillaries of the brain will be plugged and blocked because the malaria parasites will cling to the walls of the blood vessels."

"Is it not a fact that malaria brings on chills and fever?"

"Yes."

"And the presence of these tends to lower resistance to other diseases, does it not?"

"I don't wish to answer yes to that without comment. I had seven cases like that where malaria patients got typhoid fever. Only two died, a mortality that was no higher than the rest of the camp. So you cannot say."

"I hand you a card marked prosecution's exhibit 131 and ask whether you have ever seen that before."

Schilling looked at the card in disbelief. All such medical files were supposed to have been destroyed before Dachau was handed over to the Americans.

"This is a compilation of the cases I treated with pyramidon—nineteen cases."

"And of those, don't you know as a fact that four of them died?"

"I might say the following about these cases. These experiments were of greatest importance to the entire problem of immunization, as they determined that pyramidon can decrease the temperature so that the patient doesn't feel anything of his fever—he has a normal temperature, even though the parasites are in the blood. After, I determined that I could give up to two grams of pyramidon without any harmful effects on the patient, so I gave this to five people who were in the first stages of malaria. My records were burned, but if I remember correctly, in three patients the temperature rose. I examined them and found two had the characteristic symptoms of typical, real typhus. It was my duty to remove them from the malaria ward. From these five, two recovered and three died, so far as I recall."

"Of the three who died, how much pyramidon had you given them?"

"Two grams per day."

"Never more than two grams per day, is that correct?"

"It is possible that I gave maybe one of the patients three grams."

"At the time you gave the three grams, you were experimenting with him by giving him an overdose, were you not?" Schilling may well have wondered how Denson had managed to assimilate so much information about a highly specialized field of medicine. So far, he disposed of more detail than Schilling himself could recall.

"These were all experiments. This was nothing unusual."

"Three grams was more dangerous than two grams, was it not?"

"Not necessarily."

"As a matter of fact, didn't you give those five men three grams of pyramidon and direct that they receive three grams for the next ten days?"

"That was the intention, to give pyramidon as long as—" then, perhaps realizing the risk in so frank a response, Schilling backtracked in midsentence. "I don't remember that anymore."

Denson leafed through his notebooks until he found a particular reference. "On page three of prosecution's exhibit 134, I will ask you whether or not on February 20, 1945, this man Luzinski was inoculated with five cubic centimeters of blood from a man named Sowa. And on the fifth day of March," Denson said, showing Schilling the exhibit, "this man Luzinski was transferred to the typhus fever ward."

"It says so here."

"How many other men can you recall who were infected with blood from this man Sowa?"

"I cannot remember that."

"You remember an Italian by the name of Calderoni, don't you?"

"I remember the name, yes."

"Isn't it a fact that on twentieth February he was infected with Sowa's blood and that within a few days thereafter he developed typhus fever?"

"That is possible, but with so many people having typhus it is possible he received it not from the injection—and that is what the prosecutor is driving at—but through a natural infection."

"Don't you know that on fourth March the man Calderoni died?"

"How should I know that?" Shilling shrugged. "I cannot remember individual cases."

"So many died that you can't remember any individual cases?"

"No, I don't mean that."

"We'll go to something else. Does malnutrition play a part in determining the frequency and size of doses of neosalvarsan that a person may receive?"

"If a man were suffering from recognizable malnutrition, certainly I would give him smaller doses."

"Your patients received six-tenths of a gram of neosalvarsan at a time, and a number of them were suffering from malnutrition, were they not?"

"Not so severely that neosalvarsan was contraindicative. I had no hesitation giving such a dose to a man suffering from a light case. In the treatment of syphilis, for example, neosalvarsan is given to the patient twice a week until he receives six grams of neosalvarsan—but I never used such amounts."

Denson removed a leaflet from the pile of exhibits and handed it to Schilling.

"Prosecution's exhibit 134B. I ask you to state what it is."

"This is a leaflet which is included in packages of neosalvarsan, issued by the Bayer I.G. Farben company."

"I call your attention to paragraph seven and ask you to read that to the court."

McKeown had no idea where this was going. "I object to the witness reading from a document not in evidence and which the court knows nothing about. Bayer Pharmaceutical Company puts together a lot of drugs that are sold over the counter, and they all contain instructions for public consumption. I submit that instructions to a physician would be entirely different. Even a firm like Bayer would not attempt to instruct physicians in the use of its drugs."

"The objection is overruled."

"'In between doses,'" Schilling read, "'spaces of time should be permitted to elapse, from three to seven days.' These are instructions for the treatment of syphilis," he said. "They are without importance for malaria."

"Read paragraph five, please."

"'Such caution in the use of neosalvarsan is also recommended for patients suffering from a high degree of malnutrition, severe anemia, diabetes, thyroid diseases, goiter, tuberculosis, diseases of the lungs, heart, kidneys and liver. At first, trial doses should be given. Only if it is satisfactory should additional doses be given. The same procedure should be followed for persons suffering from syphilis or complications of the central nervous system.'"

"The document does not confine itself to syphilis, does it?" Denson asked. "It also says to be careful with respect to doses given to people suffering from malnutrition, doesn't it?"

"It says people suffering from 'a high degree' of malnutrition. I did not use neosalvarsan with people suffering from a high degree—high degree, that is the important point."

Denson again leafed through notes in his three-ring binder. "Do you remember a man named Grabowski?"

"I remember the name but I cannot visualize the person."

"To refresh your recollection, in the summer of 1942 isn't it a fact that this man got two or three injections of neosalvarsan and then developed skin disease?"

"How am I to remember that?"

"Did you have an assistant, Adam Cierkowicz?"

"Yes."

"Isn't it a fact that Cierkowicz brought this man to you and told you he should not receive another injection of neosalvarsan?"

"If I could see Grabowski, possibly I could remember it."

"And isn't it a fact that you instructed Cierkowicz to give him another injection of neosalvarsan and that this man broke out in running eczema all over his body—and ultimately he suffered from locomotor ataxia?"

"Yes—but he recovered completely. He recovered from his locomotor ataxia. . . ."

"Do you remember a Polish priest named Stachowski?" Denson asked, stepping up the pace.

"Yes."

"You treated him with neosalvarsan, didn't you?"

"I don't know that anymore."

"When he died, you went over to the morgue to be present when Dr. Blaha performed the autopsy, didn't you?"

"I cannot state that anymore."

"As a matter of fact, did you not order that Father Stachowski's internal organs be sent to the University of Frankfurt?"

"I did not order that."

"You were not an SS man, were you, doctor?"

"No."

"You were not subject to their control?"

"No. I was a free, independent research man."

"And you selected Dachau as the place to perform experiments, rather than another camp, did you not?"

"Yes. I picked Dachau because it was near the place where I was born . . ."

"While you were here, you knew these prisoners were being beaten and executed, did you not?"

"There were all sorts of rumors, but as an outsider I never knew what was going on. . . ."

"It was happening all around you, wasn't it, doctor?"

"No," Schilling said adamantly. "At nine o'clock in the morning I went to my laboratory. It was my principle not to concern myself about things that were not my business."

Testifying later at Nuremburg, Schilling took his claims of ignorance further. "When I came to Dachau," he told the Nuremberg tribunal, "there was a certain rumor, but my will was to not occupy myself with what did not concern my laboratory. I did not work in the camp and didn't look right or left. When I read these descriptions, I said, how is it possible that I never noticed anything?"

―――――――

"These prisoners were guinea pigs upon whom you performed experiments, were they not?" Denson asked, building to the conclusion of his questioning.

"I ask the prosecutor to not use the expression 'guinea pigs' any more," Schilling replied. "It is debasing."

"The only reason you didn't use animal guinea pigs is because malaria cannot be transferred to animals, is that correct?"

"That is correct."

"Instead, you used human guinea pigs, is that not correct?"

"I could not use an animal guinea pig—it would have made no sense. . . ."

"So you substituted humans instead, is that correct?"

"It would not have made any sense to use animals . . ."

"Just answer my question, doctor."

"That is my answer."

"No further questions."

————

Bates rose for redirect. "You infected one Father Wiecki with malaria, did you not? And he is alive and sitting in the courtroom today, is he not?"

"Yes, I saw him today."

"You gave him the same amount of neosalvarsan that you administered to other patients suffering from the same degree of malnutrition?"

"Yes. May I say something?" Schilling stood and faced the tribunal. "I have worked out this great amount of labor—it would be really a terrible loss if I could not finish the report about my experiments, as this report could be the substance of further research. It could be of enormous profit for humanity. I don't ask you as a court. I ask you personally do what you can do to help me finish this report. It is two-thirds already complete. I need only a table and a chair and a typewriter, and then I could finish this report. It would be an enormous help for science, for my colleagues," then turning to the prosecution, he added, "and a good way to rehabilitate myself."

Schilling enjoyed an international reputation for his medical research. Pleas for clemency on his behalf arrived from universities around the world. One might assume that he had initially wanted to do good, to find cures that would benefit mankind. He accepted Himmler's offer to work at Dachau because it meant having access to more facilities than any hospital in wartime Germany could offer—and access to victims for his experiments. Schilling could not have avoided seeing the crimes that were daily being committed around him, and if he were to protest he risked losing the facilities and "human guinea pigs" at his disposal. Whether his silence was motivated by fear, indifference, or ambition to be the one who went down in history for having discovered a cure for malaria, he had turned his back on what was too obvious to ignore. And that, along with his own crimes, made him in Denson's view—and the estimation of the tribunal—part of the common design.

––––––––

In his later years Denson often spoke of another physician tried at Dachau. Hans Eisele was a decent enough doctor before the war. Then he was sent to the Russian front, where he was wounded and transferred back to serve in the camps. His first assignment was concentration camp Sachsenhausen, where he was known as "the Angel." Whenever a prisoner came to him suffering from exhaustion, Eisele prescribed rest and rehabilitation and excused him from further work details. He made no distinction: Jews, Czechs, all received fair treatment. After transfer to Dachau, Eisele's behavior changed. He began to cuff prisoners around and once kept a transport standing on the roll call place without food or water for two days. Later he was transferred to Buchenwald where he "exceeded every possible baseness" and where he was known as "the Butcher." Instead of treating a prisoner's infected finger, Eisele cut it off. The longer he lived inside the camps, the crueler he became—"like a snowball rolling down a hill," Denson explained to students at Touro Law School years later, "getting greater and greater and greater," until Eisele was resectioning stomachs of living prisoners, without anesthesia, for practice. He had become cruel because cruelty had become commonplace. When speaking of Eisele, Denson never failed to mention that he was the son of a Lutheran minister. His point was that, under certain circumstances, it could happen to anyone.

Five years after his conviction in the Buchenwald trial, Eisele was pardoned by the U.S. government and released from prison. The province of Bavaria loaned him ten thousand marks "for losses due to the war," and the Butcher went back to medical practice in Munich. In 1955, when fresh evidence of his sadistic experiments surfaced, he fled and was granted asylum in Nasser's Egypt. Hans Eisele settled in Cairo, built a lucrative practice, and peacefully lived out the rest of his life.

10

The Clock
of Civilization

I f December 12, 1945, had been a normal day, Denson would have risen, shaved, showered, listened to the news on the radio, marveled at the rising paranoia over Communism, then descended to the dining room, breakfasted on toast and marmalade, and set out for his Dachau office fifteen kilometers to the west. If it had been a normal day he would have driven through the gates of the camp, arrived at his office, studied notes from yesterday's proceedings, prepared a pot of coffee, received his crew, handed out assignments, and taken a deep breath before entering the courtroom for another procession of horror stories. But December 12 was not a normal day, and Denson had again not slept. This was the final day of the Dachau trial, and he had spent the night writing his closing remarks.

There are two versions of Denson's closing comments. One is hand-written in pencil. The other is the one he gave spontaneously in court, transcribed and deposited with the National Archives in Washington. The handwritten version is a laudable piece of prose, succinct, professionally framed, and reasonably argued. The extemporaneous remarks he delivered in court, however, are memorable.

————

Douglas T. Bates and his defense team had also prepared powerful closing remarks: strong statements to summarize an equally strong showing in the courtroom. During the four weeks of trial, they pleaded that the camp was established and run on the orders of Himmler and the Reich Security Main Office in Berlin; that rations, clothing, medical and other supplies conformed to standards set by these superior agencies; and that Dachau was a good camp "as concentration camps go." They provided evidence that some defendants were no longer in Dachau when their crimes were supposedly committed; that others were rumored to be present at a beating or torture, but never actually seen. Above all, they argued that the accused only did what all soldiers do: follow orders. Nonetheless, the outcome was clear. None of the defense lawyers believed they would win acquittals. Their strategy was to convince the tribunal that superior orders weighed heavily on actions inside Dachau, and that the prosecution's evidence was mostly hearsay and insufficient to justify death sentences.

————

Before Denson could offer prosecution's closing remarks, Bates made a surprising motion. "If the court please, I have a newspaper article here from the *Daily Journal* dated October 19, 1945, reporting that a husband got ten lashes for beating his wife under a sixty-four-year-old statute of the Maryland law, and I offer that in evidence. . . ."

"And I object," Denson said, "on the grounds that it is irrelevant and immaterial."

"If the court please," Bates replied, "some of the accused are charged with beatings on orders that came down from official sources. I submit that beatings so imposed have the same efficacy in law as the beatings given under a sixty-four-year-old Maryland statute."

"Before this Maryland flogging was imposed," Denson said, "this man had the right to be tried by a jury of his peers or other tribunal where justice was dealt out—not by the Gestapo."

Bates would not let go. "Mr. President, you yourself stated just a minute ago that this court is being governed by the laws of humanity. These men were obeying a law which was then in existence in Germany. They were no more inhumane than the persons who administered the beatings in Maryland."

Lentz shook his head. "The objection is sustained. Continue."

"May it please the court, at this time I will offer into evidence *Life* magazine dated October 22, 1945, with particular reference to the caption: 'Bizarre Bookbinder in Brooklyn Uses Skins from Snakes, Skunks, and Humans.'"

Denson was up again. "Objection, may it please the court. Irrelevant and immaterial."

"If the court pleases," Bates said, "there has been a great deal of testimony as to the alleged atrocity of skinning human bodies for gloves, slippers, and so forth. A man in the United States of America uses human skin as bookbinding. Is that an atrocity, or are we being governed here by selective rules of humanity?"

Denson was adamant. "That has absolutely no comparison with the facts presented in this case. This skin was taken from prisoners put in here against their will, who died of mistreatment and starvation, which these people," pointing to the accused, "inflicted upon them. If a man walked around Dachau with a good-looking tattoo on his chest, he was marked for the hangman. There is no comparison whatever."

"The reason we offer these articles," Bates continued, "is because a charge of atrocity has been made. If the use of human skin for any purpose, be it bookbinding or handbags, is going to be considered as an atrocity here in Dachau, then it is certainly an atrocity in Brooklyn."

"The objection is sustained," Lentz again ruled. "The article will not be received in evidence. Colonel, your closing remarks?"

————

Denson rose. The penciled document lay on the table before him. He let it lie there and began speaking.

"May it please the court, this case has been long. This court has heard the oral testimony of over one hundred seventy witnesses and we make no apologies for the testimony of any of them. From the crowned heads of Europe to the lowliest criminal, we feel that each and every one has respected his oath and delivered himself of the facts as he knew them to be.

"It may be pointed out by defense counsel that some testified falsely, that on a certain date they saw Becher beat a priest so brutally that he died, and Becher states he was not at that place at that particular time. And the witness may indeed be in error in that respect. Monday was not the nineteenth of December but just another day filled with the execution of young Russians and the hanging of loyal Poles who would not stoop to don the SS uniform of infamy. Such events made their impression. Certainly that was the case when the crippled lad who testified here met his father who had been beaten to death. You can't expect that boy to remember the date on which this occurred, but he would never forget the name of Willy Tempel as it came from the lips of his dying father. It is only logical that these persons would confuse dates, living in holes in the ground amid indescribable filth and without access to any kind of calendar.

"I wish to emphasize that these forty men are not charged with killing. The offense is in a common design to kill, to beat, to torture and starve. True enough, the testimony introduced here stamps Mahl and Tempel as most brutal and sadistic murderers. But we are not trying these men for specific acts of misconduct. We are trying them for their participation in this common design.

"That there was such a common design is illustrated by the magnitude of the operation. The record shows that between 1940 and 1945, 161,939 prisoners were processed through Dachau. It is inconceivable that this operation could be done without the cooperation of those whose participation brought about the recorded deaths of over twenty-five thousand in the same period. I say 'recorded' because it appears from the testimony that thousands of other deaths were not recorded. It is ridiculous to contend that these deaths were isolated cases of misconduct and not the product of a common design.

"The defense will argue that under Weiss, conditions were different. But this change was not the product of any kindness on the part of Weiss. Conditions in Germany were different when Weiss came here. Manpower and labor were sorely needed to satisfy her demands for a war that was to rage on more than one front. Why waste this pool of manpower? The frugal yet sadistic mind of the Nazis again exerted itself. We have witnesses who testified that prisoners worked longer under Weiss, a minimum of eleven hours a day, and received less food. No regard was had for the fact that total exhaustion and ultimate death were inevitable.

"It is ridiculous to contend that these deaths were not the product of a common design. The segregation of the Jews and the systematic looting of their valuables and clothing, the invalid transports that took thousands to their deaths, the mass killings at the crematory and rifle range, the evacuation transports that left Dachau and the transports that brought prisoners to this indescribable hell, the cannibalism on some of these transports that resulted before a man was blessed with death, the overcrowding, lack of sanitary facilities, starvation, disease, destruction of human dignity, and utter disregard of all human rights as evidenced in particular by the experiments that were conducted here—all point with unerring accuracy to the presence of this barbaric common design.

"Each one in the dock was a link in the chain. Without the performance of each one, that chain and the entire scheme would have been broken. It is contended that a doctor had to attend every execution. Puhr, Eisele, Witteler, all testified that the killing could not have been carried out without their participation. The more that is made of the fact that they had to attend, the greater becomes their culpability. For obviously if they had refused, the killing would not have occurred."

He extracted a legal form from the pile of documents on the prosecution table. "I call the court's attention to a case decided by the Theater Judge Advocate's Office, which involved the rape of a girl by three soldiers. One soldier never had intercourse with the victim but merely acted as her jailer, yet he was also convicted. The opinion states: 'This accused gave direct assistance to the first two in the raping of the girl. Distinction between principals and aiders and abettors has been abolished by Federal statute.' These guards, the jailers of the prisoners in Dachau, are as guilty as the principals. And may it please the court, from the evidence it is apparent that each and every man sitting there in that dock had his part to play in the ultimate execution of this common design or scheme.

"It might be urged on the court that some of these accused did not participate in this common design because they had no knowledge of it. Such a contention is absurd. Any man who had a chance to observe the prisoners in Dachau could see starvation literally scream from their faces. To say that these people were not aware of this design is utterly contemptible."

Having disposed of defense's lesser arguments, Denson attacked their main contention. "It will be argued that these men were soldiers and as such were required to carry out their orders. This type of defense has been referred to as superior orders and has been rejected for obvious reasons as a defense. I call the court's attention to volume one of Wharton, paragraph 376: 'The fact that a party accused of crime did the act as the agent of another cannot be set up as a defense. Such person cannot relieve himself of the criminal responsibility of the act.'

"Now, in the realm of international law, I call the court's attention to page 180 of the seventh edition of Wheaton's *International Law*: 'Men who have committed violations of international law are not entitled to the privileges accorded to honorable prisoners of war, and the fact that they acted under orders cannot furnish valid excuse. By such shifting of responsibility we arrive at the conclusion that millions, including responsible officers of higher commands, are to be held free from blame regardless of what orders they have perpetrated. One person is answerable, namely the monarch or the president of the belligerent state, as the case may be. This is a conclusion which neither reasoning nor humanity can accept.'

"Practically every prisoner in Dachau was there because he had the intestinal fortitude to refuse to obey the orders of sadistic Nazis. If the prisoners were willing to endure killings, beatings, tortures, starvation, and death to prove the courage of their convictions, why should this court permit a lesser standard of courage to be applied to these murderers, that they may escape punishment for their inhuman offenses? And that is what this court would be doing if they gave credence to the fact that they may have received superior orders.

"This court is determined to administer justice, and I say it is only just to require each of the accused to have said, 'No, I will not participate in this nefarious scheme, regardless of the consequences.' These men's victims suffered, countless thousands of them, because they had the courage to refuse to do what, to them, was wrong. Then why in heaven's name should any of these men who are responsible for those deaths and starvation and suffering and distortions in body, mind, and soul receive the slightest mercy for failing to refuse to do what was obviously wrong? The answer that 'I was ordered to do it' has no part in this case."

By now even the most incredulous members of the tribunal must have been converted to Denson's side. While he may have referred to paper notes, his comments were emerging spontaneously, from conviction, in unscripted bursts. His team must have been equally impressed: an impassioned William Denson had taken command of the courtroom.

"These accused have committed a war crime that has shocked the sensibilities of a civilized world. These acts were committed by individuals who profess to belong to that civilization, but it is enough to make one stop and wonder whether they are not beasts. Certainly they cannot lay claim to being human in any respect. These accused will have turned back the hands of the clock of civilization at least a thousand years if this court in any manner condones the conduct that has been presented to it. And I am sure that this court will impose a sentence by which the world at large can understand that such crimes will not be again tolerated on this earth. I believe, and am convinced, that every man in that dock has forfeited his right to mingle in decent society."

Lentz cracked his gavel. "This court stands adjourned."

————

The following day at nine o'clock, Lentz called the court to order and German defense counsel Von Posern rose, holding a sheet of paper. Though thin, his face was round and his forehead wide, with a balding scalp and deep, heavyset eyes that peered out from a history that others were not invited to share. He spoke in broken English, preferring direct contact with the American tribunal to relays through a translator.

"May it please the court, *Befehl ist Befehl*—an order is an order. It had to be obeyed, however its quality was. This was not only a custom in the Third Reich, where the duty to obedience was more severe, but the USA seems to have a great attention to this. Studying the country war order of the USA, I found the following text: 'Individuals of armed forces will not be punished for these offenses, violations and customs and laws of war, in case they are committed under the orders or sanction of their government or commanders.' If the USA gave their GIs the upper-mentioned protection, it must appeal as equitable and fair to give the same protection to the victims of National Socialism, those who had to keep quiet and obey, for they too were the victims.

"Here is defendant Mahl," he announced, gesturing behind him, "who was told he had to take part of an execution. He gets led up to the execution place and receives the order to place the rope on the neck of a man who shall get hanged. If he had not obeyed to the order, his own execution would have taken place. I beg and propose for a discharge in this case for the reason of actions in state of necessity. And how many others are from this same nature and deserving to be discharged?

"High court, a trial looked on by the whole world is nearing to its end. In this chapter of history I am standing alone as the only German defending Germans before you. I stood up for my former comrades, whatever the world may say about them, because a ring of fellowship grew around us in those days of need. If some of the actions of the defendant prisoners seem incomprehensible for you, I beg you to account how long these men were kept behind electrically loaded fences, what sufferings *they* went through. All this obviously affects the nerves, changes opinions, alters actions. Gentlemen of the court, find your judgment in the heart and not in public opinion. In your hand life and fate of these men is lying who have suffered immensely for the sake of justice."

———

Von Posern resumed his place at the defense table and Capt. Dalwin Niles stood, no doubt more puzzled than encouraged by his co-counsel's remarks.

"I am not exactly sure just what is to be said on behalf of these defendants. As the court will recall, at the beginning of this case we asked what the charge against the defendants was. I find myself wondering the same thing at the conclusion of the case. Where is the alleged common design? Who made it? Where did it take place? When? If that common design has not been proved, how can we prove that common design has *not* been made?"

Niles was making a critical mistake by calling common design "the charge against these defendants." The defendants were in fact not charged with common design but with violations of the laws and usages of war. The phrase "common design" appeared in the particulars of the charge, which proposed that the defendants had acted "in pursuance of a common design" to violate the laws and usages of war.

"The prosecution has stated," Niles continued, "that if this court should condone the acts of these defendants, it would turn the clock of civilization back a thousand years. I submit that if an American court fails to judge each one of these defendants on proof of acts that he committed, the clock of civilization and of American justice will likewise be turned back a thousand years. And what is proof in any court, including a military court? Proof is not vindictiveness or prejudice. Proof is fact, shown beyond reasonable doubt. Let us look at the 'proof.'

"As to Welter, there was an absurd attempt to state that he might be responsible for certain deaths. This was brought out by Dr. Blaha, but he stated that the only deaths he could remember took place in 1944—the year after Welter had left. It has been proved that Welter was not here voluntarily but was placed here by the German army and did his duty as a soldier would anywhere.

"In commenting on superior orders, counsel for the prosecution quoted from the criminal code. But this case is being tried under international law, and we have no exact precedent for superior orders. Chief Justice Jackson expressed his opinion: 'Undoubtedly there is a circumstance under which the notion of obedience to superior orders should be sustained. If a soldier is drafted because of service duty and is ordered to an execution detail, he cannot be held responsible for the legality of the sentence he is carrying out.'

"I submit that that is the case of Eichberger. The court heard his testimony. He was a soldier. You saw him on the stand. He was wounded and is without his leg at the present time. Because of that disability he was ordered to Dachau. He had nothing to say about that. He had nothing to do but to carry out orders.

"Then we come to Lausterer. I ask the court: What is his act in furtherance of a common design? One witness, Opitz, testified against him but could not identify him in the dock. What credence can be given to such testimony? The prosecution would also have the court believe that because Lausterer was present on a transport, he is responsible for anything that happened there. He attempted to get billets, to get food, to do anything that might relieve their condition. Is that the act of a brutal man, as every one of the defendants has been characterized by the prosecution? Is there any proof that he aided or abetted any of these crimes in Dachau, in any manner? I submit that there is not one single thing that can be ascribed to Lausterer.

"As to Trenkle, he has been charged with participation, by his own statement, in executions of men convicted of sabotage and looting. Under the law, these were capital offenses, and he had orders to carry out. He stands in a position of carrying out superior orders which, as far as he knew, were the orders of competent superior authority.

"As to Niedermeyer, the only charge is working in the crematory. I submit that working at the crematory was the same as the job of grave digger. Niedermeyer performed no more than disposing of bodies in a sanitary method. There is no indication or proof that he knew of any common design, or plan, or that any act of his was criminal.

"Eichelsdorfer was never even a member of the SS. He was a member of the Wehrmacht and stands in the unfortunate position to have gotten sick, and as a result was transferred to Dachau. He was placed at the Kaufering camp and told that he was commanding officer. I submit that if there is anything that can be ascribed to him, it is merely that he was an old, sick man and failed to take the corrective action that a young, vigorous man might have taken.

"As to Tempel." Here Niles hesitated. "It is admitted by Tempel that he beat prisoners on some occasions with a cable or a rubber hose. That is in the court's province to decide the degree of culpability and the punishment. The other accusations against him—there have been attempts to ascribe to him certain deaths. No proof, again, of those deaths—only accusations."

Niles sat and Capt. John May stood to speak on behalf of the accused under his charge. Like Denson, May's thick Southern drawl rolled out across the courtroom. "May it please the court, I would like to say at the outset with respect to the address delivered by the chief counsel for the prosecution, I am sure that all the members of the defense agree wholeheartedly with his indictment of Nazis. As wonderful as it was, the speech should not have been delivered at Dachau but at Nuremberg. That is where Nazism is on trial, where the big frogs are and not the little polliwogs.

"Also, he amused us with his treatise on orders. I did not know that in this new era of things we didn't have to obey orders. Had I known that when Colonel Straight ordered me to come on the defense, I would have been a happier man to know that I didn't have to come. Because on the defense—the unpopular side in this case—we four have had to walk alone. Ridicule and shame have been heaped upon us because we represent the defense, through no choosing of our own. Little did we know that we didn't have to obey.

"But since it was an order that we understood had to be obeyed, I thought of the words of Robert E. Lee when he said, 'Duty is the sublimest word in the English language.' If it was my duty to defend Nazis, then it was my duty to defend them with all my vigor and power. We could have sat idly by, made a feeble objection now and then for the record, and let it go. But that is not my idea of duty. When called upon to defend, it was our duty to defend with every power we knew and all the legal training and experience we had. I think we've done that.

"I don't think I have to explain that I am a Southerner. I am the grandson of a Confederate soldier. He would be a war criminal today because he guarded some Yankee prisoners—and not a one of them escaped.

"There is a thing called conscience," May said. "And in the wee hours of the morning when we can't sleep, I am glad that we defense counselors can say that the blood of nobody will be on our conscience. We have stood here, with all the power and law that we knew to be right and just, to defend what we think are innocent men.

"Take old Grandpa Lippmann—they referred to him as 'grandpa.' He didn't have part in any scheme. He's innocent. Nor will the blood of Degelow, whose identity was mistaken, be on my conscience. The blood of Schulz, the simple carpenter who had to do a job, will not be on my conscience. What about Filleboeck? Relative to the testimony that he was present at the execution of the ninety Russians, one witness says yes, six witnesses say no. Filleboeck says he wasn't there. Shall the word of one prejudiced man be the cause of the execution of this man, when all the evidence shows that he never attended, simply because this one witness thirsts for revenge on the SS?

"Kirsch and Kramer are charged with beatings. Consider the witnesses: all out for vengeance. No proof. One witness says, 'He slapped somebody who was then taken to the hospital, and he died two days later.' The next witness: 'Slapped a prisoner, took him to the hospital, died two days later.' Over and over the same story of a man being slapped and two days later he was dead. Pass sentence on Kirsch? Nothing definite was proved against him. All is supposition, inference.

"So there are weak links, and also some missing links, in that so-called chain of common design. Hitler is one of the missing links. He started it. Himmler is another. But you can't bring them in, so you pick forty Germans and accuse them of common design. What about Dr. Blaha? He was a prisoner here. He was forced to do things that I presume he didn't want to do. Blaha admits that he performed operations and took hearts out of people—hearts that were still beating. Do you suppose that he wanted to do that? No more than Mahl wanted to put the noose around the neck of others.

"What about Seybold, the prosecution witness? He was just like Mahl, a *kapo*, a prisoner ordered to do these things. Why don't they bring him in and make him a defendant? Is it because he was willing to turn state's evidence that he went free, and Mahl is sitting here accused? Somebody has to pay for Dachau, so we go out and pick forty people—it doesn't matter who they are. You can go into the courtroom and pick out forty Germans, and get the same thing. Somebody must pay for Dachau.

"Yes, the prosecution has had the popular side. They had everything on their side. Their witnesses came eagerly seeking revenge. 'From the crowned heads of Europe to the lowliest criminal,' to borrow a phrase from our distinguished chief prosecutor, it was easy for them to get witnesses. Everybody wants to punish somebody.

"In the words of Justice Jackson at Nuremberg, what we do here history will judge us for tomorrow. In the mad cry for justice, let us not stain our flag with innocent blood. If somebody must hang for Dachau, let's hang him on the truth, not on vengeance."

Lentz struck his gavel. "The court will adjourn until eight-thirty tomorrow morning."

11

Judgment at Dachau

"The court will come to order."

Defense counsel Major McKeown stood and addressed the tribunal. "Mr. President, gentlemen of the court. As has been said by Captain May, some of us were a little perturbed by this assignment. But General Eisenhower made a statement that the occupation forces are over here not to govern Germany but to oversee and guide the German people in the methods that we know are democratic in principle. For that reason, I take a different outlook on my association with the defense of SS men—of Nazis, so to speak. Because we are *all* here on orders. Can this court say definitely to the American public and to the world at large watching this case that superior orders of an army officer are not to be followed?

"A great hue and cry has been sent up by the prosecution that doctors attended executions. How atrocious! We do the same thing in the United States. No execution in any of the thirty-six states that recognize capital punishment is performed without the presence of a doctor to certify as to death. In New York, in the Tombs where there are electrocutions, a doctor is sent there by the governor. It is the same in Pennsylvania. In New Jersey twenty-three witnesses are required, including newspapermen.

"If the court please, there is a statement which is indicative of the difficulties with which the defense has had to contend. The witnesses testifying against Langleist stated that he took a prisoner and threw him in the gravel pit, as a result of which that prisoner died. I asked him what he had to say about that. To me, never a truer word was spoken in any courtroom. He said, 'The witness is mistaken, but for me that mistake is a fatal error.' I think the court will remember his words, 'A fatal error, that mistake.'

"To be fair. That is all we want to demonstrate to the world. That regardless of the pain and suffering and tortures of hell that some men have gone through, that we can still be fair. That is what we have to do today, if it please the court. To demonstrate to the world that we Americans can fight a war, can win a war, and still be fair with the conquered, regardless of their position in that war. People have suggested to me personally that we Americans are putting on a show, that this is only a theater. That is what we have been accused of. That is the reason that I take pleasure in my role as assistant defense counsel, because it hasn't been theater.

"As to Dr. Schilling, he is a scientist, a man seventy-four years of age, who spent his life studying science, studying tropical diseases. At the beginning of this conflict he was called upon to discover, if possible, something that would relieve the troops suffering from malaria. Back in 1902, Walter Reed was called upon by the American army to discover the cure for the scourge that was affecting the American troops—yellow fever. Walter Reed experimented on human beings. He paid them each two hundred dollars for their submission to his experiment. He used immigrants, some of whom probably didn't understand or know what he was talking about, but for two hundred dollars probably would do anything. And people died under the inoculations of yellow fever performed by Walter Reed.

"The court has indicated, prior to the time this case started, that it would consider the doctrine of reasonable doubt. Where there is reasonable doubt, it should be resolved in the favor of a defendant. We on the defense feel that we have done our duty, and hope that the court feels the same."

––––––––

Denson came out swinging. "May it please the court, it is an insult upon the administration of justice in the United States to compare the executions that took place here with executions that take place in the thirty-six states that have capital punishment. How in the world could counsel sincerely contend that determinations of the Reich Security Main Office, where a man never had the opportunity to be heard, can be compared with an execution that our judicial courts determine, arrived at through the principles of due process of law and in the courts of your own country? It is an insult to the intelligence of this court to make such a comparison."

Denson's team shared his outrage. Unlike the public, who learned of concentration camps from flickering newsreel images and printed magazine photos, no screen separated the prosecutors from what had occurred. They reached out and touched evidence with their own hands and, like liberation soldiers, faced the raw reality of Nazi Germany. But unlike soldiers, who could immediately respond to what they found—shoot guns or carry prisoners to freedom—Denson and his team arrived too late to pull a trigger or care for the wounded. So they fought here before the tribunal with the weapons of logic, legal precedent, and passionate speech.

"An appeal was made here with respect to Dr. Schilling. They say that he was just a scientist. No, may it please the court, he was nothing more than a common murderer. I believe it is a disgrace upon the memory of Dr. Walter Reed to mention Schilling in the same breath. They told about the use of individuals in the United States as human guinea pigs. The only answer is that in the United States they do have a regard for the personal rights of the individual. In the United States a man is used as a result of his own consent, not forced into a ward where he is involuntarily subjected to Dr. Schilling's needles and mosquitoes.

"I hate to go back into a discussion of each man individually, because I do not want the court to feel that it is necessary to establish individual acts of misconduct to show guilt or innocence. If he participated in this common design, as evidence has shown, it is sufficient to establish his guilt."

Knowing that the defense would offer reasons why the tribunal should be lenient in their findings, Denson now argued against any mitigation of sentences.

"Every man who is sitting on the court unquestionably has sympathy for people who are married, who have children—but sympathy has no part in this case whatsoever. Think of the thousands of individual prisoners who also had wives, children, whose families were absolutely exterminated by the operation of this common design, which would never have been possible except for the participation of each and every man in that dock today. I am satisfied that this court cannot ever be charged with being soft in the rendering of its findings and the sentences in this case."

————

Douglas T. Bates rose and stood silently for a moment, hands folded. "There have been stormy days," he began slowly, "and quiet days. Irritating moments and bland moments. By and large we consider that we have been treated at the hands of this court with tolerance and understanding."

Then a harshness entered his language that had not been there throughout the trial. "Counsel for the prosecution has indulged in quite a display of epithets. That indulgence was the theme throughout this process. Epithets—vicious, sadistic, savage, murdering epithets."

Stenographers and reporters, war crimes staff, operations officers, everyone who followed the proceedings knew there had been tension between the prosecution and the defense. But a formal professionalism had kept their exchanges in court civil despite occasional flare-ups. All bets were off now, and with these few lethal opening remarks Bates made it clear he was about to challenge the capacity of the court to conduct a fair trial.

"There has been a concerted effort on the part of counsel for the prosecution to supplement glaring deficiencies in the proof by the use of strong adjectives and adverbs. I submit that the court will not be deceived into thinking such epithets anything other than what they are: bald and otherwise unconvincing statements.

"The surest safeguard against totalitarianism is uncompromising adherence to the administration of justice, which does not humor heat and revenge but rather protects men from them—and before I go too far, it is necessary for me to presume that the court recognizes the forty men who are defendants in this trial as men and not as beasts.

"From all directions is heard a primitive cry: 'Blood, for the atonement of Dachau!' It matters not whose blood, so long as it is German. Preferably SS. This court is sitting by authority of our country and under its flag, and it has the heavy responsibility of protecting these forty individuals from such unrelenting bitterness and hate.

"The most talked-of phrase has been 'common design.' Let us be honest," Bates proposed, "and admit that common design found its way into the judgment for the simple expedient of trying forty defendants in one mass trial instead of having to try one each in forty trials. Where is the common design? Conspicuous by its absence, established for the purpose of trapping some defendants against whom there was a shortage of proof—by arguing, for example, that if Schoepp was a guard in the camp, then he was equally responsible for everything that went on. There are guards at each gate of this American post today. Is it not far-fetched to say they are responsible for crimes that may be committed within the confines of this large area? If every one of the defendants is guilty of participating in that large common design, then it becomes necessary to hold responsible every member of the Nazi Party and every citizen of Germany who contributed to the waging of total war—and I submit that can't be done.

"I read this in *Life* magazine today: 'Justice cannot be measured quantitatively. If the whole of Germany is guilty of murder, no doubt it would be just to exterminate the German people. The real problem is to know who is guilty of what.' Perhaps the prosecution has arrived at a solution as to how an entire people can be indicted as an acting part of a mythical common design.

"And a new definition of murder has been introduced along with common design. This new principle of law says, 'I am given food and told to feed these people. The food is inadequate. I feed them with it, and they die of starvation. I am guilty of murder.' Germany was fighting a war she had lost six months before. All internal business had completely broken down. I presume people like Filleboeck and Wetzel should have reenacted the miracle at Galilee, where five loaves and fishes fed a multitude.

"There has been a lot of impressive law read by the chief counsel, and it is good law—Miller, Wharton. The sad thing is that little of it is applicable to the facts in this case. Perhaps we have not been diligent enough in seeking applicable law. Some think the prosecution has found applicable law in the Rules of Land Warfare on the doctrine of superior orders. We have no intention of arguing that executions by the German Reich were due process. Nevertheless, we contend that executions were the result of law of the then recognized regime in Germany and that members of the firing squad were simple soldiers acting in the same capacity as in any military organization in the world."

With this unembellished deconstruction of Denson's main charge, Bates reached his peroration. "I quote a speech by Justice Jackson in which he warns against the use of the judicial process for nonjudicial ends and attacks cynics who 'see no reason why courts, just like other agencies, should not be policy weapons.' If we want to shoot Germans as a matter of policy, let it be done as such. But don't hide the deed behind a court. If you are determined to execute a man in any case, there is no occasion for a trial. The world yields no respect for courts that are organized merely to convict.

"If law cloaks a bloodbath in Germany, the idea of law will be the real victim. Lynch law, of which we have known a good deal in America, often gets the right man. But its aftermath is a contempt for the law, a contempt that breeds more criminals. It is far, far better that some guilty men escape than that the idea of law be endangered. In the long run, the idea of law is our best defense against Nazism in all its forms.

"In closing, I ask permission to paraphrase a great statesman. Never in the history of judicial procedure has so much punishment been asked against so many on so little proof."

The court adjourned and the tribunal withdrew to determine its verdicts.

———

Winter had turned cold. The courtroom windows were closed, and a strangling compression in the air blended with clouds of cigarette smoke to keep spectators shifting in their seats. Guth, who had never been part of a prosecution team before, sat calculating. He knew the facts were on their side, but if the tribunal was not convinced of the common design idea, they might find evidence against some of the accused flimsy. Guth figured those would get off. Denson kept a stolid face. One hour and thirty minutes later, the tribunal resumed their places at the long wooden table beneath the Stars and Stripes. It had taken them less than three minutes per defendant to arrive at verdicts in one of the largest judicial actions ever organized. Even if history looked back and judged his work charitably, Denson might have imagined one hour and thirty minutes to be a shockingly short time in which to determine the fate of forty men.

"The court will come to order," Lentz announced. "The court cautions the audience that it will tolerate no expressions of approval or disapproval.

Will the accused and counsel rise?" The accused stood. The lawyers and officers behind the prosecution and defense tables stood.

"The court in closed session, at least two-thirds of the members concurring in each finding, finds all the defendants guilty of all particulars and charges. You may sit down."

The announcement came as no surprise to Denson. No one had doubted that a U.S. Army tribunal would find Nazis guilty of war crimes. The true determinant of his team's success—the sentences—would not be known until the following day. One by one the defense lawyers introduced pleas for clemency, as Denson had anticipated. McKeown explained that Weiss had lost everything, that his mother was seventy years old and depended on him for her support; that Schilling was seventy-four and that his work might still be of some use to humanity. John May went next, listing reasons why the defendants he represented deserved consideration. Dalwin Niles followed, listing his clients' extenuating circumstances. Then it was over.

"Nothing further," Bates told the tribunal.

"Court is adjourned until nine o'clock tomorrow," Lentz said, "at which time sentences will be announced."

Tribunal, accused, witnesses, and spectators filed out of the courtroom. Only Denson and Guth remained, putting away papers. The room was empty. Denson put a hand on Guth's shoulder. The two men embraced.

"Amazing grace," Denson said quietly. "Amazing grace."

————

"It is the desire of this tribunal," Lentz said the following morning, "to announce sentences in open court. We will do that only if the audience demonstrates its ability to maintain complete silence.

"The evidence presented to this court convinced it beyond any doubt that the Dachau concentration camp and its by-camps subjected its inmates to killings, beatings, tortures, indignities, and starvation to an extent and degree that necessitates the indictment of everyone, high and low, who had anything to do with the conduct and operation of the camp. This court reiterates that it sits in judgment under international law and under such laws of humanity and human behavior that are commonly recognized by civilized people.

"Many of the acts committed at Dachau," Lentz said, "clearly had the sanction of the high officials of the German Reich and the de facto laws and customs of the German government. It is the view of this court, however, that when a state sets itself up above reasonably recognized international law, or transcends civilized customs of human behavior, then the individuals effecting such policies must be held responsible for their part in violating international law and the customs and laws of humanity.

"The accused and counsel will stand. The accused will present themselves before the bench individually in the order in which they are numbered." Number one, Dachau's former commandant, made his way down from the prisoners' dock and presented himself at attention before the tribunal.

"Martin Weiss, the court in closed session, at least two-thirds of the members present at the time the vote was taken, concurring, sentences you to death by hanging at such time and place as higher authority may direct." One by one, the Germans presented themselves to receive their sentence.

"Doctor Klaus Carl Schilling, the court in closed session, at least two-thirds of the members present at the time the vote was taken, concurring, sentences you to death by hanging at such time and place as higher authority may direct.

"Johann Kick—death by hanging . . ."

In solemn, staccato tone the tribunal announced thirty-eight death sentences. Lentz finished reading the sentences and turned to Denson.

"Does the prosecution have anything further to be presented to the court?"

"The prosecution has nothing further at this time."

"I have a request," Bates said, rising from the defense table. "Lieutenant Haulot, the Belgian officer, represents an international association of former inmates at Dachau. The request is for him to have an opportunity to be heard at this time."

"May it please the court," Denson said, "unless he is of counsel in the case or unless he appears as amicus curiae of this court, I do not think it would be proper—unless the court feels otherwise."

Lentz consulted with others on the tribunal, then said, "The court does not desire to hear Lieutenant Haulot at this time. The court will adjourn."

Denson watched as across the aisle, one by one, the defendants filed out from their rows of seats, walked somberly past their lawyers and out the door to the holding cage. Some of the Germans wept. Bates sat on the edge of the table, shaking hands, nodding in sympathy, acknowledging their appreciation. No one looked toward the prosecution table. Denson turned back to his own team, shook hands, accepted sober congratulations from spectators and politicians, promised to return for dinner that evening, mounted his jeep, and left.

A crowd gathered in the officers' mess that evening and bobbed around Denson, toasting and congratulating and filling his ear with names of people he should meet and gossip about how big the press will be. The path to democracy had been traversed and the free people of the earth had been heard. Now came the sweaty handshakes and boisterous accolades for points of law brilliantly played, and senior officers touching his shoulder just for the vicarious feel of his achievement. Paul Guth stood close by, speaking to an attentive crowd of 3rd Army staff.

"Every one of them in that group was a certified murderer—at the very least certifiable gangsters. You had to have two left hands and two deaf ears to find someone in that first group unjustly accused. . . ."

Exultation over what they had accomplished gave way in Denson to a numbing realization that for him this was not yet over. Mauthausen was next, considered by many to be one of the worst camps in the history of the Greater Reich. But the odds of again winning unanimous convictions would not be as good. The prosecution's legal weapons were on public display now, their tactics and strategies available for examination by the Mauthausen defense team. He would need more time to adequately prepare, more time and more staff. He would ask Guth to stay as long as he could, but Denson had promised him his discharge. Heller, Lines, and McCuskey had earned their points now and would leave within the week, and he would be on his own to confront defense lawyers a thousand times better prepared and the uncertainty of a new prosecution team. Still, this first trial had been a successful journey of discovery: researching applicable laws and charges, creating systems for organizing mountains of evidence, excavating credible testimony from the ruins of memory. The discovery had taken place within as well: shaking off a provincialism ingrained from childhood, watching himself perform effectively on a world stage, realizing with satisfaction that righteousness had not required him to compromise legal integrity.

Along the way he had discovered, too, that these trials were layered with agendas unrelated to due process. Some were clear to everyone involved: the army's need to reach convictions swiftly, to show the world that America could do its job. Others were deeper, more obscure: the line between justice and vengeance, the frustrating tension between the letter and the spirit of the law, the challenge of conducting an aggressive prosecution while respecting Christian intent. He had grown up in a home that believed in the inherent goodness of men and the mercy of God. The work he had taken on at Dachau should by all rights have validated that belief. Instead he had discovered that charitable beliefs and Christian intent were not always consonant with legal justice, and that revelation had begun to harden him. Was he wrong to recommend that Haulot not be allowed to speak at the end of the trial? Had his determination to win convictions interfered with the defense's pleas for clemency? Somewhere along the way, had righteousness turned self-righteous?

––––––––

Paul Guth's final duties as administrator for the prosecution included paying witnesses their fees. Among them was a woman who had offered important details concerning the children's transports. Guth extended an envelope containing one thousand marks. The woman shook her head.

"Don't be silly," Guth protested. "You're not in a good economic position. Take the money." She shook her head again.

"There is something I did not tell you," she said. "My son was on one of those transports."

She opened her purse and took out a photograph so worn the image of her son was barely visible. She tore the photo in half, gave one piece to Guth, shook his hand, and left.

––––––––

The day after sentences were announced, chief defense lawyer Douglas T. Bates received a phone call from a member of the tribunal. The judge asked Bates to meet him that evening and to not mention their appointment to anyone. Bates agreed.

New York Times, December 14, 1945

Dachau Nazis All Convicted of Atrocities

*40 Defendants Will Hear Sentences Tomorrow
for Camp Tortures*

Death Decree Means Noose

*Guilty Verdict Reached by U.S. Court in
90 Minutes—SS Men Asked Clemency*

Dachau, Germany, Dec. 14 (AP)—A United States Military Government court today convicted Commandant Martin Weiss and thirty-nine fellow defendants, on a charge of committing atrocities at the Dachau concentration camp. Hanging is the penalty prescribed by United States Army headquarters for any sentenced to death for the regime of starvation, torture and murder at the Nazi horror center overrun on April 30.

The eight-officer court, headed by Brig. Gen. John M. Lentz, received the case at noon and deliberated only ninety minutes before reaching the verdict. The defense wound up the twenty-four-day trial with pleas for mercy for several defendants most of whom were SS guards, although five were camp doctors and three were prisoners used in official capacities.

Audience Apathetic

The defendants received the verdict stoically. There was no visible reaction from German civilians and others in the audience of more than 300. . . . Decapitation had been regarded as the probable fate of any of the Dachau war criminals sentenced to death, but United States Army instructions have reinstated hanging as in the case of common criminals.

"Colonel Bates, I have been thinking over the trial and I believe we have made a terrible mistake," the judge told him. "I just wanted you to know that. I'll be writing a dissenting opinion. That's all."

The next morning Bates's phone rang again. "Colonel," the judge said, "that discussion last night never took place." The following day Bates wrote to his wife in Centerville, Tennessee.

December 16, 1945

My Angel,

Thursday was a day that I'll never forget, though I would very much like to. Thirty-six of the forty defendants [sic] were sentenced to death. It shocked everybody. One cannot work night and day with forty men for six weeks without having a feeling of comradeship. The happenings of Thursday tore my heart completely out. After the court adjourned, the defendants filed by and shook our hands, thanking us for the fight we lost. Strong German men with tears in their eyes and streaming down their cheeks, but not sobbing, telling us American officers that they could not have had better defenders from anywhere. God, Kitty, can my heart stand much more. A German newspaperman came up to me later and said, "Colonel, we've watched the gallant struggle you've made, we see and understand how you are moved by the sentences. The German people admire you a great deal." Well, I excused myself fast. Even for a tough hombre like me there is a limit beyond which I might act like a baby.

Friday night a phone call informed us that Defense Counsel, Court, and Prosecution were expected to lunch with Gen. Truscott, Patton's successor . . . Gen. Lentz, the president of the court, told Gen. Truscott that I was one of the finest soldiers he'd ever known. I sat on Gen. Truscott's left, the place of honor. There were about thirty officers present. Three of us spoke, Truscott, Denson and me . . .

Shortly, Beloved, I'll start that sentimental journey home to the most wonderful woman in the world and to what I hope is a peaceful life . . .

Love, Douglas

———

At the end of December 1945, G. M. Gilbert visited Landsberg prison near Munich, where the Germans sentenced to death in the Dachau trials awaited execution. Gilbert was prison psychologist before and during the Nuremberg trial and had the unique prerogative of personally observing and questioning Nazi criminals. Landsberg, the prison where Adolf Hitler wrote *Mein Kampf*, featured two rows of cell doors. Prisoners could put their heads through portal openings in the doors and converse with one another. Gilbert described the Germans "talking and laughing to each other across the corridor, making it look as if they were being pilloried before the execution and enjoying it. Bored GI's stand around playing with their carbines, comparing points for redeployment."

Frank Trenkle, an overseer and executioner at the Dachau camp, acted helpless and wore a woebegone expression. Denson had questioned Paul Guth on the stand concerning Trenkle's statement, and Guth swore it had been obtained without threats or violence. "I just did the shooting on command of Gauleiter Giessler," Trenkle told Gilbert. "I couldn't prevent the atrocities—I could only execute commands, or I would have been stood up against the wall. The *Führer* and *Reichsführer* SS [Himmler]—they brought all this about and now they are gone—Glücks got it from Kaltenbrunner [head of the SD], and finally I got the orders to do the shooting. They can all pass the buck to me, because I was only a little *Hauptscharführer* [equivalent of a sergeant in the SS] and couldn't pass the buck any further down the line, and now they say I am the murderer. . . . I hope none of those bastards in Nuremberg gets away with it. That would be a terrible injustice."

Gilbert interviewed Dr. Schilling, who told him—contrary to his claims on the witness stand—that he was not sure he had achieved anything with his malaria experiments because he had not been able to obtain accurate reports on the causes of death. Schilling admitted seeing the results of the freezing water experiments: naked Gypsy women waiting to be placed in bed next to the frozen subjects in order to revive them. "Warming them back with 'animal heat' of the women," Schilling scoffed. "Just sexual sadism!" His own experiments, he told Gilbert, were more scientific. In May 1946, Schilling was hanged at Landsberg prison and buried in an unmarked grave.

PART THREE

Mauthausen

―――

Blessed is the man that walketh not in
the counsel of the ungodly,
Nor standeth in the way of sinners,
Nor sitteth in the seat of the scornful.
But his delight is in the law of the Lord;
And in His law doth he meditate day and night.

—Psalms 1:1–2

12

Christmas, 1945

The end of the Dachau camp trial meant that Denson's team could at last return home. Capt. Bill Lines returned to his law practice in Florida, Capt. Phillip Heller to his in New York. Capt. Richard McCuskey resumed duties as general counsel for Hoover vacuum cleaners in Canton, Ohio. Dalwin J. Niles went on to become a New York state senator. Col. David Chavez Jr., brother of a senator from New Mexico, had been a chief investigator at Dachau. Two days after his departure he sent Denson a letter commending him for the way he handled the prosecution. "From every quarter," Chavez wrote, "I hear nothing but praise for your splendid work. As one officer from Wiesbaden expressed it, 'Not even Jaworski [later of Watergate fame, and Mickey Straight's predecessor as war crimes head in Europe] could have done any better.'"

Chief defense counsel Douglas T. Bates returned to Centerville, Tennessee, where he was branded as a Nazi lover and excluded from public office. He persevered and succeeded in building a small private practice with offices overlooking the town square. Until his death in 1996 he consistently maintained the position he had taken during the Dachau trial: if the Germans were guilty of a common design, so was every citizen of

Germany who had contributed to waging total war. Due process was not only for Americans, and the defendants had to his mind been denied their God-given right to a fair trial. "John Adams did not create the Bill of Rights," he would often say. "He just wrote it."

Guth relocated to an inn five minutes away in the town of Dachau, then set out to spend Christmas with his family in Vienna. With the holding cage still filled, Denson's own return home would not come for months. He moved into Guth's apartment two blocks from the Dachau courtroom. Preparing the Mauthausen trial would take every minute he could find, and the move eliminated a twenty-minute commute from Munich. With Guth in Vienna and his other friend O'Connell back in the States visiting family, Denson accepted an invitation to Nudi von der Lippe's Christmas party.

As always, he came with gifts—fruit and liquor—and a radiant smile that charmed the room. When speaking with other guests, he concentrated on them, never looking over their shoulder to see if someone more important stood nearby. He took pleasure in knowing people, heard their stories with rapt attention, and acknowledged their willingness to let him share the experiences of their lives. Encountering another human being in the simple, civilized context of a holiday gathering provided him with respite from the complex, uncivilized world in which he worked. His interest heightened their attraction to him, and the crowd drew him to their center and loved him for his modesty and charm.

Huschi was there. "Hello, Colonel Denson," she said.

"Please, call me Bill," he said.

They spoke, as they had at their first meeting, of childhood. She told him that her mother, Princess Lily, had been impressed by Hitler's *Mutter und Kind* programs but that her father, Hans Clemens, could not stand the Nazis. He had traveled extensively and knew a little more of the world than Lily. After they separated in 1934, he settled in Austria to live an aristocratic life, driving in a chauffeured Mercedes and dining with the Duke and Duchess of Windsor.

The castle where Huschi lived as a child had been part of her family's lavish Upper Silesian estate. Their thousands of acres of land bordered other aristocratic estates and were serviced by peasants from the nearby village of Zyrowa. Huschi was twelve in 1935 when Hitler renamed the village Buchenhöh, not wanting any Polish names in the Third Reich. She had been raised with an English governess and a French tutor, and her own opinions of Hitler were closer to her father's than to her mother's. In 1936, Hans Clemens visited from Vienna and took his thirteen-year-old daughter to the Berlin Olympics. As a young man he had been as far as Alaska on hunting expeditions and proudly led the German shooting team to victory in the 1928 Olympics. The 1936 spectacle was quite another affair: lavish military parades, propaganda filmmaker Leni Riefenstahl and her camera crews positioned around the stadium, thousands of Nazi flags, and constant repetitions of "Heil Hitler."

"This is nauseating," he told his daughter.

Huschi shared with Bill the one good memory she had of that outing: seeing American runner Jesse Owens win his race to the embarrassment of Hitler and laughing about it with her father. That visit was the last time Hans Clemens set foot in Germany.

Then Huschi told Bill the story of how she surrendered the village of Velden an der Vils. In May 1945, having survived the bombing of Dresden, she finally arrived in Bavaria, where she was reunited with her mother and seven-month-old daughter, Yvonne. Three days later she was biking to a nearby farm to get milk for her baby when she saw U.S. Army tanks cresting a hill in the distance. The Americans were liberating towns and villages across Europe, often with heavy gunfire and civilian casualties. Huschi turned around and raced back to alert the villagers. They were terrified and begged her to speak to the Americans in English and get them to occupy their village peacefully. She positioned people on the road with white flags, and when the tanks approached she held up her hand. The convoy stopped. From the hatch of the lead tank emerged a bemused GI.

"There are no soldiers here," Huschi announced in impeccable English. "We surrender this village to you!"

The American, dumbfounded, saluted and gave the order: no shots were to be fired. Later, Allied soldiers handed her a huge box filled with chocolate, cigarettes, and Spam.

"Bill," she said, "that box was so big we lived off it for months."

Denson reciprocated by telling her about lavish Sunday dinners his mother would serve up, after which he was expected to recite verses memorized from the Bible.

"I got five cents for every verse recited without error," he said. "That was just enough for a frosted bottle of Coca-Cola. My prize for each Bible verse went up as I grew older, first ten cents, then fifty. When I got to twelve years, my daddy gave me a car, a Willys-Knight hand-me-down, back then there being no concerns by the Sovereign State of Alabama over the age of licensed drivers. . . ."

He was glad to be there with her, glad for the easy banter and companionship at holiday time. Denson had had girlfriends since coming to Germany. There was Nudi, whom Huschi described as "a real party girl." There was a Hungarian blue blood named Carola who had been his secretary for a time and ran with the Munich crowd. But that evening's flirtation was one to which both Bill and Huschi felt immune. I'm married, he said. So am I, she said. Then both with equal candor confessed that their marriages were not going particularly well. Denson's wife had thought she was gaining a social partner from an aristocratic family, not a legal missionary who would run off to prosecute Nazis, and had filed for divorce. Huschi's dilemma was different. She had married the boy next door, who happened to be the son of Germany's most decorated tank commander. After sustaining wounds at the Eastern Front, he had returned home and lapsed into a bitter self-pity from which he refused to emerge.

A man of different sensibilities might have been ill-at-ease fraternizing with the daughter-in-law of a highly decorated German tank commander. Denson felt no such discomfort. The yardstick by which he measured people, in and out of the courtroom, was their personal behavior. Caution may have dictated that he not mention Huschi to fellow JAGs or discuss the trials with her, but nothing could diminish his attraction to this elegant young woman with the spunk of a field officer, whose material losses had not diminished her wealth of character. She had saved her family from rampaging Russians, walked away from one of the worst bombings in World War II, liberated a Bavarian village, and still held on to her sense of humor. Friendship with Huschi, he decided, deserved the same integrity of purpose as his mission in the courtroom. So despite their mutual attraction, Bill and Huschi spent a thoroughly platonic evening together. Before they said goodnight, Huschi called him "my honest American," and Bill promised to come see her again when the Mauthausen trial ended.

The year 1946 began with the first session of the United Nations in London. High on the U.N.'s agenda was Soviet Russia's aggressive expansion across Europe. In November 1945, Communist governments had been elected to power in Yugoslavia and Bulgaria. In January, Albania proclaimed itself a Communist republic. "Half, maybe all of Europe might be Communist by the end of next winter," Averell Harriman, ambassador to the USSR, told Navy Secretary James Forrestal. Soviet forces were establishing puppet governments wherever they could. Ellery Stone reported from Rome that a Communist putsch was imminent. William Donovan, head of the Office of Strategic Services (the OSS, reorganized as the CIA in 1947), urged, in light of the terrifying reports flowing in from across Europe, that Western defenses be immediately coordinated. At the Moscow Conference of Foreign Ministers in December 1945, Secretary of State James Byrnes reported back that Russia was "trying to do in a slick-dip way what Hitler used to do in domineering over smaller countries by force."

In January 1946, as Denson began preparing the Mauthausen trial, President Truman took a firm stand. "I do not think we should play compromise any longer," he told the press. "I am tired of babying the Soviets." Shortly after, Winston Churchill came to Fulton, Missouri, and delivered a now famous speech that included the words, "From Stettin in the Baltic to Trieste in the Adriatic, an Iron Curtain has descended across the continent of Europe." He exhorted America and her allies to immediately strive for "an overwhelming assurance of security." Polls indicated that a permanent military alliance was supported by 81 percent of the American people.

American isolationism had at last been interred forever—and with it most of the perceived value of the war crimes program. Nuremberg verdicts were yet to be handed down, but many in the U.S. government felt the expensive and time-consuming trials were absorbing resources better used to combat the Red menace. Secretary of State Byrnes added that subsequent trials might do nothing more than alienate Germany's new leaders at a time when their support against the Soviet Union would be critical.

Washington's position on dealing with Nazis was undergoing a dramatic metamorphosis. In public, the government continued to favor trials. Privately, officials were working to quickly end a war crimes program that no longer fit America's foreign policy.

13

Preparations Begin

eturning from their brief vacation, Denson's young staff threw themselves into preparing a case that would dwarf the one that had just ended. The Dachau camp case had convicted forty defendants, already a staggering number. The number of defendants in the Mauthausen case was rising past sixty. The large number of accused obliged Straight and other JAG seniors, undoubtedly against their will, to allocate a full three months to prepare. Only one month had been allotted for Dachau. During those three months Denson and his small team worked nonstop readying for a trial of disproportionate size. To put their task in perspective, Robert Jackson's team at Nuremberg, prosecuting twenty-two Nazis, included more than 640 staff members. At its height, Denson's team, prosecuting sixty accused, numbered twenty-two.

Joining Denson as co-counsel for this second trial was Lt. Col. Albert Barkin, a lawyer from Boston who had managed the office of Gen. Lucien Truscott at JAG HQ in Munich. As reward and a kind of dowry for Barkin's future civilian career, Truscott had him appointed to the Mauthausen prosecution. At first Denson and Guth were concerned: Barkin was senior to Denson both in age and army rank. Might he try to take charge of the case? Their fears were without grounds. Barkin proved to be cooperative and polite and, despite his lack of legal experience, worked diligently with Guth to bring in witnesses and identify more on his own.

Another prosecution lawyer for the Mauthausen trial was Baron Hans Karl von Posern, who had served as co-counsel for the defense in the Dachau case. Also joining the prosecution team were Capt. Charles Matthews of Texas and Capt. Myron N. Lane of New York, experienced criminal lawyers, mild-mannered and industrious. Like their predecessors in the Dachau trial, Denson's co-counsel came to admire him as a real-life Jefferson Smith, the idealistic lawyer portrayed by Jimmy Stewart in the 1939 movie *Mr. Smith Goes to Washington*: lanky, virtuous, innocent of politics.

That confidence nourished his staying power. On a professional level he was self-contained: Denson knew law the way a farmer knows his fields. But on a personal level appreciation from those under him kept him energized. Growing up in the Depression, he had witnessed privation and sickness face-to-face and sought sincerely to make the world a better place. After completing school with an exemplary record, he did not ask himself what he wished to do: he was ready to work, to begin trials, to begin fighting the good fight. For five years he practiced civil law in his father's firm as though his clients were his family. He was human and made some mistakes, but in those five years there was not one complaint about his manners or morals. His community applauded him, his clients adored him, and if his father had been a taskmaster who never knew how to express his love, the affection of those for whom Denson labored made up the loss. The legal circle was not a profession for him: it was his larger family bound by a shared dedication to justice—and now by a shared desire to convict history's worst criminals through due process. That bond was sacrosanct. Whatever Washington's agenda might be, Denson was not about to compromise his standards or those of his teammates.

By March 1946 the prosecution was ready for trial.

14

186 Steps of Death

I n 1938, soon after Germany's invasion of Austria, Himmler ordered that two hundred prisoners from the Dachau camp be sent to the little town of Mauthausen, twelve miles outside Linz, Austria. Their task was to build a new camp that would supply slave labor for the *Wiener Graben*, or stone quarry. Himmler's intention was to establish his SS as a separate economic empire, and revenues from the quarry would add to those of his other slave-labor enterprises. These included the German Earth and Stone Works (*Deutsche Erd- und Steinwerke* or *DEST*) and the German Equipment Works (*Deutsche Ausrüstungswerke* or *DAW*). Mauthausen included the usual array of atrocities, but the quarry was what set it apart from other camps. The stone provided Himmler with a thriving business. Huge granite slabs were sold to build the streets of Vienna, the city from which the quarry drew its name.

The two-hundred-foot-deep quarry also provided the SS with one of their most brutal arenas of punishment. Prisoners were divided into two groups: one that hacked into the granite walls and a second that carried the slabs up 186 *Todesstiege*—steps of death—to the top. One torture required prisoners to run up the steps shouldering stones weighing as much as two hundred pounds. The SS called those who fell, were pushed, or leaped into the pit *Fallschirmjäger*: parachute troops. In one instance, the SS ordered an Italian Jew known for his beautiful voice to stand atop a rock mound and sing Ave Maria. Charges were laid around the rock. In midsong an SS officer pressed the plunger, blasting the prisoner into the sky. Among the more notorious German guards in the quarry was one nicknamed "das blonde Fräulein," who hacked to death a contingent of eighty-seven Dutch Jews while they dug into the quarry's granite walls. Life expectancy for inmates in the quarry was at most three months.

The earliest concentration camps, including Mauthausen, were not originally intended as extermination camps even though tens of thousands died there. Rather, their function was to isolate groups considered hostile or dangerous by National Socialism—primarily Jews, antisocials, homosexuals, Gypsies, and other minorities—and to create cheap SS-controlled slave labor. Then, after the outbreak of war, camps were divided into three categories graded according to difficulty of living conditions. Category I camps were considered the mildest. Category II had harsher conditions. Category III camps were the "death factories."

Mauthausen became a Category III camp: the fiercest kind, meant for prisoners termed *Rückkehr Unerwünscht*, "return not desired," and *Vernichtung durch Arbeit*, "to be exterminated by work." This camp was one that prisoners knew to avoid at all costs. An estimated 195,000 people passed through Mauthausen between its opening in 1938 and its liberation on May 5, 1945. Of these, an estimated 150,000 lost their lives. A public road led directly through the camp, and residents of the nearby town of Mauthausen regularly witnessed atrocities. Eleanore Gusenbauer, a local farmer, filed a complaint in 1941: "I am sickly, and these sights make such a demand on my nerves that in the long run I cannot bear this. I request that it be arranged that such inhuman deeds be discontinued, or else done where one does not see it." Objecting to the ways of Mauthausen had its risks. A town resident named Winklehner was caught throwing bread and cigarettes to inmates and was himself imprisoned at Dachau, where he died.

The road to Mauthausen passed through quaint villages and thick woods, up high hills that looked out on the Danube valley below and the Alps in the distance. Flat brown fields gave way to green hills that surrounded the camp. Due to the immense number of prisoners pouring in,

Mauthausen commandant Ziereis ordered fields to the north and south to be ringed with wire. Here, Hungarian Jews and Russian soldiers, among others, were kept in the open year round. For all prisoners, wake-up in summer was at 4:45 A.M. and an hour later in winter. The workday ended at 7:00 P.M. Work revolved around the quarry and the underground tunneling at the subcamps of Gusen (I, II, and III), a few miles to the west; Melk, built in the shadow of a hilltop monastery; and Ebensee, in the wooded region of nearby Salzkammergut. Nearly sixty subcamps emerged during Ziereis's time, each with its own brand of torture and death. The death toll in the Gusen complex was so high that each barrack was divided into two parts, *Stube A* and *Stube B*, with *B* reserved for the sick, wounded, and those too weak to work. No food or water reached *Stube B*, where prisoners lay on the ground, or on one another, covered in their own excrement, until they died.

As elsewhere, conditions in Mauthausen worsened after 1943. Hitler's invasion of the Soviet Union resulted in an overwhelming influx of prisoners from the East. Disease reached epidemic proportions, and toward the end of the war more than two hundred people were dying each day. Even as late as April 1945, killings continued in the gas chamber. From April 21 to 25 alone, 650 prisoners were asphyxiated in the course of "cleansing operations" in the sick bay. On May 3, 1945, the last morning roll call took place in Mauthausen. After that the SS guard squads deserted the camp, leaving prisoners in the hands of a unit of the Vienna fire brigade. On May 5 an American tank patrol accompanied by a Red Cross delegate arrived at the main camp, disarmed the remaining guards, and liberated the camp. That same day American soldiers also liberated Mauthausen's subcamps.

During the six years of its operation, thousands of SS guards and administrators served in the Mauthausen complex. American forces captured less than two hundred. From these and other arrestees in the Dachau holding cage, Guth and his interrogation team identified sixty-one men who would stand trial for war crimes at Mauthausen.

All pleaded not guilty.

15

A Hollywood Soldier

The Mauthausen trial began on an unusually warm day in March 1946. Morning sunlight slanted in through high windows, painting bright crosshatches on the wooden courthouse floor. Visitors from U.S. Army Headquarters, former camp inmates, and local citizenry packed the room. Verdicts in Nuremberg were still six months away, and the international press had once again returned to Dachau. Photographers gorged themselves on the spectacle of sixty-one accused arraigned together in the dock.

"I assure the court," chief defense counsel Ernst Oeding began, "that I have conscientiously tried to get the defendants to understand the charge against them—but I don't understand it myself, and I've practiced law for many years."

Born and raised in Brooklyn, Oeding had attended St. Johns College on a basketball scholarship and had played center when St. Johns won its first NCAA title at Madison Square Garden. "Stretch," as he was known, stood six-foot-three and looked like John Wayne with a receding hairline. Oeding did not object to defending the Germans and had in fact wanted to be there from the outset. His parents were of German descent and he spoke German fluently. Despite his confidence in his own abilities, he knew he would lose. What mattered to him was providing the defendants with due process. He and Denson were waving the same flag.

"The defense moves to quash the charges and particulars. Common design is not a crime," Oeding said, "and in fact could be entirely lawful. Try a man for murder, for instance, and you set in motion a common design: the police who make the arrest, the attorneys, the judge, jury—all working with a perfectly lawful common design.

"One of the purposes of the occupation," he said, "is to show the Germans how the ideals of American justice work. And exactness in defining crimes is not an unnecessary technicality. We appreciate that there is eagerness for punishment of guilt and that these cases must be conducted quickly. However, a court's function is to apply existing laws, not make new ones."

"May it please the court," Denson said, reacting to a now familiar insinuation that the prosecution was party to victors' justice, "I would like to be of assistance to defense counsel. There is a definition of common design in Black's *Law Dictionary*, also in Bouvier, as well as in *Miller on Criminal Law*. . . ."

"Motion is denied," Maj. Gen. Fay B. Prickett ruled, saving Denson the trouble of having to read anything. Possibly the oldest JAG officer in Dachau, Prickett peered out over the courtroom like an owl surveying its prey. Oeding was not deterred and responded on behalf of his clients.

"Defense respectfully points out that we have sixty-one persons jointly charged. The offenses alleged specify eighteen areas—killings, beatings, tortures, and so on—covering three and a half years. Each accused is, we submit, entitled to know what it is he is supposed to have done, where, when, and to whom he is alleged to have done it."

"Now, these accused," Denson countered, "know better than anyone else whether they were in Mauthausen between 1942 and 1945. They know better than anyone else whether they tortured or beat or starved people there as described in the particulars."

"Motion is denied," Prickett ruled again. Oeding mustered his forces.

"May it please the court, this is the last motion of the defense. We move for a severance based on the unwieldy number of accused sitting here. Now, we are not trying to delay bringing any guilty man to justice. We are entirely willing to sit with the prosecution and work out smaller groupings of the accused on a practical and fair basis . . ."

"Motion is denied. Does the prosecution desire to make an opening statement?" Oeding sat, the court's leaning clear to him and his defense team.

"May it please the court," Denson began, "we expect the evidence to show that the victims of Mauthausen and its by-camps were gathered from countries at war with Germany or overrun by the German army. We expect the evidence to show that these victims constituted in the main the intelligentsia of continental Europe, persons who had the intestinal fortitude to stand up against the Nazi yoke of oppression. We expect the evidence to show that somewhere between 165,000 and a million and a half persons were killed in the camps of Mauthausen; that these prisoners were used in such a manner as to derive the greatest economic value from their services and were fed a diet that was calculated ultimately to end in their death. . . ."

The wide latitude in Denson's estimation of how many prisoners were killed in Mauthausen reflected an uncertainty in 1946 as to the number of Mauthausen prisoners who had died in the Castle Hartheim gas chamber. Most official records had been destroyed by the SS before they fled the camp. In his deathbed confession, former Mauthausen commandant Franz Ziereis had estimated more than a million. Historians today accept that figure as greatly exaggerated.

"Mauthausen and its by-camps," Denson continued, "were nothing more than a many-headed hydra of extermination—and these sixty-one men on trial before this court encouraged, aided, abetted, or participated in a common design to subject its prisoners to killings, beatings, and tortures. Prosecution calls Lt. Jack Taylor."

Taylor, a lieutenant commander in the U.S. Navy, had been a prisoner in Mauthausen during the final months before liberation. Within hours after arrival of American troops, he was interviewed on film inside the camp. A portion of the interview was included at the beginning of a fifty-minute film shown at Nuremberg titled *Nazi Concentration Camps*. The film had been shot and edited by Lt. Col. George C. Stevens, a Hollywood director who is remembered for having later directed *The Diary of Anne Frank*.

Crime scene photography was well established in Anglo-American courts, but this was the first time a motion picture had ever been used in a court of law, and it was a turning point at Nuremberg. Gasps of horror, fainting, sobbing, and cries of outrage filled the darkened courtroom. The judges were so disturbed they retired at the end of the day without their usual announcement of the time set for the next session. *Reichsmarschall* Hermann Göring, who had been winning laughs by verbally manipulating Chief Prosecutor Robert Jackson, later commented, "It was such a good afternoon, too, until they showed that awful film—and it just spoiled everything."

"I'm from Hollywood, California," Taylor explained in the film. He added almost shyly, "Believe it or not, this is the first time I have ever been in the movies." The camera moved from his boyish face to mass graves while Taylor described in voice-over the many crimes he had seen at Mauthausen. Knowing the impact his interview had produced at Nuremberg, Denson made Taylor his opening witness.

"When did you come to Mauthausen, Commander Taylor?"

"April first, 1945. There were thirty-eight in my transport. We were marched up the hill and lined up with much slugging, slapping, and spitting—do you wish me to go into this, sir?"

"Please continue."

"We were lined up alongside a wall and more of the same sort of intimidation was done by several SS—'Where are you from?' 'Who are you?' 'Why are you here?' Every time an SS asked a question, he would hit you over the head."

"And how long did this type of conduct continue?"

"About two hours. Then we were taken down below the laundry where we were stripped and had all the hair shaved off our bodies. After a shower, we were assigned to prisoner barracks. Each barracks was designed normally for two hundred and twenty men. At the time we arrived they were holding four hundred."

"Were you assigned to any work detail?"

"Yes, sir. My first job was setting tile in the new crematorium. They were very anxious to have it completed because all the bodies from hanging and beating had to be cremated to destroy the evidence."

"Did you at any time receive any threats," Denson asked, "with respect to the completion of this new crematory?"

"Yes, sir. Prellberg and Roth, who were heads of the crematorium, threatened us because the work was going too slowly. We knew that the only thing that kept the number of violent deaths down was the fact that the crematorium couldn't take care of any more. And we knew that as soon as we finished, the rate would accelerate tremendously because it was a more efficient oven. I say 'violent deaths.' You must remember that each day there were at that time between two hundred fifty and three hundred dying of starvation alone. This is separate from all the executions and beatings and so forth."

"Do you have any judgment, commander, as to the number that died daily by violent means?"

"Only that the regular procedure for the gas chamber was twice a day, one hundred and twenty at a time. I would say that the new crematorium increased the facilities to two hundred and fifty a day."

"Now, when was this crematory first used?"

"On Sunday, April tenth. Three hundred and sixty-seven prisoners, including forty women, arrived from Czechoslovakia. They had been marched overland, straight through the gate to the crematorium. This particular group had so much more fat—so much more fat," the words coming with difficulty, "than ordinary prisoners that the flames from the crematorium were going straight out the top of the smokestack. Ordinarily it was a pale brown smoke, heavy with the smell of burnt hair, and it wafted over the camp. It seemed to go up, then settle down. As hungry as we were, we had a hard time eating sometimes."

"Can you describe the gas chamber?"

"Yes, sir. It was rigged up like a shower room with shower nozzles in the ceiling. New prisoners thought they were going in to have their bath. They were stripped and put in this room naked. Then gas came out of the shower nozzles."

In fall 1941, to better mechanize the mass murder of sick and unproductive prisoners, a ten-foot-square room in the basement of the "hospital" building was outfitted to look like a shower. Prisoners were made to construct a tiled floor and walls and install airtight doors and ventilation. The gas was discharged from a thick metal box in the adjoining room.

Roughly a foot-and-a-half square with an airtight lid that locked shut with thick wing bolts, the box was large enough to hold several open cans of gas along with a hot brick that accelerated evaporation of the prussic acid. Valves were welded to the sides of the box, one that controlled an electric ventilator, the other leading to an enamel tube that released the fumes. Victims were led to a changing room where they were ordered to remove their clothes. Then SS men wearing white doctors' coats put a spatula into the victims' mouths to see whether there were any gold teeth. If yes, an "x" was marked on their back before they entered the shower room. From the partial logs Denson had read, at least 3,400 people were killed in the ten-foot chamber.

———

"I hand you a photograph marked prosecution's exhibit eight and ask you to state what that is, if you know."

Taylor took the photograph and studied it for a moment. "This is a picture of the electric fence along the north side, showing a number of dead who had grabbed the electric wires to commit suicide. As I heard the story, too many of them grabbed at once and the current was not strong enough to kill them all. So they were shot down by a machine gun."

"How many different forms of killings did you come in contact with there in Mauthausen?"

"Gassing, hanging, shooting, beating. There was one particular group of Dutch Jews who were beaten until they jumped over the cliff into the stone quarry. Some that were not killed on the first fall were taken back up and thrown over to be sure. Then there was exposure. Any new transport coming in was forced to stand out in the open, regardless of the time of the year, practically naked. Other forms of killing included clubbing to death with axes or hammers and so forth, tearing to pieces by dogs specially trained for the purpose, injections into the heart and veins with magnesium chloride or benzine, whippings with a cow-tail to tear the flesh away, mashing in a concrete mixer, forcing them to drink a great quantity of water and then jumping on the stomach while the prisoner was lying on his back, freezing half-naked in subzero temperatures, buried alive, red-hot poker down the throat. I remember a very prominent Czech general who was held down in the shower room and had a hose forced down his throat. He drowned that way."

"What if anything did you learn concerning the extraction of gold teeth from the heads of prisoners?"

"I questioned the chief prisoner dentist when the Americans liberated us, and he gave me a very complete report on the whole racket. Every corpse had to be examined by a member of the dental staff for gold teeth before it could be cremated. One of the accused, Dr. Hoehler here, can give you complete data on this, I am sure."

"Commander Taylor, would you describe to the court your physical condition at the time you were liberated by the Americans?"

"Yes, sir. I weighed one hundred twelve pounds. I could not stand at the roll call for any length of time without becoming faint. I never expected to live from the first, and my mental condition was, if anything, worse than my physical condition. At this time, just before liberation, it was very dangerous. We had heard that Churchill, on visiting Buchenwald, had broadcast to the Germans that if they found similar conditions in any other camp . . ."

That brought Oeding to his feet. "I object to the answer of the witness strenuously, bringing in Buchenwald and hearsay at the same time. Evidence of this type is inflammatory—I don't want to detract from the intelligence of the court or the prosecution, but we are all human beings and subject to becoming emotionally aroused, myself included. Unless the testimony has some bearing on the guilt of an individual accused, we submit that it is not relevant to the function of the trial."

"Objection overruled," Prickett said.

"Please continue, lieutenant."

"We were extremely worried that they would try to kill us all to remove the evidence. I only mention this to show the state of mind that all the prisoners were under in these last days. We had heard that Commandant Ziereis wanted to annihilate all the prisoners."

––––––

Throughout the Mauthausen trial the accused referred to this one man as the real demon, the one whom the court should hold responsible for the horrors of Mauthausen. Franz Ziereis did not look like a sadistic murderer—his nickname was "Baby Face"—but camp records confirmed reports by staff and prisoners alike: Ziereis had been among the worst. He ordered prisoners thrown alive into the crematory fires. He ordered the kitchen staff to overturn pots of soup so he could watch starving prisoners lick the spillage before it was absorbed in the dirt. He staked inmates out as shooting targets. For his son's twelfth birthday in 1943, Ziereis had twelve men tied up by the killing wall. "Here is my present," he told the boy, "one for each year." The boy raised his rifle and fired twelve times, executing them all.

When the American liberation forces arrived on May 23, 1945, Ziereis fled but was discovered at his hunting lodge in Upper Austria. While attempting to escape, he was shot. The following night on his deathbed, Ziereis was interrogated by army officers and former prisoners, among them Hans Marsalek, who later testified in the Mauthausen trial.

"I, myself, am not a wicked man," Ziereis professed, "and I have risen through work." He went on to provide condemning evidence against many who would later stand trial at Dachau. It was SS chief doctor Krebsbach, Ziereis told his captors, who ordered that gas chambers be built. It was Dr. Wasitzki, he said, who had ordered that other prisoners be killed in a specially designed "gasmobile." Ziereis told the Americans that August Eigruber, civilian leader for the Nazi Party in Upper Austria, had refused to provide food for new arrivals to camps in his zone and had even ordered that 50 percent of camp Mauthausen's potato stock be turned over to him. "I know more, too," Ziereis said, "about other camps. In Buchenwald, I saw how SS leader Hackmann stripped Jews of their valuables, then arranged for a big car and dressed himself up in a tuxedo, with stolen diamonds on his fingers. . . ." Ziereis died shortly after his confession.

———

"Commander Taylor," Denson said, "will you relate to the court how you escaped being killed?"

"The day before we were scheduled to be executed," Taylor replied, "the camp was liberated."

Among those who spoke with Jack Taylor at liberation was Staff Sergeant Albert J. Kosiek, attached to General Patton's 3rd Army, 11th Division, 1st Platoon. "On May fifth, we came upon Mauthausen," Kosiek told the military magazine *Thunderbolt*. "The camp was surrounded by a wire fence charged with two thousand volts of electricity. Behind that fence were hundreds of people who went wild with joy when they first sighted us. It's a sight I'll never forget. Some had just blankets covering them, others were completely nude, men and women. I still shake my head in disbelief when it comes to mind. They hardly resembled human beings. Walking in first, I was greeted with the most spectacular ovation. I felt like some celebrity being cheered at Soldier Field in Chicago.

"One of the prisoners stepped forward and introduced himself as Capt. Jack Taylor of the United States Navy, and he showed me his dog tags to prove it. He told us he never expected to see Americans again.

"There were prisoners from thirty-one nations in Mauthausen. We managed to get all the people in the courtyard with an English-speaking representative from each nation and explained that they if they would please stay in their quarters that would facilitate our clearing the camp of the German guards and then the camp would be in the command of the United States Army.

"Some of the refugees were setting up a band down in the courtyard. The first representative to speak was Polish. When he finished, he asked for three cheers for the Americans and the response was thunderous. Each representative went through this procedure. Then the band played 'The Star Spangled Banner,' and my emotions were so great that the song meant more to me than it ever did before. Many of the refugees were crying as they watched our platoon standing at attention presenting arms. When we dropped our salute, we found out that Captain Taylor had taught the band our national anthem just the night before."

———

Denson knew the story. If fortunes had reversed them, would he have been like Taylor, able to withstand Nazi torture and teach fellow prisoners to play "The Star Spangled Banner"? He gave Taylor a slight nod of thanks. "No further questions."

———

"Did you see any of these sixty-one defendants while you were in Mauthausen?" Oeding asked on cross-examination, seeking to move the tribunal past the emotion of Taylor's testimony.

"Well, maybe five or six. It's been about a year. In their uniforms they looked different."

"Can you say for certain that any of these five or six whom you think you recognize committed any of these alleged atrocities while you were in Mauthausen?"

"No, sir."

"Commander, you made certain statements concerning Dr. Hoehler, the camp dentist. When did you first see Dr. Hoehler?"

"I'm not positive. I only recognize him from pictures that I uncovered."

"Then this is actually the first time you have ever seen Dr. Hoehler?" Oeding asked, discrediting the prosecution's star witness.

"Yes, sir."

Oeding could have left well enough alone but instead pushed the point. "You were mentioning about teeth being extracted from corpses in the camp. Was this your own knowledge, or is that also hearsay?"

"When the liberation forces came in, they asked me to help interview prisoners, and I got a sworn statement from the prisoner dentist who worked under Hoehler. . . ."

"It's not of your own knowledge, then?" Oeding asked, point made, prepared to dismiss the witness.

"Well, to this extent, that at the same time that I interviewed him, the prisoner dentist gave me the last day's collection of extracted teeth with the gold in them."

16

Death Books, Doctors, Sick Camp

Denson progressed from Jack Taylor's description of how people were killed in Mauthausen to evidence in death books of how many were killed. His next witness, Ernst Martin, had been a clerk for the camp's head physician. Martin made entries in the death books, filled out autopsies and coroner's reports, and logged tens of thousands of death certificates.

"Mr. Martin," Denson said, "the death certificates of persons who died while allegedly trying to escape—were they true or false?"

"Hardly a dozen people ever actually tried," Martin answered. "Escape from Mauthausen was practically impossible. These people were in reality driven into the chain of guards, or else beaten to such an extent that they could find their only salvation in a quick death."

"What happened to a guard in Mauthausen who showed a reticence with respect to killing?"

"Usually," Martin replied, "he was transferred."

The witness was providing important testimony about a complex issue. If a German soldier could avoid taking part in killing prisoners simply by requesting a transfer, then claiming he had followed orders would not get him excused. Soldiers, even under German law, had an obligation to refuse to obey an illegal order, unless by refusing he put his own life at risk. For a plea of superior orders to stand, the defendant had to prove that disobeying would have put him at risk of imminent death or grievous bodily harm. In a lecture delivered at a Touro Law Center symposium in 1995, Denson offered the following explanation.

"There never was one scintilla of evidence that anybody was ever shot for not obeying an order. If that occurred, it never appeared in any record of the trials, and they had every opportunity to put it in if it was true. In the Dachau trial, there was an incident in which an SS officer was ordered to inject several female prisoners with a phenol solution because they had become pregnant as the result of their activities in the concentration camp bordello. The SS doctor declined to carry out the order—and he was not shot, neither was he even reprimanded officially. The sole consequence to him was a transfer to one of the out-camps. In all of these trials, no witness ever came forward to testify that any subordinate was punished for failing to obey orders that were illegal on their face. I think it is fair to say that superior orders never was and never is a complete defense for an act which calls for the unlawful killing of human beings."

An elaborate analysis of the Nuremburg trial included this caveat: "Let it be said at once that there is no law which requires that an innocent man must forfeit his life or suffer serious harm in order to avoid committing a crime which he condemns. . . . No court will punish a man who, with a loaded pistol to his head, is compelled to pull a lethal lever."

But what if a soldier does not realize that the act he is called upon to perform is a crime? And what exactly constitutes "crime" for a soldier? The efficiency of an army, American or otherwise, depends on discipline, obedience, and a willingness to follow orders. The issue was complex, and while superior orders was never considered an absolute defense, the war crimes review committees considered it a factor in mitigation of sentences.

———

Denson took a large bound volume and approached the witness. "Mr. Martin, I hand you prosecution's exhibit fourteen and ask you to state what it is."

"This is the death book that was kept by me in 1942 and 1943. Around April 20, 1945, an order was issued to burn all papers concerning the prisoners and the SS, among them also these death books. The papers concerned approximately seventy-two thousand deaths and burned without interruption for eight days. Because it was such a long procedure, I was able to hide these death books. After the liberation by American troops, I turned them over to Lieutenant Taylor."

"Was there at any time an escape from block twenty?"

"Yes. In February 1945. It was talked about in camp that sixteen or seventeen prisoners got away. All the others were killed."

While escape from Mauthausen may have been nearly impossible, several hundred officers broke out of the camp's Russian block and disappeared into the surrounding forest. Most were recaptured. Those who made it to freedom did so thanks in part to a handful of local inhabitants daring enough to aid "enemies of the Reich."

"Do you know," Denson asked, "what treatment these escaped prisoners received after they had been recaptured?"

"They were shot or beaten to death."

———

"Mr. Martin," Ernst Oeding asked on cross-examination, "directing your attention to the sixty-one men accused in this case, did you ever see any one of them shoot anybody?"

"No."

"Did you ever see any one of these sixty-one people gas anybody?"

"No."

"Did you ever see any one of these sixty-one people inject anybody?"

"I did not see that."

"Did you ever see any one of these sixty-one men drive anybody into the electric fence or beat anyone to death or push anybody into the stone quarry?"

"No."

"Thank you. No further questions."

Denson called his next witness, Dr. Bratislav Busak.

"I am a professor of law, University of Prague. I was brought to Mauthausen on February 18, 1942, and remained until the end on fifth May 1945. I came in a group of Czechs, chiefly intellectuals, university professors and doctors."

"Will you describe the treatment you received, please, doctor, upon your arrival?" Denson asked.

"On the way from the railroad station we were severely mistreated by the SS with rifle butts. After we came into the camp we waited in front of the bathhouse for approximately one and a half hours. Then a group of SS men came whom we later recognized as camp commandant Ziereis, camp physician Dr. Richter, post physician Dr. Krebsbach, and several others. Then Commandant Ziereis made a speech. 'Here in Mauthausen you work, or else you die.' Afterward we went into the bath, where we were again beaten."

"To what detail were you assigned, doctor?"

"The so-called Russian camp, where leveling work was done. Next to the stone quarry, it was the worst place of destruction in the entire camp. It was winter, very cold at the time. We had insufficient clothing. SS troops were constantly among us, so that we never had an instant in which to rest. There was not only constant beating going on, but also every day between thirty and sixty people were driven into the chain of guards and shot down. People were also crushed to death—it was true destruction."

"Doctor, how were bodies of the prisoners who died there carried out?"

"The corpses were undressed and put on one cart and the clothing on another cart. The reason was that before, when the people had not been undressed, the bloody corpses froze together to such an extent that the bodies could not be separated and had to be hacked apart with axes and chopped to pieces."

"Did you receive any injury while you were working on this detail?"

"Two of my ribs were broken. I was working with four or five comrades, and we were supposed to remove a huge granite rock weighing approximately two hundred kilos. It was impossible to remove that stone for physically healthy people, not to speak of us in the condition we were. When we attempted to use axes as levers, we broke the handles. As punishment we were beaten up. Then the sick camp was opened, and I first came as block clerk, and later on as camp clerk."

"Will you describe this sick camp to the court, doctor?"

"The barracks were nothing more than stables," Busak said. "For the entire personnel of two hundred people there was one toilet in the court-yard. For patients to go from the barracks to toilet in the courtyard they had only underwear, and toward the end many were completely naked. They had to do this in all sorts of weather. The people were so weak that I saw some of them fall down on the way from the barracks and die. For patients inside the barracks there were three large pails. Weak patients sometimes fell into this pail full of fecal matter. I ask your pardon for having to go into unpleasant details, but this was what life was like in the sick camp."

"Were the beds kept clean and sanitary, doctor?"

"Since people were suffering all kinds of diseases, the blankets and mattresses were full of dirt and filth. The bunks were in very poor shape. It sometimes happened that the top layer, containing six people, collapsed and fell down on the second layer. Then the second layer collapsed and fell down on the bottom. The result in one such case was one dead person and two people with broken arms. It also happened that people in the upper bunks who were too weak to get out in order to relieve themselves preferred to remain where they were. The stuff fell down on the people below them. The stench and the noise in these barracks was terrible."

"Was there a period known as the starvation period in the sick camp?"

"Yes. That was three weeks in the spring of 1945 when there was no bread at all. During this period we received one loaf of bread for twenty people. The people became what we called in camp dialect *muselmann*. These were people who sank from a weight of eighty to forty kilograms, liv-ing skeletons who would just fall down one day and die. I saw several cases where a man who two minutes ago still looked alive, suddenly died. These people ate anything they could find—leather straps, grass, coal—things which it would appear impossible to eat, those people ate."

"Prior to the time that the SS left Mauthausen, did they destroy any of the facilities that were present there?"

"Yes. I think it was on the second of May, the SS destroyed the water pressure pump. As a result, the secretions from the upper camp came down into the lower camp and remained there for more than ten days, under the sun on the hot ground. The main camp had almost fifteen thousand people at the time. One can hardly imagine the stench."

"Can you stop there, Mr. Prosecutor?" Prickett asked. Even the tribunal had been worn down by the incessant descriptions of conditions in Mauthausen. Denson, it seemed, could have gone on all night.

"Yes, sir."

"The court will adjourn until eight-thirty tomorrow morning."

17

Christ's Rebirth

"Dr. Busak," Denson continued the next day," will you describe to the court what transpired the day that the Americans came?"

"The Americans came in on May fifth at exactly one-fifteen. Five armored cars drove up past the front gates of the concentration camp. I know this exactly because the front line was quite near, on the other side of the Danube about fifteen kilometers away, and for hours I had been looking from the hill on which Mauthausen was located to see what was going on in the battlefield. In front of the sick camp was a large sports field. Along the edge of the sports place and up to the main camp went the main street, which made a large curve. At the moment when the Americans came in, inmates flung open the gates to the sick camp of Mauthausen. I will never in my life forget the following impression. Thousands of patients hurried out into the sports field—it was terrible. They were chiefly naked people, crawling on all their four parts, and those who had no legs dragged along their paper bandages with them. They hung to the armored cars like bees. Then the second wave came, and that consisted of women from the two women's blocks. Many of the women were hysterical and became unconscious. It was like . . ." grasping for words, "it was like the—like the youngest day of Christ's rebirth. I remember standing there and looking on and thinking of the misery of the past years. At that moment I looked up to the camp and saw a white flag flying. It was one-thirty and Mauthausen had capitulated. Around three o'clock the American flag was put up and we were free."

"No further questions."

18

Witnesses for the Prosecution

The one German lawyer on Denson's team rose from the prosecution table and took the stand.

"Tell the court your name, please," Denson asked for the prosecution.

"Hans Karl von Posern, born in Dresden, occupation lawyer. I was in Mauthausen from July 1941 up to the liberation. I had to take care of civilian law matters for the SS."

"In the course of your work, did you have access to the secret files of these individuals?"

"In part, yes. I have here, for example, a copy of a secret order of Zeller issued in the beginning of 1942: 'Don't give a piece of bread to any prisoner: that will prolong his life. Don't give a cigarette butt to any prisoner: he will take several of them and make a new cigarette for himself and will enjoy it. See in every prisoner your personal enemy who will kill you if he has an opportunity to do so. Always remember that the prisoner is excluded from society: he is a common criminal who was sent here to be destroyed. If we did not take his life in spite of that, then this is only due to our strength of character.'"

"Mr. von Posern, did you later see a secret order from the defendant Glücks?"

"Yes. Schiller came over to me just before liberation and said, 'Well, you know the Americans will come and all our comrades will be finished.' Then he said, 'Black things are in store for me. There are too many foreigners around, and they will try to get revenge. I will make you a proposition. I will get you out of the camp tonight and quarter you in the troops' quarters, and I will save your life in that way. When the Americans arrive tomorrow, then you will try to cover up for me.' Then Schiller gave me this radiogram that said, 'When the Americans approach, the prisoners are to be taken to the woods in order to "gather flowers and buds." Signed Glücks.' I asked Schiller what all this nonsense was supposed to mean, and Schiller explained to me that it was code words for the extermination of the prisoners."

"Do you know a man by the name of Eigruber?"

"Of course. Eigruber was *Gauleiter*, provincial governor of the upper Danube. He was a friend of Commandant Ziereis and frequently inspected Mauthausen. I recall toward the end of '42, Eigruber toured the camp with Ziereis, Bachmayer, Schultz, and several others. They passed by the execution grounds where Eigruber saw the folding chair, which had become famous in Mauthausen for hanging executions. This chair had a release pedal. Apparently he was interested in the mechanics of it and tried it himself several times. Then there was conversation between them, which I did not hear. Bachmayer went away and returned with four prisoners who were executed using this chair. In one case Eigruber himself pushed down this release pedal. I would like to say that four isn't much for an execution in Mauthausen—just unpleasant for the people concerned."

Denson ignored the attempt at sarcasm and asked, "Do you know a man by the name of Werner Grahn?"

"Yes. He arrived in early '44. We learned he had been SD—*Sicherheitsdienst*, the much-feared security service of the SS. We prisoners mistrusted anyone who had been with that group, so I took Grahn under observation. Grahn arrived in the morning, disappeared into the bunker and left again in the evening. He made some comment about setting up a translation office there. What made us mistrust him was that his work was always accompanied by the screaming of women. A friend of mine who worked in the crematorium showed me bodies of women whose breasts and thighs had been whipped and their eyebrows beaten open. 'These are translations,' he said. We estimated the number of Grahn's victims at approximately seven hundred."

"Mr. von Posern, do you know a man by the name of Willy Eckert?"

"Willy Eckert was *Hauptscharführer*—an SS master sergeant—and work detail leader of the laundry in Mauthausen."

"Did you ever see him kill a man?"

"A Russian prisoner of war, an invalid, who had arrived on a sick transport. Both his legs were missing up to here, and he moved around on two boards strapped down there. One arm was missing from about here, the other arm was entirely missing. Actually, there was only the torso of this man. Eckert kicked him with his feet and rolled him along in front of himself like a football, then he picked up the handle of a shovel and beat him to death. When he saw that I had been watching, he came past me and said, as if to excuse himself, 'Terrible, such things without any members.'"

———

Denson had come face-to-face with a similar expression of disdain for the physically disabled during his pretrial interrogation of Eduard Krebsbach. After completing his doctorate at the University of Bonn, Krebsbach worked as a pediatrician before applying for membership in the SS in 1937. In 1941 he became chief doctor at Mauthausen, where he conducted mass killings of prisoners through lethal injections *(spritzen)*, earning himself the nickname "Dr. Spritzbach."

"When I began my service," he told Denson during the interrogation, "I received an order to kill—or have killed—all those unable to work or hopelessly sick."

"And how did you carry out this order?" Denson asked.

"As far as the hopelessly sick were concerned or those absolutely unfit for work, most of them were gassed. Some of them were killed through gasoline injections."

"To your knowledge, how many were killed while you were there?"

Krebsbach did not answer. Denson rephrased his questions.

"So you were given orders to kill the *Lebensuntuchtigen*?" he asked, referring to "those unfit for life."

"Yes," Krebsbach replied. "I had the order to have this kind of individuals killed if I thought that they would be a burden to the state."

"Did it never occur to you that you were dealing, after all, with human beings? Human beings who had the misfortune of being prisoners, or who had been neglected by nature?"

"No," Krebsbach said. "Things are similar between human beings and animals. Animals born crippled or which are otherwise unfit for life are killed immediately after birth. One should do the same with these human beings—out of humanitarian considerations—and we would prevent a great deal of misfortune and misery."

"This is your view," Denson told him. "The world's view is quite different. Did it never occur to you that the murder of these persons was an abominable crime?"

"No. It is the right of every state to protect itself against antisocial individuals, and those unfit for life are part of this."

"So, the thought never occurred to you that this was a crime?"

"No. I followed my orders to the best of my knowledge and conscience because I had to follow them."

———

Cross-examination of Von Posern was conducted by 1st Lt. Patrick W. McMahon, a New York state assistant attorney general. McMahon had been with the war crimes program since its inception and knew that some Germans had avoided trial by agreeing to cooperate with the prosecution. "How long were you a prisoner of the Americans here in Dachau, Mr. von Posern?"

"From October last year to February of this year."

"And did you then, starting this past February, go to work for Lieutenant Guth of the prosecution?"

"Never. But I do know Lieutenant Guth from the first Dachau war crimes trial when I defended some of the accused."

"How many times have you been in the lieutenant's office since your release?"

"May it please the court," Denson said. "I object on the ground it is absolutely immaterial and not within any scope of cross-examination."

"Objection sustained."

"With the court's indulgence," McMahon replied, "regardless of this witness's statement, he is an employee of Lieutenant Guth. And regardless of the fact that he calls himself a witness, he has been hour after hour and day after day since February in the office of Lieutenant Guth and other members of the prosecution."

"May it please the court," Denson said. "In the preparation of any case people operate to secure facts. Whether this man is an employee of Lieutenant Guth or not is utterly immaterial to the issues in this case."

"I am attacking the credibility of this witness," McMahon said, "and I am at perfect liberty to attack in any respect whatsoever. The court will have abundant proof that the matters which I am proceeding upon are very, very material—not only to the case but to the fundamental issue of each and every one of these defendants."

"Objection sustained."

Oeding took over for the defense. "Are you being paid anything for your assistance in this case?"

"Now just a minute," Denson interrupted. "May it please the court, I object to this whole line of questioning. In the first place, this man is not on trial. In the second, these questions are not pertinent, the insinuations are improper, and none of it should be permitted."

"Sustained."

Oeding tried another angle. "Did anybody ever threaten you that either you agree to become a witness for the prosecution or else become yourself a defendant in this case?"

"Objection on the same grounds," Denson said.

"Sustained."

McMahon gave up his attack on Von Posern's credibility and reverted to specifics. "What was the date of this folding chair hanging when Eigruber was present?"

"That, I think, was late in 1942."

"Who all was present?"

"Ziereis was present, Bachmayer, Schultz, and a few more."

"Ziereis is dead, isn't he?" Oeding said.

"Yes."

"Bachmayer, he is dead, isn't he?"

"That is what they say."

"So as to this folding chair hanging, it's your word against Eigruber's, that so?"

"I am a witness and nothing else. I have nothing to do with collecting other witnesses."

———

To secure a conviction against Eigruber, Denson wanted to introduce further evidence of the folding chair and called upon a former prisoner to testify. Wilhelm Ornstein had been assigned to the crematory in Mauthausen. "I used him extensively," Denson recalled in an interview forty years later, "because one who worked in the crematory usually had a life span of about three or four weeks. They got rid of the people who knew a lot—and this man knew more than most."

"My name is Wilhelm Ornstein. I was born in Drohobycz, Poland. I came to Mauthausen as a prisoner on the tenth of August 1944 and was liberated on fifth May 1945. In the crematory detail there were different rooms. There was the room where the people took off their clothes. There was another room in which an SS man played the role of a doctor. He told people to open their mouth, presumably to see if they were ill, but in reality to see if they had gold teeth. Those prisoners with gold received a cross on their chest. Then there was the gas chamber, which Lieutenant Taylor described."

"Mr. Ornstein, what was the room next to the gas chamber?"

"That was a very narrow pass that led to the place of execution, where the so-called neck shots were performed." Prisoners to be executed were positioned in front of a wall that had a discreet slit at neck level. On cue, an executioner hidden on the other side fired his pistol through the slit. "The neck shots were carried out in different ways on Americans in high office, women, and prisoners," Ornstein said. "In the case of American officers and women there was always a screen put up, like in a photo studio, and after every neck shot the SS would get rid of the blood so that the next one coming in would not see the blood. In the case of other prisoners, there was no such pretense. Eight to ten were executed in succession, and only after that the blood was removed. The SS who took part had their various functions. One SS in the clothing room sent the people in. Other SS were in the hallway from the clothing room to the execution room. One was at the door and called out, 'Next one.' One was at the camera and called out 'Photograph.' One prepared the ammunition and loaded the weapon. Others held the innocent victims by the arm if they struggled."

"Will you describe, please, the method that was followed in the hanging of prisoners while you were in Mauthausen?"

"Yes. On an iron rod there was a rope wrapped around, and three people at a time were hanged. Under the rod there was a chair set up with springs in it. Those sentenced had to stand up on the chair and put the rope around their own necks. One SS man secured the rope, pressed the spring, the chair fell down, and those sentenced remained hanging in the air. They hanged about ten minutes on the rope and afterward were taken into the cooling room."

"Mr. Ornstein, what was the next room?"

"Ovens."

"I hand you an object marked prosecution's exhibit number seventy-one and ask you to state what it is, if you know."

"That is an identification tag which I turned over to Captain Taylor after the liberation. I took it off a corpse on twenty-sixth January 1945, after an execution."

"And what is the name that appears on that?"

"Nelson Bernard Paris."

"Do you know how this man met his death?"

"Yes. He was shot in the neck during the execution of American officers in the Mauthausen crematory. At that time there were fourteen men executed. They had all been executed by the so-called neck shots. Various SS men took part."

"Do you see any of these men sitting over in the dock?"

"Yes. Altfuldisch, Niedermeyer, Riegler, Eigruber."

"Nothing further."

"Mr. Ornstein," Oeding said on cross-examination, "did any prisoner in Mauthausen ever die a natural death?"

"Even if he did die a natural death," Ornstein replied, "one should ask what got him to the state in which he died a natural death."

"No further questions."

———

In some instances, evidence that led to convictions in the Dachau trials would not have held up in regular American courts. A few witnesses offered illogical testimony, with an obvious purpose of exacting retribution against someone who had done them harm. No one blamed former victims of the camps for wanting to see their tormentors convicted, but some moments in the prosecution's case breached the limits of credibility. One such moment occurred when court reconvened on April 12, 1946.

"All right," Prickett said, "call your witnesses."

"Efraim Sternberg," Denson announced. The witness took the stand.

"I was born in Kolo, Poland. I was a prisoner in Mauthausen when I was sent there from the Krakow concentration camp. I was liberated by the Americans."

"Did you know a man by the name of Keilwitz, Mr. Sternberg?"

"The older people, Spaniards and others who had been there for some time, told us Keilwitz was a very cruel man. He received a group of our people who came in a transport. There were several thousand. When they had to undress, he practiced boxing on them, hitting them in the stomach. Those who fell down he immediately kicked with his feet or else hit with an oxtail whip until they were dead. He is the one looking at me, that dog, the thin one with the long nose."

"Now, did you know anybody by the name of Guetzlaff?"

"Yes. He was a guard in the tower. He shot at prisoners from the tower. The tower at the top of the steps—that was the best place to shoot prisoners from. They did that all the time."

"Now, walk over to the dock and see if you can identify the man you knew by the name Guetzlaff. Walk over and . . ."

"That is the one!" Before anyone could stop him, Sternberg leaped from the witness chair, sprinted to the dock, and began pummeling the defendant, yelling in his ear.

Prickett stood. "Stop that!" he shouted.

Guards rushed over to restrain the witness. Denson grabbed Sternberg by his arms. "Sit down," he ordered, shouting over the witness's invective. Denson turned to the translator. "Tell him to not do this. He is not to touch anyone." McMahon and the other defense lawyers were on their feet. Sternberg was subdued and brought back to the witness chair.

"Will the court direct the interpreter to translate what the witness was saying?" McMahon said. "Let the record reflect what he said."

"Does the interpreter remember the words he spoke?" Prickett asked.

"I can remember some of them, sir. 'That's the one,' he said. 'That's the one who is spreading the new German culture.'"

Oeding rose at the defense table. "Are you an Orthodox Jew, Mr. Sternberg? Do you know what an oath is?"

"I am a little religious, and I know what an oath is."

"What is an oath?"

"When you take an oath you are responsible for it to God."

"And you have taken an oath here this morning to tell the truth?"

"Yes, all is the truth."

"What would you say if you were told that Guetzlaff was not in Mauthausen during 1944 or 1945?"

"He was in Mauthausen."

"No further questions."

19

"The Pigs Must Perish"

Nazis who operated concentration camps forced inmates to execute their orders and maintain discipline in the barracks, or "blocks" as they were also called. Inmates deputized by the Germans to carry out these tasks were called *kapos*. These prisoner-guards, many of whom had been convicted as common criminals and sent to a concentration camp, sometimes received privileges for performing their duties well and often faced severe consequences if they did not, with the result that many *kapos* became as cruel as their German captors. With this scheme to protect them, senior SS personnel could frequently remain aloof from the daily workings of the camps. Prosecutors in the war crimes trials consequently faced a dilemma in attempting to connect certain senior officers to specific crimes.

August Eigruber was one of forty-three *Gauleiters*, or civilian provincial governors, in Nazi-occupied territories. He joined the Nazi Party in 1927, making him one of Hitler's earliest followers. Three years later, at age twenty-three, he was appointed head of the local Hitler Youth. His rise to *Gauleiter* followed Germany's invasion of Austria in September of 1939. Eigruber was an enthusiastic Nazi who enjoyed close relations with Hitler and Martin Bormann, Hitler's deputy for Nazi Party affairs. On his arrest after liberation, Eigruber went silent and offered not one word concerning his activities or those of his acquaintances during the Nazi period. War crimes investigators in Germany shrugged their shoulders and gave up interrogating him. Eigruber was sent to Washington, where further questioning also failed to elicit the slightest cooperation. When Paul Guth was preparing his list of defendants for the Mauthausen trial, Eigruber's whereabouts were unknown. Then word came that he had been sent to Nuremberg, and Denson placed a call to Robert Jackson.

"Send me Eigruber," he told the chief prosecutor. "I'll hang him high as Haman," referring to the antagonist of the biblical story on which the Jewish holiday of Purim is based.

"Well, sir," Jackson replied, "that's pretty high."

Eigruber arrived in Dachau on February 18, 1946, and the following day Guth began the toughest interrogation of his career. Getting a statement from Eigruber would be a turning point: through the echelon, no one else had succeeded. Guth had a strategy. Through family connections the young officer was acquainted with Austria's business elite. He reasoned that Eigruber must have had dealings with some of those same men and, after a round of calls, succeeded in enlisting the help of mutual acquaintances. During the interrogation, Guth played to Eigruber's vanity, conversing about everything other than atrocities and concentration camps, and plying him with a limitless supply of coffee and other refreshments. Eigruber frequently excused himself to go to the bathroom, where he happened upon these former associates.

"Who's your interrogator?" they asked with seeming innocence.

"Paul Guth."

"Oh, he's easy," they assured him. "Throw him a bone or two and he'll be happy." In their own minds, many German officers imagined gradations of guilt: someone who had killed a thousand people felt he would do well admitting to killing only three—particularly if the three "were of no consequence," Poles or Jews, for example. As a skillful interrogator, Guth used that tendency to advantage, knowing well that in the eyes of the tribunal killing three or three thousand bore the same consequences.

Eigruber broke his silence, offering what he believed to be innocuous admissions about his jurisdiction and involvement with camp functions, and signed a statement. He was held at Dachau for trial, and Guth burst into Denson's office waving the paper. The chief prosecutor was speechless.

———

Denson's investigators had found witnesses to Eigruber's participation in atrocities in Mauthausen. Hans Schmeling, a former camp inmate, testified, "I had to go with three other prisoners to get laundry for block twenty. Between the laundry and the wall, several new arrivals were standing. Eigruber was telling them, 'You have come here in order to work—to work,' he said, 'until you rot. Anybody who has not rotted will be beaten to death. My men will see to that.' Then the incoming prisoners were taken to the blocks and beat so badly that some of them went into the fence out of pain or fear."

Prosecution witness Richard Dietel also spoke about Eigruber. "I was sent to block sixteen in the nude. We slept on the floor—fourteen men, one blanket. The next day at about four o'clock we had to fall out again and were told that Gauleiter Eigruber would come to inspect us. Eigruber, Ziereis, Zutter, Trum, and several other officers came in. Eigruber stepped up and shouted, 'You dumb fools! You idiots! You thought the war was over, but you made a mistake. It hasn't even started yet.' Then he turned to Colonel Ziereis and said, 'My people work well. When they are through with them, we can still use them to work. But as far as life is concerned, they are through.'"

"Would you recognize Eigruber if you saw him in the courtroom today?" Denson asked.

"Yes, I would. Number thirteen."

———

Ernst Martin, who had been a clerk in the physician's office in Mauthausen, also offered testimony concerning Eigruber.

"Did you have occasion to hear conversations between Eigruber and Ziereis," Denson asked, "with reference to the treatment of the recaptured Russian prisoners?"

"Yes," Martin replied. "Eigruber said, 'All these pigs must perish.'"

"Nothing further."

———

"The conversation that you testified to hearing between Ziereis and Eigruber," Oeding asked on cross-examination, "where did that conversation take place?"

"I was going to the hospital on the morning after the escape. Eigruber and Ziereis were standing together about four meters from me."

"Exactly what did you hear?"

"'The pigs must perish.' I heard only that one thing as I passed by. I was careful not to stop, because that would have been a death sentence for me. I had to assume it was connected with the Russians from block twenty who tried to escape, since they were going there to look things over."

"Of your own knowledge then, you do not know what Eigruber meant by the word 'pig,' is that correct?"

"Obviously he didn't give me an explanation, but I heard that sentence."

———

"The prosecution calls as its next witness Lieutenant Guth. Did you interrogate August Eigruber on or about the nineteenth of February 1946?"

"Yes, sir."

"And before, did you tell him that he did not have to make a statement?"

"Yes, sir."

"Did you threaten Eigruber in any manner to make a statement?"

"No, sir."

"I hand you Eigruber's statement. Did he sign this in your presence?"

"Yes, sir. On each page."

Major Oeding stood and said, "Defense objects to this statement on the grounds that it fails to meet the requirements of USFET Circular No. 132, Subject: Investigation of War Crimes. There is no witness, no authentication of any kind."

"May it please the court," Denson replied, "we have here a letter written and signed by Col. C. B. Mickelwait, Deputy Theater Judge Advocate, Subject: Admissibility of Reports of Investigation in the Trial of Suspected War Criminals. In part this letter reads, 'It is the position of this office that such testimony procured by an investigating officer may be introduced in evidence without further authentication.'" Denson was not going to let Eigruber slip through the prosecution's hands because of some technicality and had come to court armed with the authorizations needed to make sure his statement would be admitted.

"With great respect to Colonel Mickelwait," Oeding said, "that is merely his opinion. The document to which defense has referred has the direct authority of the USFET commanding general."

Notwithstanding the authority of Oeding's document, the judge advocate's letter carried greater weight. The directive, dated August 25, 1945, stated that military commissions, while obligated to see that accused received "a full and fair trial," were not bound by general rules of evidence. "Such evidence shall be admitted before a military commission," the directive stated, "as has probative value to a reasonable man." A. H. Rosenfeld, who was serving as law member, said, "The rules of procedure in military government courts are the rules which guide this court during trial. As such, the written evidence produced by prosecution will be admitted. The motion is denied."

Oeding made one last move, this time to minimize the danger of Eigruber's statement to the other defendants. "Defense moves that the statement be held for naught as to any allegations made therein with respect to the other accused. In that connection, I quote briefly from Underhill's *Criminal Evidence*: 'Testimony as to statements of accessories made after the conspiracy has ended and out of the hearing and presence of the accused is inadmissible.'"

"I don't wish to be tedious," Denson offered, "but in view of what counsel has said the court might be under misapprehension with respect to the opinion of deputy theater judge advocate of the European theater. The text from which counsel read was obviously written prior to any such time as trials such as these were contemplated."

"I respectfully urge on the court," Oeding replied, "that the nearer they can stay within the established rules and still accomplish the purposes of the case, the more closely we hew to the lines of Anglo-American justice."

Denson must have felt strange hearing defense counsel echoing his own arguments.

"The court will give such value as it sees fit," Rosenfeld ruled. "The motion is denied."

"May it please the court," Denson said, "I ask permission to read the English translation of Eigruber's statement."

"Proceed."

———

"I, August Eigruber, born on the 16th of April 1907, residing in Steyr, Upper Austria, declare herewith: In June 1938 I was made Gauleiter *(state leader) and in 1943* Reichsverteidigungskommisar *(Reich defense commissar) of Upper Austria. The District Food Office was under my supervision. From 1942 on, I had a steadily increasing influence on the District Work Office with the goal of building up the armament industry of Upper Austria.*

"The purpose of the concentration camp was, first, the education of the prisoners. From 1939 until 1942, its purpose was guarding inhabitants of occupied countries who had offered resistance to German occupational troops, in that manner preventing all further resistance. From 1942 on, with the increasing need for armaments, prisoners were supposed to be employed in armament productions to the greatest possible extent.

"Steady increase of Mauthausen concentration camp made necessary frequent discussions with camp commandant Ziereis, about administration, health, and industrial questions which served to insure the existence of the camp and the nourishment and distribution of prisoners for armament production.

"I came into somewhat closer contact with the Mauthausen concentration camp by inspecting the gravel pit several times and the gas chamber once. I also participated in the execution of ten prisoners of unknown nationality, which occurred at night during March or April 1945. At the end of 1944, the Upper Austria Security Organizations under my order participated in the search for Russian prisoners who had escaped from Mauthausen.

"In 1939 I leased to Reich Leader Philipp BOUHLER, who had an order of the Führer that mental patients who were incurably ill or unable to work were to be killed, the Castle Hartheim for the execution of the Leader's orders. In the Gau *(State) of Upper Austria, I was the only one who knew officially what Castle Hartheim was to be used for.*

"This statement was made by me on three pages on the 19th of February 1946, in Dachau, Germany, of my own free will and without compulsion. To save time, a clerk wrote it down on a typewriter. I have read through it, and I have made corrections that appeared necessary to me.

"The above declaration contains my statements, and I swear before God that it is the entire truth. Signed, August Eigruber."

———

Denson finished reading and looked at his team. They had met all the items on their checklist, had brought to the stand witnesses to speak against each of the sixty-one men on trial, and entered into evidence confessions to which, for reasons known only to themselves, the accused had sworn and then signed. There was nothing more to do here but prepare for whatever surprises the defense might have in store.

"The prosecution rests."

20

Case for the Defense

Maj. Ernst Oeding announced, "The defense calls August Eigruber."

"You are advised," tribunal president Prickett said, "that the court may draw such inference as the circumstances justify from your refusal to answer or from your failure to take the stand in your own behalf. Are you now willing to testify?"

"Yes."

"In any of the official positions that you held," Oeding began, "did you have any jurisdiction over Mauthausen concentration camp?"

"No."

"Did you ever send any orders to Mauthausen relative to the treatment of prisoners?"

"Since I was not in charge of it, I could not give any orders. No."

"Did your office receive any reports relative to the number of sick or any type of statistical reports relative to Mauthausen?"

"No, with one exception. The administration of the camp requisitioned their monthly food ration cards at the food office."

"And who determined the amount of food that would be authorized by this certificate?"

"That was done by the Reich Food Minister for Germans, according to the harvest and circumstances published by the various food offices."

"Was the quantity of food called for by these ration cards always available in the market?" Oeding asked. Denson noted to himself to make sure the tribunal understood it was the quality, not just the quantity, of food that made the Mauthausen prisoner's diet grossly inadequate.

"Usually, with the exception of the later days. In the later days, it was not that the food wasn't available but that food could not be transported. In addition, there was a large number of refugees. During February, March, and April a half million refugees came to my *Gau*, especially when the Russians advanced toward the Reich border."

"Did you know that four or five hundred Russian prisoners escaped from Mauthausen concentration camp in February, 1945?"

"Yes."

"Did you at any time in camp say, in reference to those escaped Russians, words to the effect, 'The pigs must perish'?"

"The witness heard from a distance of several meters somebody say something about swine or pigs," Eigruber proposed, "and probably imagined what it was supposed to have meant. However, I was not in Mauthausen at that time."

"Did you ever visit the prison compound in Mauthausen?"

"Yes. With its large population, Mauthausen had needs like any other city. It would have been impossible from an administrative point of view to close it off entirely. It required water, lighting, sewers, construction material, and so on."

"Did you ever see the collapsing chair that was allegedly used in Mauthausen to execute people by hanging?"

"No. That is the testimony of Von Posern. He said that I liked this chair so much I had four prisoners called and hanged with this apparatus. However, his only witnesses are dead."

"Did you ever visit the stone quarry in Mauthausen?"

"I was in the quarry once with Himmler and once, I believe, with Reich Minister Speer. The witness Wahsner claimed that I put a sixty-kilo rock into the hands of a weak, starved Jew in the quarry, and that I said this rock was too light and then gave him a rock weighing ninety kilos."

"Did you ever pick up a stone weighing ninety kilos?"

"I don't think I could pick one up that weighed sixty," Eigruber said.

"Did you ever tell any of these co-accused that it was your goal to see that as many prisoners as possible were killed?"

"I never spoke with any of these accused even a single time about the internal affairs of Mauthausen. In fact, I met 90 percent of the accused for the first time here in the bunker—particularly those who have made statements against me under oath."

"Did your office have jurisdiction over Castle Hartheim?"

Near Mauthausen stood Castle Hartheim, one of six institutions where the Nazi euthanasia program was enacted. The program took its inspiration from neo-Darwinian theories of eugenics, which held that society was weakened by the presence of "inferior elements" and could protect itself from "degeneration" only by practicing "racial hygiene," a euphemism for killing people deemed inferior. In 1939 the Reich Interior Ministry sent a list of such "inferior" types of people to every hospice and asylum in Germany. The list included, among others, anyone suffering from epilepsy, senility, Huntington's disease, anyone who had been in a hospital for more than five years, foreigners, and all those falling under National Socialist race legislation. This last group included people defined as "defective" because of their race—in general, Jews.

On June 6, 1940, the first victims were asphyxiated in Castle Hartheim with carbon monoxide gas. On August 24, 1941, Hitler ordered the program discontinued because of protests from the Church and influential private citizens, but in those fourteen months more than seventy thousand human beings had already been gassed. Castle Hartheim was then supplied with new victims: SS leader Himmler issued instructions that "sick and ailing" prisoners from the concentration camps (including Mauthausen, Gusen, Dachau, Ravensbrück, Buchenwald) were to undergo "special treatment" at Hartheim. After the gassing, the corpses were incinerated in crematorium furnaces. Body parts littered the surrounding countryside and tufts of hair flew out of the chimney, but neither these nor the smell of burning flesh were sufficient to cancel the castle's annual candlelight festivals. At the end of 1944 the technical installations of the gas chamber were removed and the castle was returned to its original state.

———

"No," Eigruber answered. "In 1939 my office leased Castle Hartheim to Reich leader Bouhler, who was looking for a building in that vicinity in order to carry out an order of the führer."

"What was that order of the führer?" Oeding asked.

"The order stated that incurable German mental patients were to be killed there. Bouhler showed this order to me. Otherwise, I would never have given him the castle."

"Did you know that prisoners from Mauthausen were gassed at Castle Hartheim?"

"No."

"Did your office ever procure prison labor for use in the armament industry?"

"As Reich defense commissar, one of my tasks was to increase armament production. From 1943 to 1945 there were continuously fifty to sixty thousand open jobs in the armament industry. Like other officers, I attempted to get prisoners from Mauthausen into the armament works."

"Commander Taylor testified in this court that there was a four months' supply of potatoes in Mauthausen when it was liberated. Do you know why it wasn't fed to the prisoners?"

"I do not know. I was not the cook at Mauthausen. At least the food supply was sent there, but why it wasn't distributed I don't know."

"No further questions."

———

Denson had presented witnesses attesting to Eigruber's personal involvement in camp atrocities, and he expected the tribunal would recognize them as credible. But it would be their word against Eigruber's. He also had Eigruber's sworn statement establishing his participation in the common design at Mauthausen. No doubt defense would make noise over the way they thought Guth had obtained it, and to depend on Eigruber's statement for a conviction was risky. Now he had the man himself on the stand. What could Denson accomplish? At the very least he could bring out his arrogance and utter lack of sympathy.

"Are you aware," Denson began on cross-examination, "that Mauthausen was a class three extermination camp?"

"That phrase 'extermination camp' I heard here for the first time. That didn't exist. It's a fairy tale."

"A fairy tale. What other phrase would you use?" Denson asked.

"Just a moment, I didn't finish. I did hear that Mauthausen was a severe camp and that is why—you may believe this or not—I tried to get the prisoners into armament works. At least there I knew they would receive the same conditions as German workers. However, I had no influence so far as the quarry or other work done in the camp."

Despite his correct assessment that Mauthausen was not technically classified as an extermination camp, Eigruber's cavalier minimizing of its severity more than warranted Denson's incredulous reaction. Over time some camps changed status, and by the end Mauthausen had gone from bad to worse, becoming one of the most feared among the Category III camps. In footage at the National Archives, Eigruber's appearance—frequent smiles, small, shrewd eyes, casually crossed legs—appears intentional, the portrait of a small-town mayor rather than the master of Upper Austria, a recalcitrant philistine who could not have rubbed Denson any harder the wrong way if he had tried.

"It was up to you to maintain Mauthausen as a going institution, is that not a fact?" Denson asked.

"A 'going institution'?"

"Yes. It was up to you to supply those essentials that were necessary to maintain Mauthausen, is that not so?"

"For example, what? Prisoners?"

"Yes, prisoners. What about the fifty-one that you sent to Mauthausen from your own concentration camp?"

"I do not know what you are talking about," Eigruber said. "I never had my own concentration camp. Why should I have my own concentration camp when, according to your statements, I was in charge of Mauthausen?"

"I will explain that. Do you know a man by the name of Franz Kubinger? Did you not run a concentration camp with him?"

"No."

"You never had any connection with the concentration camp located at Weidermoos?"

At this revelation, shouts erupted.

"Let's have order in the court," Rosenthal demanded.

"Weidermoos," Eigruber reflected. "First of all, this camp was constructed in 1940 and closed in 1941. Therefore, it is before the time that concerns the charges in this trial. Secondly, this was a work camp, not a concentration camp. It was conducted by the Gestapo, and when they constructed their camps they did not require my consent."

"Well, those that were created in Upper Austria were created with your consent, were they not?"

"No, I was not asked about it. Himmler never asked me . . ."

"Did they beat the prisoners there?"

"Yes. That is why it was dissolved. I myself saw to it that the five or six SA men who were responsible for the beatings were arrested and turned over to a court. Thereupon the State Police dissolved the camp."

"And is it not a fact that the dissolution of that camp was nothing more than a transfer of its surviving inmates to Mauthausen?"

"I don't know what happened to the prisoners. I think only fifty or sixty people were concerned there, anyhow." Eigruber's casual dismissal of "only fifty or sixty people" must have registered on Denson's face, as Eigruber was quick to distance himself from the remark. "I was never there," he said. "I never saw it."

But it was too late. Like so many of his cohorts, Eigruber was a contemptible murderer whose only redeeming quality may have been his avoidance of pretentious ideology. He offered no excuses, no presumption of lofty faith in the vision of Adolf Hitler, despite their friendship and Eigruber's look-alike square mustache. Not one of the hundreds of Germans who took the stand during the Dachau trials touted the superiority of National Socialist doctrine. Not one attempted to argue the merits of the Nazi Party or, with the exception of Krebsbach, defend its beliefs. The twenty thousand pages of trial transcripts are a tedious panoply of excuses, pretexts, obfuscations, and denials. The more devout could have argued, "You are missing the logic in what was done." None did.

———

"Do you remember a man by the name of Dietel?" Denson continued.

"I remembered him from when he was sitting on the witness chair here," Eigruber said.

"You remember that he was in the group you sent to Mauthausen, do you not?"

"I did not send any group to Mauthausen. . . ."

"And while in that group he was beaten in your presence, was he not?"

"No. Prisoners were never beaten in my presence. It wasn't like that."

"What was it like?"

"In my presence, or Himmler's presence, or the presence of leaders who accompanied me, there was never anyone beaten, there was never anyone killed. There wasn't even an SS man with a dog whip. That's what it was like."

"Did you not tell Ziereis he should 'work these Communists to death,' that their lives had 'already been written off'?"

"I made no such speech. And Ziereis did not do things in my presence. I did hear about it frequently from the mayor of the Mauthausen community, and I asked Ziereis whether these things that the *Burgermeister* told me were true. In reply, Ziereis three times showed me Himmler's order that prisoners should not be beaten and swore that he was adhering to this order."

"Did you make any further investigation to ascertain the truth or falsity of the charges?"

"I do not wish to say much more about this since the people concerned are no longer alive," Eigruber said with feigned reverence, then added, "In 1942 or 1943 when Himmler was at Mauthausen I did clearly tell him what was on my mind, but to do something against Himmler? I did not have strength enough for that."

"And yet you continued to bring water and electricity and other essentials to Mauthausen, is that correct?"

"Should I not have brought them? Should I have had the water and the electric current shut off?"

"You answer the question," Denson demanded, stepping up the pace.

"That can be the only reply. If thousands of people are there, without my having done anything to bring them there, as an official I am nonetheless responsible to see that the essentials regarding their life are provided insofar as it is under my jurisdiction."

"And if you had stopped in 1939, there wouldn't have been a camp in 1941 or 1942, is that not correct?"

"I object to that question," Oeding said, "as argumentative."

"May it please the court," Denson replied, "he stated that nothing he could do would have prevented this camp from being operated, and that it would have been even worse if he had adopted the plan suggested by the question. I submit it is perfectly proper."

"Objection overruled."

"If the Reich railroad office or some other organization which was not under my supervision wished to construct something," Eigruber said, "how could I fight against it? Above me was the entire Reich government. I was not the one who instituted Mauthausen."

Eigruber's first blunder had been allowing his old business cronies to talk him into making a statement. He had just made his second by adopting the posture of someone helpless against the cruel Nazi machine. It was the opening Denson had been waiting for. Eigruber's elusiveness over the months since his capture drew strength from its neutrality: without declaring what his intentions had been, his role had no purchase, nothing that could be attacked. A crack had appeared now in the edifice, a reaction that Denson could use as a starting point to bring down one of Hitler's top officials.

"Are you trying to tell the court that the only reason you contributed to the maintenance of Mauthausen was because you received orders to do so?"

Eigruber answered carefully. "I did not help legally in the creation of Mauthausen, nor in its continuance. I merely did things, like any other state or city official, which my office had to do. Even against my will, Himmler would certainly have succeeded in getting for Mauthausen the water, the electricity, the sewers. . . ."

"But you wouldn't have had a part in it, would you?"

"I had to do it. Or do you think I was stronger than Himmler? Perhaps you don't think that Himmler was Himmler, but that I was Himmler."

There was the phrase that could hang him—*I had to do it*—patently a lie. "Is it not a fact, then," Denson said, "that you lacked the courage to tell Himmler that you would not participate in the operation of this camp?"

"I object to the question," Oeding said, perhaps sensing that Denson had maneuvered his client into a corner, "as argumentative."

"And I submit, may it please the court, that it is not. People were confined to Mauthausen because they did have the courage of their convictions and were willing to stand up for what they thought was right."

"Objection overruled."

Eigruber knew that the chief prosecutor had him in a potential checkmate. If he admitted to having voluntarily participated in the operation of Mauthausen, then he was part of the common design—and there wasn't a shred of evidence supporting his argument that he "had to do it." Denson was holding his own against a man who had confounded investigators and given up nothing in more than a dozen interrogations in America and Europe.

"I don't answer such questions," Eigruber said.

"Do you refuse to answer the question?"

"I will not answer such a question."

That was good enough for Denson. Refusal to answer a question would be sufficient indication for the tribunal. "No further questions."

––––––––

August Eigruber was found guilty and hanged at Landsberg prison. In 1981, Denson met a captain in the corps of military police that had presided at Eigruber's execution. The captain stated that as the rope was being placed around his neck and the trap was sprung, his last words were "Heil Hitler!"

"Eigruber," Denson said, in later years, "was a Nazi to the bitter end."

21

Life and Death in the Block

As the trial entered its second month, exposure to the constant description of atrocities was wearing everyone down and JAG HQ arranged for some distraction: the Radio City Rockettes toured the camp, attended a cocktail reception and dinner in the officers' mess, then performed for the Americans in a club in Munich. The city had been heavily bombed during the war: seventy-one air raids had hit Munich between 1940 and 1945, and more than seven million cubic meters of debris littered the streets. Enterprising speculators had built clubs from bombed-out restaurants and shops, patching up walls with wood planks and sheets of tin. Music blared from record players, and occasionally local musicians plucked out simulations of American hit tunes. The war was over and celebration, however crude, couldn't happen fast enough. Libidos that had lain dormant for years from lack of food and an abundance of misery resurfaced with a vengeance. Denson did not attend the Rockettes' performance. While obliged on occasion to attend army functions, he had no interest in or time for the frivolity of chorus lines. Even opera, more to his liking, held no appeal with the trials in full gear. When called upon to entertain a visiting VIP, Denson would ask Guth to do the honors. "I must have seen *Tales of Hoffmann* thirty times," Guth groaned. "Ask me anything."

It was the beginning of May. Fields throughout Bavaria blossomed.

––––––––

"During your time, did you know that these alleged atrocities were being committed?" Defense counsel Oeding was questioning defendant Viktor Zoller, former adjutant to Mauthausen commandant Franz Ziereis.

"Partly," Zoller replied. "Of course everybody was very careful not to commit any illegal acts in my presence, but from the testimony of some prosecution witnesses one might assume it was perfectly normal for prisoners to be mistreated and shot. That was simply not the case. There was one basic order: only the Führer can decide whether a prisoner is to live or die."

"Didn't you hear a witness testify that you mistreated prisoners in a dental clinic?"

"I heard that, yes, and I am not surprised. In the spring of 1945, I went to the dental clinic and found that prisoners had stolen gold, large quantities of food, fur jackets, cigarettes. I did not touch the prisoners. I only now heard that they were beaten severely by Ziereis and Bachmayer. Now Ziereis is dead, Bachmayer is dead, and I can easily understand that all this anger is directed at me."

"Were you ever interrogated by a member of the prosecution?"

"Yes."

"Was any attempt made to elicit a statement out of you by duress?" Oeding was again raising the specter of coercion in an attempt to minimize the value of statements signed by the defendants prior to their trial.

"Yes. In January, I was interrogated by Lieutenant Guth, and at the beginning I was treated decently. At first I had to relate my life in the SS. When I started telling about Mauthausen, Lieutenant Guth told me that Gauleiter Eigruber had an important position there, that he had power to issue orders. I told him no, and Guth yelled at me, 'Degenerate pig! Stupid man! My orderly is more intelligent than you.' Then he ordered me to stand at attention and say, 'I am a liar, I am a liar.' He spit in my face and called me a criminal. I answered that I was not a criminal. He told me to shut up and only talk when asked. Then he told me, 'I hope I have time for you next week. We will start with knee bends.'

"On fifteenth February I was again interrogated. Lieutenant Guth told me, 'I received special permission and can have you shot immediately if I want to.' He asked me if I wanted to make a confession. I told him that I had not committed a crime and did not have a confession to make. He said, 'Your friend Wolter broke down and told me some nice things about you. All of them have broken down. Riegler, Altfuldisch, Drabek, they testified nicely against you.' He put his hands in his pockets and I heard a noise, as if a pistol was taken off safety. He walked closer and said quietly, 'Zoller, what do you think is going to happen right now?' I remembered a proverb from my priest, that if someone is meeting a sudden death, such as falling off a cliff, and has no opportunity for confession, he should say the following, 'Jesus knows all. Please forgive this poor sinner. Amen.' That proverb I thought about quietly because I didn't know what was going to happen. Then Lieutenant Guth started to dictate a confession to Dr. Leiss. He left, and I told Dr. Leiss, 'I am not going to sign that. It is not true.' Instead, I put down the following: 'I won't say another word even though the court might think I am a criminal who refused to talk.' I didn't hear from Lieutenant Guth anymore after that."

"Your witness."

As troubling as the description of coercion might have been, Denson stuck to a simple line of cross-examination.

"Tell the court please, Zoller, your best judgment as to the number of people reported dead in Mauthausen from January 1942 until the time that you left."

"I really can't say. The political department compiled those lists."

"Was it more than three thousand?"

"Oh, certainly not. That was quite impossible. The lists would have been a stack that thick," he said, holding out two flat hands a foot apart.

"Well, roughly, how thick was the list?"

"Four or five typewritten pages."

"And how many can be written on one of those pages?"

"Thirty approximately, I don't know."

"Zoller, I hand you a book marked prosecution's exhibit twenty-seven, which is the death book from October 1940 to March 1942. I call your attention to entry 904 and ask you to read."

"'Shot upon order of the Reich's Leader of the SS.'"

"I call your attention to entry 990 and ask you to read."

"'Shot upon order of the Reich's Leader of the SS.'"

"And what are the dates on the entries that you just examined?"

"Both say eighteen November 1941."

"I call your attention to entry 1,322 and ask you to read."

"'Hanged twenty-second December 1941.'"

"Didn't you tell the court there were no hangings in Mauthausen while you were adjutant?"

"I didn't see any hangings."

"I call your attention to entry 25 of that same exhibit and ask you to read."

"'Executed on the fifth of January 1942.'"

"Entry 402. Please read."

"'Executed on the sixth of January 1942.'"

"I call your attention to entry 144."

"'Executed by means of eight shots in the back, twenty-sixth January 1942.'"

"And 300 down to 310?"

"'Shot upon orders of court-martial, thirteenth February 1942.'"

"So, as a matter of fact, Zoller, there were many more than two or three executions."

"According to this book, yes. But this book was not kept by me."

Denson took a moment to refer to notes in his binder. "Zoller, you were near the bridgehead in April 1945 when a transport of Polish Jews came across the river, weren't you? How many of those prisoners were pushed off the bridge in the river?"

"I don't know."

"Well, was it more than five?"

"I can't say."

"How many did you see pushed off?"

"One." That's all it took. Denson paused.

"Did you laugh at him while he drowned?"

One could almost hear the collective intake of breath as the courtroom watches a man renowned for his calm and manners edge toward kinetic anger. Every man has his limits, and Denson was rapidly approaching his. Maintaining an even keel through nearly a year of exposure of Nazi sadism, career bureaucrats, and personal trauma had started to take its toll. He faced men in the courtroom on a daily basis, men like Zoller, whose barbaric behavior in concentration camps made Denson physically ill. It had been nearly a year since his arrival at Dachau, and uninterrupted contact with such inhumanity was prompting changes in his demeanor and appearance. Appetite had left him weeks ago, and his weight had dropped dramatically. His hands trembled periodically, and on occasion, such as now, he permitted his outrage to show its face.

"No further questions."

———

To reestablish an inner equilibrium, Denson fished. Fly-fishing was his therapy, his meditation, a time to empty his mind of all else and allow the lapping of water on the side of a boat to lower his metabolism, slow his breathing. He made his own flies and kept them in a special pouch. He knew a German guide who had a good sense of where the fish were. They did not speak much. Denson stood in the boat and worked the line, casting, slowly reeling in, and tossing again, for as long as his waning energy would permit. The guide rowed, and everything went away except for the tossing and reeling in and teasing the line from time to time with a little tug. He caught fish or did not catch fish, it made little difference. This was about breathing easier for a little while. Tomorrow he would rise, dress in his uniform, pin on his bars and stars, put a fresh handkerchief in his pocket, and set out for the courtroom on the grounds of camp Dachau. Heaven only knew what fresh nightmares awaited him, so he tossed his line and reeled it in and let yesterday's nightmares evaporate in the morning mist.

22

A Ruling for the Defense

ood manners and neat appearance are not always true measures of a person's character, but in Denson's case they accurately reflected his view of life. Witnesses might lie on the stand, army brass change their tune, and his own wife turn her back and walk away. Yet the handkerchief in his breast pocket was folded and clean, his JAG pin polished, and when a lady entered the room he stood and pulled out her chair. From the top of his combed head to the tips of his shined shoes, Denson's personal style declared his conviction that how we live our life matters. Those who knew him, both young staff and older officers, frequently heard him quote the Bible and knew that the spit and polish reflected his appreciation of an elegant, purposeful universe and of the symmetries of creation. A vision of life's importance on both large and small scales also informed his diligent trial preparation. If he forfeited sleep or ignored his health or declined to take well-earned days off, it was to dedicate more time to uncovering large truths in tiny details of evidence.

How strange it must have felt, then, when the formula failed, when meticulous preparation led not to truth but illusion. Denson hated losing more than anything in the world, and one day near the end of the Mauthausen trial he lost a ruling to the defense. The case involved a farmer who had been made a *kapo* and was accused of beatings, taking part in executions by lethal injection, and shooting prisoners during an evacuation.

———

"What is your name?" McMahon asked for the defense.

"Georg Goessl."

"Will you tell this court just when you were first arrested by the Germans?"

"On the 9th of March 1933, when the Nazis took over. I had been a member of a republican association, and we were unwilling to have our building, which had been built with workers' money, taken away from us. I was inside the building with several of my comrades when SA began shooting into the windows. They rushed in and began to beat and push people and break everything. Twenty or so people were arrested. Toward the end of March we were taken to Dachau."

"Then what happened?"

"In 1935, I was interrogated by a Gestapo agent and told that if I would serve the Gestapo and betray my comrades, I would be dismissed immediately. I told him he could not expect me to betray them. I received twenty-five lashes and food only every fourth day. I was eventually dismissed."

"When were you next arrested?" McMahon asked.

"In 1936, I was taken to Gestapo headquarters and interrogated for six days. They did not learn the names of other people involved, which is what they wanted. My two fingers were put into a press until only the bone remained, and they told me that if I wouldn't talk they would shoot me. I was taken to Buchenwald, then to Mauthausen. All those who had the notes RU on their file were sent to Mauthausen."

"What does the notation RU mean, Mr. Goessl?"

"*Rückkehr Unerwünscht*: Return Unwanted. From there I was taken to Sachsenhausen and told that my brother had been shot there and that my mother and sister lost their lives in Ravensbrück. I was then taken to

Mauthausen as a medic. Toward the end of January I was called into the hospital and made *kapo* for louse control. I took prisoners for baths, gave them fresh laundry, and saw to it that they kept their bodies more or less clean. I was frequently beaten."

"Why were you beaten?"

"If a prisoner had lice, I was supposed to report him. But these men were punished with twenty-five thrashes, so I did not always report them. If the *Sanitätsdienstgefreiter*—the SS corporal of the sanitary service— found lice on the prisoners, he beat me with his leather dog whip. That wasn't so bad, I was used to it. During my time in camp I got twenty-five perhaps fifty or sixty times. Another time the camp was being disinfected, and I was supposed to push the heads of prisoners into this acid of disin- fecting solution in large bathtubs. I did not do as I had been ordered, so the SDG picked up a fire hook and beat me. That was bad."

"Did you ever hit any prisoners yourself, Goessl?"

"Yes. For example, when a prisoner would avoid a bath and when the SDG saw, I was called in and beaten. It was getting to be too much for me, so when I caught a prisoner running away from the bath I slapped him in the face."

"Why didn't you report such cases, rather than hit the prisoner?"

"The prisoner would have been beaten terribly, maybe even to death. SS like Bruckner, Buehner, Schiller—when they started to beat, they just didn't know when to stop."

"Do you remember a certain incident at the hospital on the night before the evacuation?"

"I was standing together with the physician. Buehner came in and said, 'All prisoners in the hospital will be killed by means of injections because we have no cars available to take them away. That is my order, and you know who gives orders around here.' That night forty-seven prisoners were killed by means of injections, according to the statistics I had in the hospital."

McMahon took a document from the defense table and approached the witness stand.

"I hand you prosecution's exhibit 110 and direct your attention to the third paragraph and ask you to read it aloud."

"'I prepared forty-seven patients for injections with benzine and luprex.'"

"Is that true?"

"I did not make any such preparations."

"If you didn't prepare these patients, why did you write that?"

"I made this statement in front of Lieutenant Guth. According to what he said, I was supposed to add 'and were injected by myself'—I would really have to explain in more detail my interrogation . . ."

"May it please the court," Denson interrupted, "to let him run on in narrative form is grossly improper. We have seen examples of that yesterday and the day before. Defense lets them ramble on without getting anywhere. Counsel is required to ask questions that elicit matters that are material and relevant. Those questions which do not I will object to."

Before the law member could rule on Denson's objection, McMahon turned his exasperation on the tribunal.

"During the prosecution's case," he said, "the defense time and again objected to introduction of evidence which we did not even deem to be of probative value. Here each and every one of these sixty-one defendants' lives hangs in the balance. They are literally talking for their own lives. They must defend themselves, and the only way they can do it is to best explain what did transpire in their minds and what circumstances they were surrounded by. I submit especially in the case of these statements that each be allowed to explain what they meant when they wrote and signed them and what did transpire.

"Every minute of every day," he continued, frustration mounting, "these defendants and their counsel are constantly surprised by new facts. We were never served with a bill of particulars. We had no warning whatsoever that such and such fact would be alleged—there are loosely drawn charges encircling all of the defendants under this blanket of 'common design'. . . ."

"The court has heard this argument before," Prickett said.

"Yes, but not in the same light."

"The objection is sustained. Defense will ask questions to bring out probative information and will not permit their witness to ramble on."

McMahon turned back to Goessl. "Were you interrogated by any of the prosecution's staff?"

"Yes."

"Will you tell the court—briefly—what was said?"

"I was called by Lieutenant Guth from the waiting room. I came into his room. He gave me paper and ink. He said, 'Even if the talk around camp is that we only want the big ones and let the small ones run off, that is not so.' He said I should write down what he dictated, and if I didn't want to do that the way he wanted—he stood up between the desk and myself, put his hand to his neck, turned his eyes upward and snapped his fingers."

"Let the record indicate that the witness lifted his eyes and face upward as if to indicate a hanging motion. . . ."

Denson was up. "Just a minute. I object to that altogether."

Prickett was right behind him. "Strike the whole thing from the record."

Goessl raced ahead. "I thought to myself, I have already had enough tortures by the Gestapo. I'll go ahead and write, and if I get before a court the matter will be cleared up."

"Your witness."

————

The repeated accusations concerning young Paul Guth's interrogations could not be ignored. Denson wanted his wins, but not like that, and he truly believed the rumors to be nothing more than a defense tactic.

"Goessl, you took the pen in hand and you started writing, is that correct?"

"Yes. I wrote down what was dictated to me by Lieutenant Guth."

"Do you tell the court that when you wrote it, you knew it was not so?"

"I knew that it wasn't quite correct. When Lieutenant Guth told me that these patients were injected by me, I said, 'Just a minute. It was the male nurse who made those injections, not I.'"

"Isn't it a fact, Goessl, that you made much of the fact that you pre-pared *only* forty-seven patients at the time of this interrogation? And is it not a fact that you selected the forty-seven who were the sickest to be killed by injections?"

"No . . ."

"And when you made this statement, did you not write in your own handwriting that it was made by you of your own free will and without compulsion?"

"It was like this. After the dictation was over . . ."

"Just answer my question. Did you did or did not make that statement?"

Denson's battery of questions brought McMahon to his feet. "If the court pleases, I object to his interrupting the witness."

Denson ignored him. "May it please the court, I ask for an answer that is responsive." Without waiting for law member A. H. Rosenthal to rule, he turned back to the defendant. "Goessl, did you sign this: 'I have made this statement in my own handwriting at Dachau, Germany, on the fifteenth of February 1946 of my own free will and without compulsion'?"

"I did sign it, yes. I did sign it. But I didn't read it through. . . ."

"You wrote it, didn't you?"

"Yes, I wrote it. . . ."

"Now, on this evacuation from Hinterbrühl to Mauthausen, you were dressed up like a guard, were you not? And on that march you acted as a guard, did you not?"

"I was a medic."

"But you were dressed like a guard and you carried out the orders that Buehner gave the guards, did you not?"

"I had nothing to do with those orders. . . ."

"Isn't it a fact that you shot six prisoners in the back of the neck who were unable to go along on the march?"

"I never carried a weapon. . . ."

"Isn't it a fact, Goessl, that an old Polish man was unable to go any farther and he dropped down on his knees and told you he had six children at home and begged for his life, and you shot him?"

McMahon sensed an opening and lured Denson onto the defense's turf, saying innocently, "I object to the prosecutor asking these questions unless he has some grounds to substantiate these charges."

"Sir, I certainly have." Denson lifted a small sheaf of papers and held them up. "Two sworn statements here—absolutely—taken on the twenty-fifth of May in Mauthausen."

McMahon turned to Prickett and said, "The prosecution has rested, but now he's bringing new charges that we've had no opportunity to investigate or prepare a defense on."

"I submit," Denson said, "that this is proper cross-examination with respect to his activities on this march. If he didn't do it, then that is his defense. If he did, then he should admit it and take the consequences."

"Objection overruled."

Denson again faced the witness. "Is it not a fact, Goessl, that you shot that man in the back of the neck?"

"No. This case I have to explain entirely differently."

The tribunal looked at Denson. He was the one who had raised the bar, and only he could force the witness to jump over. "All right," he said, "let's hear it."

"This Polish prisoner was ill," Goessl said, "and lay down on the edge of the road. I picked him up and he told me that he couldn't go on any farther. But he had children at home, he said, and we should not leave him. 'Try and come along,' I told him, and he collapsed in my arms. I took the prisoner to Buehner and told him he was ill. Buehner said, 'Kill him.' I said, '*Rapportführer*, I can't do that.'

"Then Buehner called Rottenführer Ruber and said, expressly pointing his finger at me, 'I don't want to see him alive tomorrow morning.' Then he said something about insubordination and how they had to watch out for prisoners dressed in uniforms. I hid out that evening with two non-commissioned officers of the air corps and the next day hid by marching between them—and that is the truth. Other witnesses can testify, too."

"So according to you then, this man was never killed at all, is that correct?"

"I don't know. I didn't see him anymore."

"Do you know a man by the name of Anton Vescadori?"

"Yes, I know him. He was in Mauthausen with me."

"Do you deny that you shot this Polish man and that he died in the arms of Anton Vescadori?"

Over four weeks of proceedings, defense scored very few clear wins on behalf of the Germans, but McMahon was about to do so, due largely to having studied the charge sheet. The charge sheet, a written act of accusation in war crimes trials, was a vaguely drafted document that indicated only generally the facts of the accusations and offenses charged. This lack of specificity did not hinder defense counsel, however, from discovering in due course what the prosecutor intended to prove. Defense became aware of the charges in pretrial examinations and, at least in the early

Dachau trials, had no difficulty obtaining the necessary information from the prosecutor, whose dossier was available for inspection by the defense—a practice contrary to that in American criminal courts. It seems that at a later stage of the trials this practice was discontinued. But in this instance it had allowed defense to anticipate Denson's mention of Vescadori. To ensure that Goessl's response would be allowed, McMahon needed to first draw a ruling.

"If the court pleases, we have gone through this. The witness has answered that with a denial and explanation. The prosecution is arguing with him."

Law Member A. H. Rosenfeld was sympathetic but not swayed. "Apparently defense counsel does not seem to understand. The witness may be cross-examined on any matter in connection with this case. If it is true, he will answer it. If it is not true, he will not. The objection is overruled."

Satisfactions for the defense team were few and far between, but that was the ruling McMahon wanted. He turned to the defendant. "Tell the court who Anton Vescadori is."

"Vescadori was a prisoner with us in the by-camp. After the liberation, I worked in the bakery shop in Lugnitz, about three kilometers away. I was returning to Mauthausen one day with two American soldiers, and on the way a girl came toward us waving her hand. We stopped, and she explained she had been taking eggs, butter, and milk to the sick camp on a horse-drawn cart when six or seven prisoners robbed her. They pulled her down off the cart and rode off."

Denson was stymied by a revelation with which he could not quarrel. "I object to all that as being immaterial and irrelevant to the issues in this case."

"Sir," McMahon said to Rosenfeld, "I submit it will be connected with Anton Vescadori and will show Goessl's motive for the making this statement."

"Defendant will continue."

"We asked her where they had gone and she showed us a country road, sort of a farmer's pasture road, and said they had gone that way. We drove there and overtook them. One of the American soldiers told me to call out for them to stop, and when they didn't the soldier shot his pistol into the air. Then the Americans jumped out of the jeep and told the prisoners to remain standing while they searched for weapons. Vescadori was there, and during this search he looked at me and said, 'Georg, we will get you for this.' At the time, I didn't know what he meant."

"Do you know whether it was Vescadori who then caused your arrest?"

"Yes, four days later."

It wasn't much. A small possible win amid the torrent of inevitable defeats, but McMahon was not about to let the slight edge disappear. He turned his attention to the charge of beating prisoners.

"Defense calls as its next witness Hans Franke. Did you ever see Goessl strike any prisoner?"

"Yes, I saw that."

"Will you tell the court the circumstances?"

"It is hard for anyone who wasn't in the camp to understand. We prisoners knew the best thing possible was to have as few SS men come in as possible. An SS man in the camp always meant not only the prisoner reported was beaten, but all the others who were connected in any manner—*kapos*, block elders, clerks, it didn't make any difference."

"Are you saying it was better for Goessl to discipline a prisoner than report it to someone else?"

"I object to that," Denson said. His case against Goessl had taken a disagreeable turn. "It is leading and suggestive."

"Objection sustained."

McMahon rephrased his question. "What was the purpose of the self-discipline of the prisoners?"

"Most of the prisoners' lives took place inside the block. There were no partitions, no walls. Between the beds was a small passage, and in that small passage six hundred prisoners on average had to move around, get their food, and so on. Toward the end, things deteriorated to such an extent that gangs of robbers operated inside these blocks. I remember a Frenchman who received a Red Cross package. Twelve Ukrainians fell on him and beat him up. If cases like that were reported, the SS would have turned the entire block upside down. Goessl had to see to it that prisoners were controlled—and in part he punished them himself by hitting them a couple of times."

"Was the degree of punishment that he rendered greater or lesser than the punishment ordinarily administered by the rapport leader?"

"I assume a couple of slaps in the face is better than twenty-five thrashes with an oxtail."

"No further questions."

"It is a fact, is it not," Denson asked, looking for anything that would salvage his prosecution of a Mauthausen *kapo*, "that Goessl did beat the prisoners?"

"Yes."

"No further questions."

Losing a battle may have galled Denson, but it did nothing to diminish his determination to win the war. "If we had the wrong sow by the ear," he told an auditorium of students years later, "a finding of not guilty was in order and an acquittal was proper. But that was an infrequent occurrence. Extreme care had been taken in the selection of the accused placed in the prisoners' dock. I didn't prosecute an accused whose guilt was doubtful."

Goessl was found guilty and sentenced to hang.

23

The Oldest Defendant

Defense counsel Charles B. Deibel rose and called sixty-two-year-old Emil Mueller to the stand.

"Do you recognize Josef Mayer, Theophil Priebel, Thomas Sigmund, Heinrich Fitschok, and Kaspar Klimowitsch as members of your company?"

"Yes."

"When were you company commander in Wiener Neudorf?"

"1943 to 1944—1944, yes."

"And how many times did you receive reports that prisoners were shot trying to escape?"

"There might have been three or four at the very most. I can't give you a definite number."

"Would it be possible for your guards to shoot prisoners without you receiving a report in your daily guard report?"

"No."

"You may take the witness," Deibel said to Denson.

"I believe you stated that you only received three or four reports of shooting of prisoners by your guards, is that correct?"

"Yes."

Denson approached the witness and handed him a bound sheaf of pages filled with names and dates. "I hand you prosecution's exhibit number twenty-two."

Mueller took the book and studied it for a moment through thick black-rimmed spectacles. "I don't know this. I have never seen it."

"Take some time, examine it, familiarize yourself with it so you can talk about it, please."

"I don't know anything about this. The rapport leader of the camp would know about this. I have never seen this book before."

"You can read. Now what is this title at the top of the page—where I am pointing?"

"'Name of the prisoner.'"

"And what is in that column?"

"I can read it—but I don't know this."

"Will you please answer my question? What does 'Art' mean?"

"That means 'The Reason'—why he died or was shot."

"And the fourth column?"

"'Day of Death.' And this word is 'Camp.' I see that."

"All right, and what is the next column?"

"'Kind of Death.' Yes, I know—'Kind of Death.'"

"And what is this?"

"'Factual Report Sent or Not to SS and Police Court.'"

"Now do you understand this book?"

"Oh, yes, I can read it—but I have never seen this book."

"Now, will you look at line 266 and tell the court where that prisoner was killed?"

"Wiener Neudorf. I see that."

"Now, look at line 270. Where was that prisoner killed?"

"It says here Wiener Neudorf."

"And 271?"

"Wiener Neudorf."

"Three thirteen?"

"Wiener Neudorf."

"And 318?"

"Wiener Neudorf."

"And 335?"

"Wiener Neudorf, it says here."

"Three forty-five?"

Mueller stopped reading and looked puzzled.

"Well?"

"That is impossible."

"What does the book say?"

"I don't know who kept this or where this comes from."

"Entry 360. Where was that man killed?"

"I don't know. I don't know these people."

"Well, where does the book say he was killed?"

"In Wiener Neudorf."

"Three sixty-eight?"

"Wiener Neudorf."

"Three sixty-nine?"

"It's impossible that so many people lost their lives there. That is impossible."

"Three seventy-three?"

"I don't know."

"What does it say?"

"Wiener Neudorf. Well, gentlemen, I wasn't in Wiener Neudorf for as long as it says here."

"But from January until March you were there, were you not?"

"Yes, I was there until March 1944, yes."

"All right. What is the date on 385?"

Mueller studied the death book again. "That is impossible, I . . ."

"Answer the question please. What was the date that number 385 died in Wiener Neudorf?"

"Twenty January—1944."

"You were in Wiener Neudorf then, were you not?"

"Yes. I don't know the reason why he was shot."

"Well, I don't know either, but will you examine 388 please and tell the court where that man died?"

"In Wiener Neudorf."

"What was the date?"

"Twelve January 1944."

"And you were still there, were you not?"

"Yes."

"And 393?"

"Yes, I was there, too, on 7 February 1944. I can bring the whole company down here to testify that so many didn't die. The doctors can say so, too, and the rapport leader who was there—he can say so."

"Do you know how many prisoners died in Wiener Neudorf during the time you were there?"

"No, I can't say, because I did not have any connection—I really can't explain this, really. . . ."

"No further questions, sir."

"I did not pay attention at all to the prison compound. Captain Schmutzler was in charge of that. . . ."

"I won't take up any more time, may it please the court."

"Witness excused. Court will recess until 8:30 tomorrow."

24

A Witness for the Defendants

D r. Otto Pelzer was a sociologist and former Mauthausen inmate who had voluntarily returned to observe the trials.

"At first," he explained for the defense, "I intended to collect material for a book I am writing and wanted to be here only as an observer. Then I recognized among the accused some SS men who helped prisoners, and I considered it my duty to testify."

"Why were you put in Mauthausen?" defense counsel Hervey asked.

"For refusing to do service during time of war. Before the war started, I emigrated to Sweden. Then I learned that steps would be taken against my family if I did not return, so I did and was arrested at the border. On April 11, 1941, I was sent to Mauthausen."

"How long did you remain there, doctor?"

"Until March 8, 1944, when I was sent to the work camp near Ebensee for about one year. Then Commandant Ziereis had me brought back to

Mauthausen to be shot because, as he put it, I had agitated among his prisoners and incited them to sabotage."

"While at Mauthausen, did you know a dentist by the name of Dr. Henkel?"

"Yes. My front teeth had been beaten out and Dr. Henkel tried to replace them."

"Did you have an opportunity to talk to other people in the dental clinic?"

"Yes. One waited in the anteroom, and there one could talk with fellow prisoners and rest."

"Did you ever hear of Dr. Henkel participating in any kind of heart injections?"

"I certainly would have heard something if that were true. We prisoners kept ourselves oriented as to who was dangerous and who was not. I knew about Dr. Henkel that he was in no respect dangerous and that one could receive help from him—even if help was not necessary and one only wanted to rest in the dental clinic."

"Do you know Dr. Henkel's reputation for honesty?"

"Yes. It was a good one. For example, at first I was mistrusting in connection with one of my gold teeth that had to be pulled. Dr. Henkel said, 'It is better that we keep it here because it can very easily be stolen from you when you mix with the prisoners.' I hesitated, but a Czech who was his assistant there told me, 'You don't need to worry. You will get it back later on.' After the liberation, I actually found this tooth among my personal belongings."

"Dr. Pelzer, when you were in Mauthausen did you know a man by the name of Wasicky?"

"Yes. I was still quite emaciated, and I suffered in the cold from rheumatism. Some of my comrades told me I could get tablets for this in the pharmacy. I went there and received them from Wasicky each time."

"How many times did you receive these tablets, doctor?"

"Approximately ten times."

"Doctor, while you were at Mauthausen did you make it your business to find out as much about the camp as you could?"

"Yes. I am a sociologist, and conditions in the camp were of particular interest to me. I noticed the differences among SS men and attempted to find out how such people who would help prisoners had come into the SS at all. I once asked Wasicky how it happened that he had come into the party. He said, 'Well, you see, I was young and I wished to work for the ideas of a greater German Reich.' I asked him, 'How can you support a party that takes such vigorous action against the Jews when you, as I can see, are humane and try to help people?' He said at that time such things were not going on yet, that he had helped Jews get across the Swiss border, that he had many Jewish friends, and that it was important to stay in the party to prevent its radical wing from winning an upper hand."

"Did you see or hear anything which would lead you to believe that Wasicky participated in any gassings whatsoever?"

"I never saw any evidence to that effect. This is why I brought his character into this. I considered it humanly impossible that he would participate in such things."

"No further questions."

––––––––

"Why were you in the hospital?" Denson asked on cross-examination.

"I suffered tissue infection as a result of severe beatings I received at work."

"From whom did you receive these severe beatings?"

"From SS guards. Also from *kapos* who, whenever an SS man appeared, to get into his good graces, began beating. Since I was especially weak, I received lots of beatings."

"Now, you stated to the court that you see in the prisoners' dock SS men who helped the prisoners. Are there SS men in that dock who mistreated prisoners?"

"Yes."

"Who are they?"

"I will object," Hervey said, "as being outside the scope of direct examination."

"Objection overruled."

Pelzer nodded in the direction of the box. "Spatzenegger, Trum, Krebsbach. I have difficulty recognizing most of them. They looked quite different in their uniforms."

"When you visited Dr. Henkel's office, you said you were in effect a bag of bones. Was your physical appearance apparent to Dr. Henkel, at that time?"

"Yes."

"What was the physical appearance of the other prisoners whom you saw resting in Dr. Henkel's office?"

"Some were just about as finished as I was, some were considerably better."

"Their physical condition was likewise apparent to Dr. Henkel, was it not?"

"Yes."

"No further questions."

———

Hervey conducted re-direct. "Doctor, I would like to have you point out in the prisoners' dock some of the accused who did *not* mishandle prisoners—people who were especially considerate."

"Those who did not mistreat prisoners and who even encouraged them from time to time included Dr. Wolter, Zutter, Blei—I can't say about any others with certainty."

"That is all."

Colonel Martin asked on behalf of the court, "Will you please state again the real reason for your coming into this court to testify?"

"We lived through much injustice. We prisoners did nothing to the accused, but they treated us badly. However, I think it is our duty to prove that we can think justly. In spite of the fact that we must oppose the entire system to which they belonged—we suffered under it—we must still differentiate and know from whom among our political opponents we received help."

25

The Youngest Defendant

"The defense calls as its next witness Willy Frey. How old are you?" Oeding asked.

"Twenty-two."

"Why were you in prison?"

"I was declared an enemy of the state at age seventeen."

"What did you do?"

"I had friends in the Socialist Democratic movement. A month before I was to be drafted into the SS, I tried to get away because my friends said that National Socialism was planning for war and that would throw Germany into the abyss. I cut open the vein in my left hand."

"Willy, do you remember the testimony of the witness Schmeling here?"

"Schmeling said that in April 1945, I beat up prisoners to death in the tent camp."

"What do you have to say to that?"

"I wasn't in Mauthausen then. I don't know where that tent camp was."

"Do you remember the testimony of the witness Marsalek?"

"Marsalek said that I was room eldest in block twenty-four and that I quieted people down in the evening by beating them."

"What do you have to say about that?"

"It's true that I was in block twenty-four—but he wants to make me responsible for the things *he* did."

"What was your position in the camp?"

"A regular prisoner."

"Were you ever made a *kapo* or block leader?"

"No. Those were older people who had been in that camp longer."

"Did you ever beat any prisoners?"

"Well, if somebody stole my bread I beat him. And he beat me. I couldn't let them steal my bread. We beat each other. That was in every camp."

"How many camps have you been in, Willy?"

"Sachsenhausen, Auschwitz, and Mauthausen."

"Did the prisoners fight among themselves in all these camps?"

"Yes. They stole food and clothing and shoes, anything they could get hold of."

"Do you remember the testimony of the witness Lefkowitz?"

"I remember. He said I made a head count in the forest camp and put people in groups of five, and a young girl wasn't standing properly so I beat her until the blood was running down her head and she fell down."

"What do you have to say to that?"

"Prisoners had nothing to do with the head count. That was a matter for block leaders. And I'll tell you now that if I didn't have this number hanging around my neck," he said, pointing to the white card suspended from his neck, "these witnesses wouldn't identify me because they have never seen me before. They were told my number before they came into court. They didn't look at my face. They only looked at my number. It's a funny thing, too, that when we first got our charge sheets, not a single one of the prosecution witnesses knew me. No one ever stopped me or called me over. But after Lieutenant Guth put us together in the bunker, all of a sudden everyone calls me 'The Kapo.'"

"Willy, I hand you prosecution's exhibit 133. Why did you put these things down if they were not true?"

"I was afraid that if I said no, I would be beaten again."

"Had you been beaten before then?"

"Yes, in Mossburg. Severely. An American officer put a pistol on my chest and said he would shoot me."

How many more accusations of coercion would there be? "May it please the court," Denson said, "I object to any further testimony along this line unless it has some connection with this case."

"Objection sustained."

"No further questions."

————

"What is the name of the officer who interrogated you here in Dachau?" Denson asked.

"Lieutenant Conn," Frey said, pointing to an officer in the second row.

"You received no mistreatment here at the hands of Lieutenant Conn, did you?"

"No, but the court really cannot have any impression of what spiritual condition I was in at that time."

"Spiritual condition" was a phrase that emerged several times in the course of cross-examination by the prosecution. Defense had clearly done a good job of encouraging the defendants to make much of their state of mind during interrogations. No one, however, had anticipated the intentional quality that phrase would acquire after multiple use.

"We are not asking you at this time about your 'spiritual condition,' Willy. At the time you signed the statement, you knew the difference between true and not true, did you not?"

"I didn't know anything."

"How old are you, Willy?"

"Twenty-two."

"How many years did you go to school?"

"Eight years."

"Did you ever engage in any kind of business before joining the SS?"

"No. I was a laborer." Some of the boy's defensive posturing had left, and he spoke as though Denson were a teacher or counselor. "My parents were dead, and the mayor of our town forced me to join the SS because he said the community had no money and could not support me."

Willy Frey turned to Law Member A. H. Rosenfeld and said, "Can I say something else?"

"Yes."

"I was imprisoned by the Nazis and the SS when I was seventeen for sabotage to the state. I don't understand how I can be accused of being one of them," he said, indicating the other accused in the dock, "in any 'common design.' I wouldn't kill any prisoners. Witness Schmeling was a worse beater. He was the worst *kapo* in camp. And he wants to make prisoners who were in the camp only a few days responsible for the evil things he did. As soon as the Americans came in, Schmeling hid at once so the prisoners wouldn't catch him because they would have killed him, too. And the witness Marsalek? I hold him responsible for German prisoners who were killed after the liberation. He went through the barracks with the first camp clerk and picked out prisoners and *kapos* and block eldests who behaved badly toward the prisoners—and he had them killed either through shooting or beating to death. But he knew I wasn't bad and he told the Russians who wanted to pick me up, 'Leave Frey alone. He came from Auschwitz. He hasn't got anything to do with Mauthausen.'

"Those two Jews, Ziegelmann and Lefkowitz?" Frey continued. "I never saw them in my life, and they were probably in the same position as I was. And they probably had very little school, too, because they couldn't even spell their names when the defense counsel asked them to. It's a funny thing when bums like that can say, 'Yes, this guy beat this other guy to death,' and they don't even know me. I will say again that, if the court would have left out the numbers, I wouldn't have been recognized and I wouldn't have been identified. To make me out as if I was worse than the *Gauleiter*—it's not true. I never beat a prisoner, and I never beat a prisoner to death. I ran away from a dead body when I saw one. That is all."

How to get at the clear light of truth through the infinite refracting shards of a concentration camp? And without truth, how to get at justice? Take a young man not yet eighteen, an orphan with little more than an elementary school education, who has already attempted suicide. Shuttle him from camp to camp for four years. Put him on trial based on reports that he beat other prisoners. Weigh those reports against his own testimony that he beat others to stop them from stealing his bread. Then decide whether he should live or die. Here, in this court, there was no middle ground. Anyone who aided in the beatings and torture was guilty of participating in the common design, regardless of personal history or age. Willy Frey was sentenced to death.

William Denson at West Point, ca. January 1945, just prior to his assignment to the Judge Advocate's War Crimes Division in Germany. "He had more legal thoughts per minute than anybody I'd ever met," said Marian Smoak, fellow law instructor at West Point and later chief of protocol to President Nixon. *Photo: Denson archive*

The chief prosecutor in later years, doing what he liked best—
apart from courtroom litigation.   *Photo: Denson archive*

26

Quarryman

enson's position on anyone who worked voluntarily in a concentration camp never wavered: such a person was guilty of participation in a common design to torture, starve, and kill prisoners and deserved to hang. "I was perfectly willing to put the noose around the neck of each one and spring the trap with my own hand," he told an interviewer in 1994.

Some of the accused in the Mauthausen trial, however, seemed to have acted with a different intent during their time in the camp. No doubt an accused in the Dachau trials would say anything to save his neck, but while many admitted their crimes—assuming that a plea of superior orders would protect them—others professed behavior that did not fit the stereotype of Nazi camp officers.

———

"The defense calls as its next witness," McMahon said, "the accused Johannes Grimm. When did you first begin working in stone quarries?"

"In 1928. I applied for a job advertised in the papers by the Hermann Göring Stone Works for a production manager. They hired me. I came to Mauthausen in 1940."

"Taking a typical average day, Mr. Grimm, what was your work?"

"We started early in the morning. After various work details had been formed, prisoners marched in groups to where they had been assigned to work. Stonecutters went to their huts, craftsmen to their different shops, persons assigned to stone breaking got their machines from the various storerooms, and in that manner everybody knew which place to go to and what work to do, exactly as in any civilian business. We worked until noon, food was distributed, then the same work was done in the afternoon. In the evening at quitting time a head count would be made by the work detail leader, who would turn the prisoners over to the security commander, who in turn would take them back to camp. That was the way a day ran."

"Mr. Grimm, what was the maximum number of prisoners who worked in the stone quarry at the time you worked there?"

"Maximum number? In 1942 it might have been thirteen hundred, depending on the season and the work to be done."

"And what was the smallest number?"

"Well, in winter sometimes maybe only twenty prisoners would work because of the snow. Also after 1944 there was less work as workers were transferred to armaments."

"Where did you eat?"

"At home with my family."

"Did you at one time maintain a vegetable garden in the quarry?"

"I had gardens both at the house where I lived and also in the quarry. The one in the quarry I fixed up in order to grow some additional food for the prisoners. I know from notes of the last gardener that in 1944 four hundred kilos of tomatoes were distributed. All other products, such as beans, pickles, and potatoes, whatever we had in the garden, was distributed to the prisoners. Commandant Ziereis once ordered me to destroy the produce from that garden, but I didn't do that. I enjoyed very much being able to give something to the prisoners as far as food was concerned."

"Did you have occasion to complain to Commandant Ziereis or other persons concerning the prisoners furnished in the quarry?"

"Yes, I often noticed that prisoners were sent down there who were too weak for stone quarry work. I didn't look upon a prisoner as a human being to be exterminated, but someone who was confined because of his political convictions or other reasons. I always behaved toward the prisoners as one human being to another."

"What was Ziereis's attitude toward you personally?"

"Just like it was toward everybody else: he thought he could do everything better. He was 'The Commandant,' and a little man like me was not supposed to make any suggestions to him."

"Now, with reference to the arrival of the American troops, did you have any contact with prisoners after the collapse?"

"Yes. I worked up until the last minute that Saturday. When the American troops arrived, I went back to my apartment, which is about two kilometers away from the camp, and stayed there. In the following days, prisoners who formerly worked in the quarry visited me daily. I went out on walks with them and we talked about all that had happened, and at that time the former prisoner Alfred Kock was with me. I asked him his opinion, whether I should report to the camp. He told me it wouldn't be necessary, that I had proven by staying that I had a clear conscience. So for ten days until I was arrested, I moved freely. If I had been guilty of something, then the same thing probably would have happened to me as to hundreds of *kapos* and others after the liberation. In the first days things were fairly wild."

"Now you heard the charges of the prosecution witness, Lewkowicz, did you not?"

"Yes. The witness Lewkowicz testified that I beat prisoners until they were unconscious. I asked my defense counsel to please let me tell about this nonsense. In the four years I worked in the quarry, I never had a stick or any other instrument in my hand to beat human beings. Thank God I was never a man like that."

"There was another witness by the name of *Lef*kowitz who testified against you."

"Lefkowitz stated that I had not allowed prisoners to drink water, that I beat him with a shovel, and that I beat another prisoner to death—which is the height of slander. In the stone quarry we had no water pipe. Furthermore, drinking stone quarry water was strictly prohibited because of danger of typhoid. I can only repeat that I never had a stick in my hand, much less a shovel. And in answer to the accusation that I beat a prisoner to death, I can only say thank God my conscience is clear. The testimony of these two witnesses is invention, lies. They did not know me in Mauthausen. I speak here not only because my head is at stake but also the honor of my name. What those two said against me was pure slander. I didn't do that. Those two witnesses named Lefkowitz and Lewkowicz are the ones who have charged most of us accused with something somewhere."

"Grimm, I hand you prosecution's exhibit ninety-five and ask if that is your signature."

"Yes."

"Read the third sentence."

"'I do not remember exact figures, but during this time about ten thousand prisoners were killed.'"

"Is that true?"

"No."

"Why did you write it?"

"I wrote this in a frame of mind that didn't allow me to form my own thoughts. The transfer from Mossburg to Dachau, with the possibility that I might be named as an accused, the nine months that I had already been held without any connection with my own family . . .'"

"Where did you get the figure ten thousand?"

"During the interrogation by Lieutenant Guth, I heard that the accused Drabek had said four thousand. Lieutenant Guth's assistant, Dr. Leiss, told me that the lieutenant was very agitated and had said to raise that figure."

"Is the change of that figure apparent on the original document now in evidence?"

"Yes."

"I draw your attention to paragraph three and ask you to read the first sentence."

"'Some prisoners, in view of their general weak health, died of the work which was demanded by us. It was much too hard.'"

"Is that your own language, Grimm?"

"No."

"How did it get there?"

"I cannot blame Lieutenant Guth because I am the one who wrote this silly nonsense. That is the only guilt that I take upon myself, and I am thanking the high court that I have the opportunity to explain. It is better to take my own error into account than to sentence others innocently by the nonsense which I wrote down."

"Grimm," McMahon continued, "was your statement dictated to you?"

"Yes. Lieutenant Guth dictated it to Dr. Leiss, and Dr. Leiss gave it to me."

"I ask you to read paragraph four."

"'I saw how killings were conducted between 1942 and 1945 by Zoller, Zutter, Eisenhoefer, Blei, Ludolf, and Altfuldisch.'"

"Did you ever see Zoller lead killings?"

"No."

"Did you ever see Zutter lead killings?"

"No, Zutter was incapable of doing such things."

"How about Emil Mueller?"

"Mueller was down there several times as a work detail leader, but I did not see him beat or kill people."

"Mynzak? Priebel?"

"I was asked about both Mynzak and Priebel by Lieutenant Guth. However, I never saw either of these two men beat or kill prisoners."

"Why did you write it then?"

"I already described my mental condition on that day. I had memories of the previous interrogations. My left cheekbone was broken and four of my teeth were knocked out. . . .'"

"May it please the court," Denson said, standing. Defending American interrogators was becoming almost a daily chore. "I move to strike that portion of the witness's testimony that concerns this alleged prior treatment as immaterial and irrelevant to the issues of this case."

McMahon, on the other hand, welcomed every declaration that would throw doubt on the legitimacy of the confessions. "If the court please, the accused is not alleging that these beatings took place here in Dachau. But I submit that it is very, very material to show the mental state he was undergoing."

"Motion sustained."

McMahon was going to get every piece of evidence in the record that he could and said to the witness, "I ask you to read paragraph seven."

"'I am now sorry,'" Grimm read, "'that I had to act in this capacity as work leader. However, I did this because as a member of the SS I had to obey the orders of my superiors.'" Grimm put down the paper and said,

"The only superior I had to obey was Lieutenant Guth telling me to write this sentence."

"Is there anything further that you would like to add?"

"I knew that by signing this statement I jeopardized my own credibility. However, I would rather take responsibility for what I signed here than have my comrades sentenced because of it. If I had been the type of man that those two witnesses Lefkowitz and Lewkowicz made me out to be, I do not see how I could continue working with a hundred prisoners right up to noon on the fifth of May. Or why prisoners would come up to me before leaving and thank me by shaking my hand for the good treatment I gave them. When I was arrested, some of them even gave me bread and cigarettes. A young Pole tossed me a pack. The American guard saw that, called me and the Pole over, and the Pole told him that as a work manager I had always been very nice and decent. A medic came into the bunker and explained that he was sorry I was under arrest. There are many other examples. I asked Dr. Albrecht, a former prisoner who was in charge of the interrogation there, what evidence there was against me. He said, 'Mr. Grimm, there is nothing whatsoever against you. On the contrary, you have a very favorable statement from prisoners on your behalf.' I am not the person others are trying to make me out to be. Thank God I can say my hands are clean and my conscience is clear. Now I ask the high court to judge me."

"No further questions."

———

Even assuming a degree of accuracy in Grimm's self-exculpation, he stayed and voluntarily worked in Mauthausen—and that was enough for Denson.

"Grimm, when did you join the Nazi Party?" he asked.

"In November 1931."

"And because of your forcefulness you were the head of the district indoctrination office, were you not?"

"I was the district schooling leader. That was an honorary office."

Denson handed Grimm a document and said, "Read the last paragraph of prosecution's exhibit 143."

"'On the tenth day of April 1942 I was inducted into the Waffen SS as an *Oberscharführer* on the basis of my volunteering for it.'"

"Is that a true statement, Grimm?"

"I never volunteered. We were drafted. It would have been much nicer for me if I had stayed in the Allgemeine SS."

"I didn't ask you that. Please start confining your answers to the questions I ask you. Was this statement true at the time you wrote it?"

"No. I did not volunteer for the Waffen SS."

"Did anyone dictate this statement for you?"

"I wrote it myself, but the circumstances . . ."

"Now, Grimm, I hand you another document marked prosecution's exhibit 144 and ask you to read it."

"'To Mr. Johannes Grimm, dated April 10, 1944. On the basis of the increase in size of the work in the stone quarry and because of your increasing duties, the chief of the department has promoted you to the position of works manager. Heartiest congratulations on this promotion in the name of the entire corporation.' This had nothing to do with the way in which the work was conducted, and nothing changed."

"So they promoted you because the work did *not* increase and your responsibilities did *not* increase, is that correct?"

"Promotions occur everywhere. Every place people get promoted."

"But did you not tell this court, Grimm, that there was very little going on in the quarry after August 1944?"

"Yes, because the prisoners were relocated to working on armaments."

"And of course you had nothing to do with armaments, did you Grimm? Is it not a fact that you exercised authority over the prisoners in 1944?"

"No, I . . ."

"I hand you a document marked prosecution's exhibit 145 and ask you what it says."

"'We hereby confirm that our works manager SS Oberscharführer Johannes Grimm has to take care of the prisoner work distribution at the Bergkristall German Earth and Stone Works.' May I explain this?"

"I haven't asked you any questions. How many prisoners were killed in the stone quarry, Grimm?"

"I can't give any numbers. I don't know."

"Is it more than you can recollect at this time?"

"I don't recollect anything. I had no control over the prisoners."

"Do you remember when Dutchmen were killed there in September 1944?"

———

Forty-seven Dutch, American, and English officers and fliers arrived at the quarry that month, some of the countless prisoners who were to disappear as silently as *Nacht und Nebel*, "night and fog," the phrase Hitler had chosen to describe the fate of those who resisted the Nazi Party. Hitler had promulgated a *Nacht und Nebel* decree in December 1941. "Court-martial proceedings create martyrs," he said. "History shows that the names of such men are on everybody's lips." The Night and Fog decree called for "the disappearance without a trace" of anyone accused of resistance. "No information whatsoever may be given about their whereabouts and their fate." Some information did surface, however, regarding the fate of the forty-seven officers who arrived at Dachau. Maurice Lampe, a French former inmate at Mauthausen, told the tribunal that the officers brought in on September 6, 1944, were led barefoot down the 186 steps to the quarry. Huge stones were loaded in slings on their backs. Then men were made to go up the steps at a trot, then forced to run back down. With each trip the weight of the load was increased. Anyone faltering was kicked and beaten with a bludgeon. All forty-seven men were crushed, pushed over the edge, or shot. "The road which led to the camp was a bath of blood," he testified. "I almost stepped on a man's lower jaw." Twenty-one of the officers died on the first day. The others died the following morning.

———

"I know about it," Grimm replied, "because during a tour of inspection I saw prisoners in the punishment company carrying heavy stones. I was told they were Dutch saboteurs. I couldn't concern myself, it was none of my business. I do not know who did the shooting or if any shooting was done. I heard shots but I didn't see anything."

The interrogation lasted for two days. Grimm provided an impressive and detailed account of his good intentions in the stone quarry. But as confident and cooperative as his presentation may have been, it did little to attenuate the force of Denson's blunt presentation of the facts. Nor did Grimm display any sign of repentance when confronted with those facts: his testimony was more plausible than that of other witnesses, but even he surrendered to the temptation of denying knowledge of what was happening around them every day. He contended that it was justifiable for him to remain as a cooperative agent inside Mauthausen. He may not have personally wielded the club, but Denson's vivid exposé of the crimes committed during those years branded anyone who remained in the camp as an accomplice.

"You were an SS man at that time, were you not?"

"Yes."

"When you received an order from Ziereis, are you telling this court you did not have to carry it out?"

"I didn't receive orders from Ziereis. In my position as works manager I was not under his supervision but that of the economic main office."

"He was a colonel in the SS, wasn't he?"

"Yes."

"You were a sergeant in the SS, were you not?"

"Yes."

"And you tell this court that he exercised no authority over you, is that correct?"

"From a purely military point of view, but in the stoneworks . . ."

"No further questions."

McMahon had a witness in reserve to vouch for Grimm. "What is your name?"

"Karl Baumgartner."

"Did you ever work for the German Earth and Stone Works in the quarry at Mauthausen?"

"Yes, writing delivery slips and selling the rocks."

"And will you tell the court any specific acts of kindness by Grimm toward the prisoners?"

"Yes. Mr. Grimm had a vegetable garden and gave gifts of vegetables, like potatoes and others, to the prisoners."

"And did you see him give other goods to the prisoners from time to time?"

"Yes, bread, butter, cheese, and on Sundays milk."

"Did you have occasion, through the years, to observe Grimm's attitude toward the prisoners in general?"

"As far as I know, Grimm treated the prisoners well. I never saw him beat anybody."

"No further questions."

———

"Your work was office work, wasn't it?" Denson asked in a brief cross-examination.

"Yes."

"You didn't go into the quarry. You don't know what Grimm did down there with respect to the prisoners, do you?"

"No."

"No further questions."

27

Closing Arguments

Paul Guth shipped home in early May. Columbia Law School registration would not wait, and papers had to be filed before close of term. He went to see Denson and shook his hand. The southern gentleman had become more than a mentor to the aspiring young lawyer: he had become a role model and friend. There were times when Guth would have given anything for the kind of faith Denson exuded, a belief that divine justice exists somewhere in the universe. Denson reassured him they would see one another again.

On May 11, 1946, Denson offered his closing arguments. The case had been long: more than one hundred witnesses had testified over a period of six weeks. Denson began by thanking the court for their time and consideration. Then he spoke to the trial's most obvious feature—the sixty-one accused—and placed that number in a context that lessened its disturbing size.

"I call the court's attention to the fact that in excess of seventy thousand prisoners were killed in Mauthausen between 1942 and the liberation in

1945. Seventy thousand dead cannot be ascribed to the conduct of any one man. One of the most compelling bits of evidence of the common design is the very magnitude of the operation itself. The record shows that, at the time of the liberation of the camp on the fifth of May 1945, there were in excess of ninety thousand prisoners within its 'protective custody.' How many prisoners were inmates from 1942 until the liberation will probably never be known. It is absolutely inconceivable that this operation was a product of a single mind, inconceivable that it could be conducted and executed without the close cooperation of all those men who sit in that dock.

"It may be argued that this was the will of Ziereis, that he was the commandant. Granted. But that would not account for the execution of the plan, and the execution of this scheme is what we are interested in at this time. The overcrowding, the lack of sanitary facilities, starvation to the extent of cannibalism, disease, the destruction of human dignity and utter disregard of all human rights—all point to the presence of this barbaric scheme. Each man in that dock was a cog in a wheel that mercilessly ground the greatest economic value out of a man, even to the taking of his very life. But for the performance of each man, the gears would never have meshed. But for the efforts of Gauleiter Eigruber, the operation of the camp would have ceased for want of the necessities that made its operation possible. Yes, to have discontinued his services may have cost him his job as *Gauleiter*. But it would have been infinitely better to forgo the buffoonery of being *Gauleiter* of Upper Austria than to continue contributing to the existence of Mauthausen, which was unquestionably one of the most shameful blots upon the history of our so-called civilization.

"The guards actively participated in this common design by keeping the prisoners confined in Mauthausen. The guards were the men who stood in readiness to prevent any prisoner from extricating himself from the place where he was likely to be torn to pieces by the vicious dogs of Altfuldisch or Bachmayer, or from the killings and beatings by Spatzenegger, Trum, or Eckert, or from the murderous needles of Dr. Krebsbach and Dr. Entress, or from the gas of Wasicky, Jobst, and Wolter. These guards—Billman, Cserny, and the others, Wilhelm Mueller, Eisenhoefer, Blei, Spatzenegger—are cited merely as examples. The very act of keeping these prisoners behind electrically charged fences under armed guards is a most heinous felony in itself. The only offense of many of these prisoners was that of being born a Jew.

"The law is very plain with respect to charging a man with having knowledge of those matters that he may observe. Those accused who testified here that they saw no beatings, no killings, no tortures at Mauthausen must have generated nothing more than disgust in the minds of every member of this court in view of the overwhelming evidence that has been presented. Each man, from Commandant Ziereis down, knew that Mauthausen was designed for extermination. Any man who contributed to the operation and maintenance of Mauthausen participated in the common design, be he the man who distributed the food or injected lethal doses of benzine into the prisoners."

Denson borrowed passages from his closing remarks in the Dachau camp trial, citing Wheaton's *International Law* to discount pleas of superior order and reminding the court that those SS doctors and guards who did refuse to mistreat prisoners were merely transferred out of Mauthausen.

"It was up to every man in that dock," he concluded, "to say, 'No, I will not take part in this nefarious scheme. No, I will not shoot a man that I know has done nothing wrong.' There has been presented to this court a course of conduct over three years which has unquestionably left a livid scar across the face of justice. I am satisfied that this court will return, by its findings and sentence, a judgment that the whole world will understand. Every man in that dock has forfeited his right to live in a decent society."

————

Lieutenant McMahon stood to deliver his closing statement for the defense. "Under totalitarianism," he began, "no man was free. And when the leader is bad and evil, the country does bad and evil things. When the leader is good, the country does good things. The difference between our kind of democracy and totalitarianism is that we can change our leaders when we judge them not to be for the common good. The people of a totalitarian nation cannot. Because no man was free, every man walked in fear of his life, his liberty, and his family, and when war came it became worse because anyone against the state was a traitor to his country. Is it not the prosecution's error here that he seeks to judge the acts of unfree Germans by the standards of free men? How can the unfree man have the obligations of a free man without the rights of a free man? We are judging these men by our standards, not their own. Accordingly, these defendants should be dismissed for the reason that the elements essential to any crime—consent to participate—are not present.

"Regarding the statements of the accused, there is grave doubt that these were freely given and, further, that they contained any language except that desired by the interrogator. Abundant proof is given by the striking similarity of language. I cite some examples. Altfuldisch's statement: 'There is no point in showing any administrative functions, since literally all the leaders continuously influenced the prison compounds.' Niedermeyer's statement: 'There is no sense to define their respective field of duties, since all those mentioned participated in all matters of the camp.' Eckert states: 'Since all leaders and noncoms in the various departments influenced the concentration camp, there is no point in ascribing the responsibility for the terrible conditions to any one leader.' Trum states: 'There is no point in attributing the responsibility for any one condition in the camp directly to one of these names, since all of us participated equally in the camp leadership.'

"Now consider the similarity in statements about shooting to prevent further escape. Priebel states: 'In both cases I shot at escaping prisoners according to orders, to prevent the escape of other prisoners.' Keilwitz: 'I shot this man. I did this to prevent the other prisoners from attempting to escape.' Barczay: 'I shot a Russian prisoner who wished to escape. I did this to make other prisoners afraid to escape.'

"And so it goes with Drabek, Entress, Feigl, with Trauner, Niedermeyer, Haeger, Miessner, Riegler, Zoller, with Blei, with Eckert, with Striegel, with Eigruber, with Eisenhoefer, with Mack and Riegler. Let the court also note the unbelievable accusations that the affiants make against themselves. It is contrary to normal human conduct. People just don't talk that way about themselves. Beyond any doubt, threats and duress were used to induce the signing of the untruthful statements in evidence.

"I speak now of common design. This indictment in effect permitted the military commission to make the crime whatever it willed, a procedure unworthy of the common ideals of mankind. The high feelings of the moment doubtless will be satisfied. But in the sober afterglow will come the realization of dangerous implications. No one in a position of command can escape those implications. Indeed, the fate of some future President of the United States and his chiefs of staff and military advisers may well have been sealed by this decision. The effect in this instance, unfortunately, will be magnified infinitely, for here we are dealing with the rights of man on an international level. To subject an enemy belligerent to an unfair trial, to charge him with an unrecognized crime, or to vent on him our retributive emotions only antagonizes the enemy nation and hinders the reconciliation necessary to a peaceful world.

"At a time like this," McMahon said, "when emotions are understandably high, it is difficult to adopt a dispassionate attitude. Yet now is precisely the time when that attitude is most essential. We live under the Constitution, the embodiment of all the high hopes and aspirations of the New World. We must act accordingly. Indeed, an uncurbed spirit of revenge and retribution, masked in formal legal procedure for purposes of dealing with a fallen enemy, can do more lasting harm than all of the atrocities giving rise to that spirit. . . ."

Denson had nothing but admiration for his counterparts on the defense. McMahon's eloquent language, however, translated to a blatant accusation that Denson had conducted his prosecution in "an uncurbed spirit of revenge and retribution." One can only imagine his disappointment. Other JAG officers may have felt as deep a love of the Constitution as his, but none deeper. Now he stood accused of violating one of its most sacred tenets and the one he had labored hardest to secure for the accused: the right of every human being to a fair trial.

"The people's faith in the fairness and objectiveness of the law," McMahon concluded, "can be seriously undercut by that spirit. The fires of nationalism can be further kindled and the hearts of all mankind embittered and filled with hatred, leaving forlorn and impoverished the noble ideal of malice toward none and charity to all."

———

Ernst Oeding stood, all six-foot-three, and presented his arguments for the lives of his clients. "It is worth noting," he told the tribunal, "that the military rank of these sixty-one people is very low. To say that men of this rank established the policy for hundreds of thousands of people is beyond the realm of reasonable thinking. This being so, we must then determine how far down the chain of command we wish to carry this responsibility. Is it reasonable to say that a private will someday be held as a criminal for following an order of his immediate superior? If so, then it is incumbent upon all fathers to instruct their sons that if they are ever called to the service of their country, they should refuse to obey any order until they have had a chance to determine whether or not it is legal. And if ever ordered to participate in an execution, they should first demand certified true copies of the record of the court and forward them to the family attorney for his dossier. And while son and lawyer are making up their minds, they must also keep in mind that when the war is over, an *ex post facto* law might be passed which would make their otherwise legal conduct illegal. The premise is ridiculous.

"Yours is a heavy responsibility, not alone for the fact that you have sixty-one lives in your hands, but because of the legal precedent you are asked to establish here. What you do here will influence military people for generations to come. This law that you are asked to interpret might well make an army an impossibility, particularly in a democracy such as ours, where men think for themselves and say what they think. We know it is a matter of practical necessity that soldiers obey orders. As boys, every American officer in this room heard 'My country, in her intercourse with foreign nations, may she always be right, but my country, right or wrong.' Well, those are my sentiments today. Regardless of what this court sets as a precedent, they will still be my sentiments."

―――――――

"Prosecution has nothing further," Denson replied.
"Has defense anything further?"
"No, sir," Oeding said.
"Court will be closed." At 2:30 on May 11, 1946, the court recessed. Ninety minutes later the court reopened.

28

The Verdicts

Ninety minutes, this time to deliberate on the fate of sixty-one accused.

———

"The court finds," Prickett announced, "that the circumstances, conditions, and the very nature of Mauthausen and its by-camps were of such a criminal nature as to cause every official, governmental, military, and civil, and every employee thereof to be culpably and criminally responsible. The court further finds that it was impossible for a guard or a civilian employee to have been employed in aforesaid concentration camp without having acquired a definite knowledge of the criminal practices and activities therein. The court therefore declares that any official, governmental, military, or civil, whether he be a member of the Waffen SS, Allgemeine SS, or any guard or civil employee of Mauthausen or any of its by-camps, is guilty of a crime against the recognized laws, customs, and practices of civilized nations and the letter and spirit of the laws and usages of war, and by reason thereof is to be punished. As I read the following names, I want the accused to rise."

One by one, the Germans in the dock rose as their names were called.

"The court, in closed session, at least two-thirds of the members present at the time the vote was taken, finds you of the particulars of the charge—guilty."

———

On May 28, 1946, twenty-eight of the forty defendants who had been found guilty in the first trial, that of personnel from camp Dachau, were hanged at Landsberg prison. The month before, eight cases had been reviewed and their sentences commuted. Denson never turned bitter over the reductions. "When you talk about conviction, that stamps a man," he told an interviewer from Steven Spielberg's Shoah Foundation in March 1996. "Punishment is when he pays. A lot of the people I tried were sentenced to be hanged. A lot had their sentences reduced by the confirming authority in these trials. The lesson was there, it had been taught. The punishment doesn't always fit the crime. But an effort in that direction is what I think we contributed to. I can't say there was one more heinous than the others. All of them stunk, and all of them got what they deserved. I don't think any received a punishment that was not merited—whether it fit their participation is hard to say."

New York Daily News,
Tuesday, May 14, 1946

U.S. Tribunal Sentences
58 Nazi Murderers to Gallows

By Joseph Dees

Dachau, May 13 (UP)—Fifty-eight of the 61 Germans convicted of complicity in the murder of perhaps 1,500,000 persons in the notorious Mauthausen concentration camp were sentenced by an American military tribunal today to be hanged. The other three were given life imprisonment. It was the greatest mass death sentencing since the war ended. The sentences must be reviewed by the Third Army and Gen. Joseph T. McNarney, theater commander.

Two Collapse on Sentencing

Major Gen. Fay B. Prickett, president of the seven-man tribunal, took only 35 seconds to sentence each defendant. Most of the defendants snapped to attention when they heard their names called, but two collapsed and had to be helped from the courtroom when they learned they were going to die.

29

The Miracle

Denson kept his promise to Huschi and came to see her at the end of the Mauthausen trial. At her suggestion, they went to see a miracle.

The miracle of the Wies had first taken place on June 14, 1738, when tears were said to have fallen from the face of a wooden statue of Jesus. The statue, depicting Jesus as the Scourged Savior, had originally been carved for use in Good Friday processions from a local monastery. So lifelike were the statue's bloody wounds that congregants removed it from the monastery and stored it away in an innkeeper's attic where it stood for eight years until the innkeeper's godmother moved it to her farm. The old woman was the first to notice drops of water emanating from the statue's face. Soon visitors were streaming in to see the weeping figure.

A tiny chapel was built in 1740 to accommodate growing numbers of pilgrims. In 1757 the brothers Zimmerman, considered the greatest artists of the Bavarian rococo era, completed construction of a masterpiece church in the statue's honor. War diminished the number of visitors, but by the end of the Mauthausen trial the church was again receiving crowds eager to see the weeping statue and the church's intricate architecture.

Bill and Huschi wandered through the pillared galleries illumined by a bright spring day. Joyful scenes portrayed in elaborate frescoes and colorful inlaid marble columns created a fairy-castle atmosphere of celebration in honor of the wooden Jesus, dressed in simple cloth, his manacled hands outstretched in forgiveness of those who had tortured him. Bill and Huschi marveled at the painted dome depicting the Resurrected Christ atop a rainbow throne with angels and prophets pointing to the gates of heaven. The marble and gold leaf church abounded with celebration of God's love, and for a few hours there were no wars or trials, and the only sounds were the harmonies of prayer.

The following week, Huschi left Germany forever. She knew her divorce would soon be approved and felt she had to get away, that there was nothing left for her or her young daughter in Germany. Selling her family jewels one by one provided money for food and travel. She went first to Davos, Switzerland, then Paris, and finally arrived in Los Angeles, where she and three-year-old Yvonne settled.

Denson took the news of her departure in stride—nothing could displace his allegiance to the work at hand—but an indication of his feelings emerged during a casual conversation with fellow JAGs about German women.

"What about you, Bill?" someone ventured. "Ever meet a German woman you'd want to marry?"

"Only one," he said.

30

Flossenburg

In one of the smaller courtrooms of the U-shaped building at Dachau, a lawyer named Colonel Clark was conducting an unsuccessful prosecution in the parent Flossenburg trial. He had made the critical error of levying murder charges against each of the forty defendants, entangling himself in an impossible task. Then, halfway through the trial, he had a heart attack and died. No sooner had the Mauthausen trial ended than Denson found himself appointed to untangle the mess next door. Undoing the errors of his predecessor and reestablishing the trial on proper footing took more time than the Dachau and Mauthausen trials combined. For six months he waded through another litany of torture, starvation, and death. By December 1946 he had lost so much weight and his hands trembled so violently that the tribunal president recessed the court.

"They said I looked more like an exhibit out of the concentration camp than anybody I put on the stand," he explained years later. "It sort of strains me to try to reconstruct these things. I started thinking about what they had to eat. These men were working all day long, not able to sleep at night, and being fed less than a thousand calories a day. Well, the same thing was happening to me to some extent. I had the shakes and couldn't hold a drink in my hand. I was skin and bones. I got down to 117 pounds. Normally I weighed 165. I was working fifteen-hour days and sleeping less at night because I was thinking—I had nightmares. I was reliving some of these experiences myself. What would I be doing under those circumstances? How would I react to this? It took a toll."

Denson collapsed in his room just after the conclusion of the Flossenburg trial in January 1947. He stayed bedridden for two weeks, getting up only for an occasional meal. One thought consoled him: his tour of duty was over and he could finally go home. The worst was over.

————

The worst was yet to come.

Colonels Straight and Harbaugh, representing JAG HQ, arrived from Wiesbaden to say they had another job they wanted him to do. Nazi commando Otto Skorzeny was in U.S. custody. Having led several successful operations, Skorzeny had earned the title "man most responsible for prolonging the war." Among other escapades, he and a handful of commandos had rescued Hitler's friend, Italian dictator Mussolini, by crash-landing their gliders outside Mussolini's mountaintop prison and pretending to have the prison surrounded. Denson had heard only good things about Skorzeny, whom many considered a hero and a gentleman. Inhumanity had no place in peace or war, and Denson held Skorzeny in high regard for having maintained exemplary behavior in his military career.

"Shoot," he told Straight, "we shouldn't try him. I think we ought to hire him."

"Well," Straight replied, "then we've got another job for you. Buchenwald."

PART FOUR

Buchenwald

———

And with the breath of his lips
Shall he slay the wicked.

—Isaiah 11:4

31

In the Shadow of Nuremberg

The Nuremberg main trial began on November 20, 1945, and lasted nine months. The court conducted 403 open sessions, called 113 witnesses (33 for the prosecution and 80 for the defense), accepted some one hundred thousand documents into evidence, and generated forty-two volumes of transcripts containing more than five million recorded words. In the end, three of the twenty-two defendants were acquitted. Eight received long prison sentences and the rest were sentenced to death. Today the Nuremberg trial is among the most revered proceedings of the twentieth century. The IMT served as the first model of an international criminal court and established critical precedents in prosecuting crimes against humanity. When the trial ended on August 31, 1946, however, it was not without its critics.

Some judges in the U.S. voiced concern that those found guilty had been given no right of appeal and protested that the Allies were only looking to achieve "victor's justice." Others critics objected to the makeup of the tribunal. How could nations guilty of similar offenses—Russia's invasion of Poland, or America and Britain's bombing of Dresden—judge the Germans? Should these nations not themselves also be investigated? Supreme Court Justice Harlan Stone remarked, "Jackson is away conducting his high-grade lynching party in Nuremberg. I don't mind what he does to the Nazis, but I hate to see the pretense that he is running a court and proceeding according to common law."

Shortly after the verdicts were announced, Sen. Robert A. Taft told a *Chicago Tribune* reporter, "About this whole judgment there is the spirit of vengeance, and vengeance is seldom justice. The hanging of these eleven men convicted will be a blot on the American record which we will long regret."

While these voices of dissent were a minority, they were vociferous. Today, more than fifty years later, appreciation for what was accomplished at Nuremberg overshadows the trial's imperfections. At the time, those imperfections raised doubt over the integrity of the war crimes program. The program suffered its greatest setback with the Malmédy case, which brought discredit to all Dachau trials, including Denson's. Seventy-four SS were accused of having murdered a large number of American prisoners in the Belgian town of Malmédy in the Battle of the Bulge. The trial began in May 1946, lasted two months, and ended with seventy-three guilty verdicts, including forty-three death sentences. During the trial, several accused claimed they were tortured into signing confessions. Their attorney, Willis Everett Jr., further charged that army personnel had illegally obtained some of the confessions by disguising themselves as priests. The charges appeared in magazines and newspapers, adding pressure to end the war crimes program quickly.

By the time of Denson's opening remarks for the Buchenwald trial, tensions were running higher than ever: Malmédy had put the army on the defensive, congressmen were poised to launch full-scale investigations, and all further executions were suspended pending their findings. Denson's insistence on meticulous, time-consuming preparation could not have been more anomalous.

———

A new closeout date for the Dachau program was proposed: December 31, 1947—nine short months in which to try fifteen hundred remaining cases. The date was overly ambitious, and pressure to finish quickly must have been palpable. Had Denson been a different kind of man, the kind that caved under pressure, he would have cut the Buchenwald case short: there were only thirty-one defendants, fewer than in the Dachau camp trial, which had taken only one month to hear. But that was not his way. He felt the weight of law too keenly to succumb to its compromise in deals or backroom machinations. Though many saw him as a senior member of the war crimes program, he had started in law at its most common and gritty—defending ordinary people victimized by poverty and abuse—and had arrived at his station through far less ambition than they might have imagined. Denson's only personal interest in the trials was due process and lawful convictions.

And there lay his dilemma. From the camps had emerged a picture of horror that would in years to come be held up as the ultimate display of man's inhumanity to man. Yet the perpetrators of that inhumanity were becoming incidental pawns of political forces much larger than Denson. Just before the end of the Flossenburg trial, Soviet scientists had achieved their first atomic chain reaction, and paranoia over the Communist threat fueled a growing desire among many in the U.S. government to complete the war crimes program as quickly as possible. No matter how great the pressure to get the job done, however, Denson would not just hang people. He would do the job he had been asked to do: probe issues carefully and proceed along lines of due process—not to vindicate inevitable guilty verdicts, but to establish their legitimacy. That, whether the army liked it or not, would take time.

Nuremberg's waning star to the north and the Soviet threat to the east had set an ominous tone for Denson's final and most controversial trial.

32

Goethe's Prophecy

popular belief held that Johann Wolfgang von Goethe, Germany's eighteenth-century master author and philosopher, would leave his Weimar residence on spring mornings, ascend into the beech forest north of the city, commune with nature, and write. The site chosen by the Nazis to build a camp for political prisoners, criminals, and later for Jews had as its centerpiece the Goethe Oak, a tree stump that marked the poet's favorite spot. This was a heavily wooded area atop Mount Ettersberg, fifteen hundred feet above sea level. Five miles south from the base of the mountain lay the city of Weimar, Germany's cultural capital, and the railway station where prisoners arrived for incarceration at Buchenwald.

The camp was originally conceived for "protective-custody" prisoners who, the SS believed, could benefit from education and reform. In July 1937 the camp opened with 149 prisoners and a handful of administrators. More transports arrived that summer, bringing an additional 600 prisoners who labored to clear deep-rooted *buchen*, birch trees, from the mountain's foggy northern slope. By spring 1938, 2,500 prisoners were clearing forest, building barracks and workshops, excavating ditches for water and sewer pipes, hooking up phone and telex cables, and laying concrete roads. Eventually Buchenwald encompassed 371 acres surrounded by more than two miles of electrically charged barbed wire.

As Germany's war efforts increased, Buchenwald's purpose shifted from reformation to production. As a result, the camp was known as a "mild" camp: its overt purpose, at least, was not systematic extermination but labor, and in a few years it grew to become one of the largest labor-exploitation centers in all of Europe. During almost eight years of operation, prisoners from more than thirty nations, including America, labored, suffered, and died within its confines. The inmates of Buchenwald included prisoners known in Nazi terminology as "antisocials": homosexuals, Jehovah's Witnesses, Communists, Gypsies, and other minority groups. Among the prisoners were doctors, lawyers, priests, rabbis, college professors, statesmen, nobility, prisoners of war, hostages—and habitual German criminals who took part in the scheme of destruction employed at Buchenwald.

The camp's relatively stable routine began to disintegrate in 1942 when Buchenwald, like other camps, started receiving trainloads of evacuees from the East. To accommodate the overwhelming influx of prisoners, tent cities were built around its perimeters. Health and sanitary conditions rapidly deteriorated. Especially awful was the Little Camp, a series of makeshift barracks earmarked for antisocials and sick prisoners who could no longer work.

Buchenwald had the distinction of being the first major concentration camp to fall into the hands of the Western Allies while it still had a full population of prisoners. When the camp was liberated on April 11 by a reconnaissance battalion of the 6th Army, it held twenty-one thousand ragged, starving inmates and cadavers beyond counting. "Hundreds of dead naked bodies in piles, piles of bones, a gallows, a row of incinerators with the charred remains of human bodies," Margaret Bourke-White enumerated after taking photos. "The sights I have just seen are so unbelievable that I don't think I'll believe them myself until I've seen the photographs." Liberation soldier Irvin Faust wrote, "I remember feeling that what we were seeing had nothing to do with war. Before this, even when soldiers killed each other, there were rules. This, even for the Hun, was out of bounds. As a soldier, *I* felt degraded."

Goethe had once prophesied that someday Fate would strike the German people because "they ingenuously submit to any mad scoundrel who appeals to their lowest instincts, who confirms them in their vices and teaches them to conceive nationalism as isolation and brutality." As the history of the camp unfolded, stories of "lowest instincts" surfaced that came to be identified particularly with Buchenwald. These included shrunken heads, tattooed skins, and the escapades of Ilse Koch, wife of the camp commandant.

————

Comparing miseries is a cruel task. Yet if there is a realm where those capable of the "worst" abominations dwell, Karl Koch is among its chief residents. And by his side stands his wife, Ilse. They met in 1934 when he was commandant of the Sachsenhausen camp. She was his secretary, a party member, ten years his junior. They married at midnight in an oak grove, by torchlight. She wore white, he wore dress uniform, according to SS ritual. Previously Karl Koch had been a bank clerk. In 1924, when both the bank and his first marriage failed, he joined the Nazi Party, then the SS, and distinguished himself by particularly bloody conduct in some of Germany's first concentration camps. As the camps became more brutal, Koch was promoted: from Sachsenhausen to Esterwegen to Lichtenburg to Dachau, then to Columbia Street prison in Berlin, renowned for its excesses of torture. Prisoners there were locked in doghouses, chained by the neck, and forced to lap up their food from a bowl. Anyone failing to bark when Koch walked by received twenty-five lashes with a cane. Koch had one prisoner beaten senseless, then ordered guards to stop up his anus with hot asphalt and force him to drink castor oil. "A hard man," the SS wrote of him, "but not too harsh, open, calm-minded, goal-directed. His achievements are higher than average: he does everything for the National Socialist ideal." For his loyalty and service, the Reich Main Security Office made him commandant of Buchenwald, where his barbarism reached new depths.

In September 1937, Pastor Paul Schneider of the Evangelical Confessional Church was brought to Buchenwald. Schneider's church belonged to a group of German protestants led by Martin Niemoller, an outspoken critic of Nazi doctrine. Koch directed a slow death for the pastor. For eighteen months Schneider lived in a lice-infested cell, ankle-deep in fetid water, sustaining daily beatings and torture. Infuriated that anyone could hold out so long, Koch ordered medical officer Sommer to poison Schneider's food with a heart-paralyzing drug. Then Sommer applied cold compresses to his chest until the pastor's heart stopped. Koch notified Schneider's wife and children and invited them to view the body. An SS barber concealed the bruises with makeup and a wig, then laid the corpse out in ceremonial fashion surrounded by flowers. Schneider's family arrived, were given a viewing, and escorted to the gate. On their departure Koch told the family with tears in his eyes, "Your husband was my best prisoner. Just when I wanted to inform him of his release, he died of a heart attack."

In 1938, a Gypsy attempting to escape was caught. For two days and three nights Koch kept him in a wooden crate lined with wire netting and long nails, then ordered him killed by a lethal injection of benzine to the heart. In October of that year, four thousand Poles arrived and were marched from Weimar station to camp under a rain of blows with rifle butts. Locals threw stones and yelled, "Strike them dead, the Polish pigs!" Koch and his fellow SS watched from his car. Waving a revolver, Koch yelled out the window, "Hands up! Sing German songs!" then sped through the ranks of stunned, terrified prisoners. Anyone stepping out of line to avoid the oncoming vehicle was "shot while trying to escape." Trucks followed behind Koch, picking up the bodies.

Koch was one Aryan who didn't help the fatherland unless it helped him, and his cruelty was exceeded only by his corruption. Beginning that year he instituted monthly "comradeship evenings" for his staff. These binges of eating and drinking began with a pompous open-air festival at Bismarck Tower on Ettersberg's south slope and deteriorated into all-night orgies. Koch funded these evenings by forcing the entire camp to go without food for twenty-four hours, a fast that netted him six to ten thousand marks each month.

Despite his illegal fortunes, Koch never seemed to be able to make ends meet. In large part this was due to his major weakness: Ilse. No request by his beautiful, voracious young wife went unfulfilled. Although strict rations on tobacco and wine were imposed for the SS rank and file, Frau Koch bathed in Madeira. For her birthday, Karl presented her with a diamond ring worth eight thousand marks. He had inmates build her a stylish villa that featured a spacious basement, private garage, and a wide terrace overlooking the Thuringian countryside. Bordering the villa was a fence of large stone slabs dragged from the quarry by columns of prisoners. Villa Koch was the largest of all SS residences. Prisoners sent to make repairs there returned with descriptions of a basement filled with racks of hams and smoked sausages, shelves brimming with preserved fruits and vegetables, and large cabinets containing hundreds of bottles of wine and champagne.

Ilse earned the nickname "Bitch of Buchenwald" for her cruelty, wanton behavior, quixotic anger, and indifference to the suffering of Buchenwald's victims. Witnesses at her trial testified that she ordered prisoners beaten for meaningless infractions of spurious rules—for taking off their hat in her presence, for instance, or for not taking off their hat. She displayed herself in alluring dress, then reported any prisoner who dared look at her. Many of those reported were never seen again. She was rumored to have amassed a collection of tattooed skins that she had made into lampshades, gloves, and other personal items. Her demands for improvements on her personal quarters were executed at an accelerated pace. Prisoners working on these personal projects were forced to carry heavy loads of earth and stone at a breakneck pace. Many of the workers died from the strain. Others were beaten for not running fast enough.

For Ilse's pleasure, Karl ordered prisoners to build a private riding hall. The building was three hundred feet long, sixty feet wide, and lined with mirrors. Thirty prisoners died during its construction. Ilse rode there for fifteen minutes or so a few times each week while a prisoner band provided music. At a time when Germany struggled under harsh wartime rationing, the riding hall was completed at a cost of 250,000 marks.

Despite Karl's obsession with Ilse, neither was faithful to the other. Karl made frequent trips out of camp in search of romance. Ilse, her biographer Arthur L. Smith wrote, "loved men in uniform." During a visit to Norway in 1940, Karl contracted syphilis. On return to camp he had himself treated by Dr. Walter Kramer, a prisoner orderly. To ensure that no one learned of his disease, Koch had Kramer and his assistant shot. The deaths were noted as punishment for conducting political discussions in the infirmary.

Karl Koch had an enemy, his superior, SS general Prince von Waldeck-Pyrmont, whose district included the city of Weimar and the Buchenwald camp. Von Waldeck was admired for having been the first member of a royal family to join Himmler's SS, in 1929. The prince noticed Dr. Kramer's name on a camp death list—Kramer had once successfully treated him—and investigating further discovered that Koch had ordered Kramer's clandestine execution. Further inquiry revealed that Koch had been embezzling huge sums of money from prisoners, in particular Jews, and selling camp supplies to civilians in the area. With so much evidence of corruption, von Waldeck handed the matter over to Konrad Morgen, an SS magistrate known as an insightful investigator. Morgen relocated to Buchenwald, where he uncovered further evidence of Koch's massive criminal activity.

Morgen's concern, like that of his superiors in Berlin, sprang not from sympathy for victims of the camps but from disgust over the corruption rampant in the ranks of the SS. Concentration camp personnel in particular were what Paul Guth called "the dregs." Most had been conscripted off the street from Germany's unemployed working class, and few espoused any pretense of wanting to sacrifice their lives for the greater good of the fatherland. "I can tell you," Guth said, "when there was need of military guards for drafting to the Russian front, invariably the commandant or someone else in a position of leadership would set up an attempted breakout by prisoners. He would have prisoners chased into the barbed wire and then shot down. Then he would issue a report to Berlin: 'These prisoners are so nasty, I can't do without my able-bodied soldiers.' The SS were selfish, lazy—not an attractive bunch."

Nazi senior officials knew that many of their chosen commandants lacked even rudimentary political instincts and made a point of warning them, for example, that while escorting outsiders such as government officials and industrialists around a camp, they should not include brothels or extermination facilities in the tour. Oswald Pohl, who headed administration of the concentration camps during the war, periodically sent mimeographed letters to the camp commandants warning them to be alert to their men's corruption. In one of these letters he complained, "Many of the guards at the camps are aware only in the faintest way of the obligations imposed upon them." A survey conducted by the SS in 1938 showed that, of 513 officers, only 128 were suitable for their jobs and recommended that at least half of the others be dismissed.

In principle, punishments and executions required approval from the Reich Security Main Office. In practice, such approvals were secondary to the will of camp commandants, whose transgressions were tolerated so long as the camps remained productive. Koch, however, flaunted a brazen disobedience of SS protocol. Taking money from Jewish prisoners ignored a clear directive from Himmler that no money from Jews should go into any officer's pocket.

Morgen laid his findings out before Himmler, and the SS chief told him to bring charges. Both Karl and Ilse Koch were arrested. Ilse reacted with hysterical screams and threats, claiming that her husband was a murderer and a rapist. Karl was found guilty and sentenced to death. Ilse was acquitted. Karl was taken the following day to Buchenwald, stood against a wall, shot, and his body was burned in the camp crematorium. After the war Ilse settled in Ludwigsburg and lived with relatives until someone recognized her in the street. She was arrested, charged with war crimes, and imprisoned at Dachau.

One of Ilse's former lovers, an officer from Buchenwald, worked in the prisoners' kitchen at Dachau. They met in the kitchen by chance, and Ilse told him where she was being held. The officer dug a hole to her barracks, and when she finally walked up to the witness chair in the Buchenwald trial, she was visibly pregnant. The press had a field day.

33

A Tour of Buchenwald

To prepare himself for the final trial of his military career, Denson drove with his West Point friend Edward O'Connell to inspect the Buchenwald camp. There he learned that during its years of operation the SS had created a series of thriving arts and crafts workshops. Among these was a studio that housed prisoner architects, sculptors, wood-carvers, goldsmiths, painters, potters, and graphic artists. From this studio emerged decorations for SS houses and a huge output of luxury items. No expense was spared providing these prisoner artists with supplies for their work. A professional kiln was installed for the porcelain painters. Large quantities of gold, silver, copper, special woods, and other raw materials were diverted from the war effort to ensure that the SS would continue to have their gift items from Buchenwald.

During his reign, Commandant Koch established a photo department that designed albums for officers and friends. Always anxious to prove their Aryan lineage, the SS built a studio where prisoner artists designed genealogical charts, replete with coats of arms and tables of ersatz ancestors. In the camp bookbindery, craftsmen prepared elaborately bound volumes, illustrated newspapers, plaques with favorite German maxims, and greeting cards. For Christmas 1939, Himmler received an inlaid green marble desk set created in the prisoner crafts studio and valued at fifteen to twenty thousand marks.

Denson and O'Connell toured the camp's former agricultural enterprises, which included a large rabbit hutch, sheep pen, poultry farm, riding-horse stable, gardening detail, and pigsty. Food intended for prisoners was frequently diverted to feed the camp's animals. In 1939 a pig was stolen. Convinced that prisoners had done it, Koch ordered that no food be given out until the pig was found. Four days later it was discovered that the pig had been stolen and slaughtered by SS men. By then more than 250 inmates had died of starvation.

Buchenwald housed a zoo. Himmler had suggested the idea, and as late as 1944, when great hunger prevailed in the camp, the bears, apes, stags, foxes, pheasants, peacocks, and other animals feasted on food from the prisoners' kitchen. While inmates subsisted on one-sixth of a loaf of bread and a handful of rutabaga, the hawks and falcons ate meat and the monkeys were fed mashed potatoes with milk. "There was a cage with a bear and an eagle," one former inmate described in a *New York Times* interview. "Every day they would throw a Jew in there. The bear would tear him apart and the eagle would pick at his bones."

By early 1947, Denson's health and energy had reached a dangerous low. His visit to Buchenwald charged him with sufficient outrage to make it through one last round.

34

The Buchenwald Report

The Buchenwald trial opened at Dachau on April 11, 1947, exactly two years from the day Americans liberated the camp. Photographers filled the courtroom, vying for position to photograph exhibits of shrunken heads, tattooed human skin, and the infamous Ilse Koch, Bitch of Buchenwald. The only woman to stand trial at Dachau for war crimes was drawing more attention than Denson's other three trials combined, and extra rows of wooden theater seats had been installed to accommodate the overflow crowd. Koch disgusted Denson. It was reprehensible enough to him that any human being should have an obsession for objects made of human skin, but worse to his mind was her complete lack of those emotions and feelings he had grown up expecting to find in women: modesty, probity, and at least a modicum of compassion for less fortunate human beings.

"If the court please," began Capt. Emmanuel Lewis, chief defense counsel, "for the past two weeks the German and American radio and press have been full of allegations against these accused. The prosecution has not missed an opportunity to brand these people as archcriminals without giving them an opportunity of answering the charges. We do not deny the right of the press to report facts, but this case was tried in the papers before being brought to this court of justice, and we ask permission to poll the members of the court individually."

"No member of the court has formed an opinion," said court president Brig. Gen. Emil Charles Kiel. "There being no ground for challenge, the court is declared properly constituted. How do the accused plead?"

"As chief defense counsel, I enter a plea of not guilty for all of the accused. Before we begin, if it please the court, there is a matter of great concern. The accused are charged with victimizing captured and unarmed citizens of the United States, and they seek to defend themselves against this charge. But despite our repeated requests, the prosecution has failed to furnish us with the name or whereabouts of even one single American victim."

Denson rose slowly from his seat. He had grown shockingly thin and his clothes hung loosely on his body. "We are unfortunately unable to comply," he told the tribunal. "The victims were last seen being carted into the crematories. From there they went up the chimney in smoke, and all the power of the United States and all the documents in Augsburg cannot tell which way they went. We are sorry that we cannot furnish their whereabouts, but we fail to see that it is material whether one American or fifty thousand were incarcerated in Buchenwald. The crimes of these accused would be just as heinous."

"Motion is denied. Opening statement?"

Denson steadied himself at the center of the prosecution table. "Two years ago today," he began, "victorious troops of the Third U.S. Army overran concentration camp Buchenwald and closed a chapter of infamy and sadism unparalleled in recorded history. We expect the evidence to show that these thirty-one accused, acting in pursuance of a common design, did aid, abet, or participate in subjecting victims in that camp to killings, tortures, starvation, beatings, and other indignities. We expect to show that these victims were the intelligentsia of Europe, prisoners who opposed Nazi tyranny and refused to don the Nazi uniform, and that these victims were subjected to conditions that are practically indescribable. We expect the evidence to show how the participation of these thirty-one accused fit into this plan of extermination. The tortured souls of Buchenwald's victims demand justice, and justice in this case can only be satisfied by the hangman's noose." In his previous three trials, Denson had proposed that the accused had "forfeited their right to live in decent society," leaving room for a variety of possible sentences. His opening remarks now left no room for doubt: he was seeking the death penalty for every accused in the dock. He sat, his energy spent.

Photographers snapped away at the defendants. Captain Lewis stood and said, "May I ask the court to refuse permission to photographers to take pictures of the accused with their numbers on? The photographers have had wide leeway . . ."

"Request is denied."

"May it please the court," Denson continued, rising again slowly from his chair, "we have here a film taken three or four days after the arrival of the Americans in Buchenwald. I think the only way this can be portrayed is by showing the film." The film had been produced by a Signal Corps film crew, headed by Hollywood director Billy Wilder.

"The defense objects," Lewis said. "Conditions three or four days after the liberation say nothing about what occurred prior to that time. Furthermore, the film carries a soundtrack. The person who made that soundtrack is not sworn as a witness, and his explanation of the scenes is prejudiced against the interests of the accused."

"Regardless of who made the film," Denson said to the tribunal, "it has received the sanction of the War Department, soundtrack and all."

"Objection overruled. Permission is granted to the showing."

Guards with white gloves and helmets closed the shutters, the projector was turned on, and a narrator's voice filled the courtroom.

"This is a pictorial record of the almost unprecedented crimes perpetrated by the Nazis at the Buchenwald concentration camp. In the official report Buchenwald is termed an extermination factory, and the means of extermination: starvation complicated by hard work, abuse, beatings, tortures, incredibly crowded sleeping conditions, and sicknesses of all types. This is the body disposal plant. There inside are the ovens that gave the crematory a maximum disposal capacity of four hundred bodies per ten-hour day. The ovens are extremely modern in design, made by a firm that specialized in baking ovens. All bodies were finally reduced to bone ash. One of the first things that German civilians from neighboring Weimar see on a forced tour of the camp is the parchment display. A lampshade of human skin, made at the request of an SS officer's wife. . . ."

The prosecution had discovered additional details about conditions in Buchenwald in the *Buchenwald Report*. This four-hundred-page typed document had been compiled by a U.S. Army intelligence team that included officers from the psychological warfare division. The team had arrived immediately after liberation, charged with creating a detailed report about the inner workings of Buchenwald for use in trials. The report had taken four weeks to write, included contributions from more than one hundred former prisoners, and is recognized today as one of the most significant documents extant on life in concentration camps.

The principal author was former Buchenwald prisoner Eugen Kogon. Born in Munich, son of a consular official to the imperial Russian court, Kogon had spent five years as chief administrator for the estates of Austrian Prince Phillippe. By the time he was thirty-five he had traveled across most of Europe and spoken openly of his opposition to Hitler—forthrightness inherited perhaps from Benedictine and Dominican monks with whom he studied as a young man, or from his university days in Munich and Florence. However he came by his voice, it earned him a place on the first German blacklist. After a year in various Gestapo prisons he was transferred to Buchenwald. Kogon managed to smuggle himself out of camp in a medical supplies crate shortly before the liberation. That opening day of trial, Denson called him to the stand.

––––––––––

"I am forty-three," Kogon said, "I am a journalist, a graduate economist, and a doctor of social sciences. I was a prisoner in Buchenwald from September 1939 until the liberation."

"What happened on your arrival?"

"I arrived with a transport of almost five hundred Austrians. When we arrived, some of us were grabbed by our ties and choked. Some had water poured on them. We had to raise our hands and stand with our knees bent. After about an hour and a half we were interrogated. Anybody who did not give the answer that suited the sergeant was slapped. Then we had to line up facing the wall and perform the so-called Saxonian salute, where you fold your hands behind your neck. It was an extremely hot day and we were exhausted: we had traveled thirty-six hours by train without food or water. As soon as someone collapsed, an SS sergeant beat him until he rose again. That evening we were taken to the bath, made to undress, stand on chairs, and everyone was shaved from top to bottom. There was a big boiler in the middle of the room that contained some dirty liquid—disinfecting liquid, we were told. After our hair had been cut off, we had to jump into that boiler. Every place where hair had been cut off the liquid burned in an indescribable way. I climbed out of this boiler with dead lice on me. Then we were given clothes and wooden shoes with sharp edges. Since we had to frequently run double time through camp we quickly developed severe wounds on our feet.

"We had not yet received any food. We got our first meal the next morning. Then we were taken to the formation square. I was assigned to tunnel detail one. I was lucky to not get the stone quarry, which was one of the very worst details in the camp. Some of my best friends, after only a few hours in the quarry, were beaten or shot to death.

"I was in this tunnel detail until the fall of 1940, then transferred to the prison tailor shop through the help of comrades. We started work very early in the morning, marching past the crematorium where flames would constantly be coming out of the chimney. This tailor shop detail was better than other details. We had a roof over our heads, we had fire, and we did not have to participate in the general formation. Formation was one of the worst institutions in camp. That was where most of the punishments took place. The beating table was carried there and the prisoner made to lie down on it. From a loudspeaker the camp would hear an announcement of the type of punishment to be administered. Two SS sergeants would approach the prisoner, one from the left and one from the right, and start whipping him. After the whipping was over, the prisoner was unbuckled from the table and made to walk away, if he was able, and then perform one hundred knee bends—allegedly to get the muscles and blood moving again."

"For what offenses did prisoners receive the punishment you have described?" Denson asked.

"For any reason the camp leaders liked. Jews received blows just for being Jewish. The only possible way to avoid being chosen for punishment was to not draw attention. Even before I was brought to Buchenwald, prisoners who had been there told me that the most important principle of behavior was to not draw attention, to not be seen by anybody."

"What was the Little Camp, doctor?"

"Unbelievable misery. Beginning 1943, many transports arrived, especially from the west in 'night and fog' actions, as the SS called them. Tens of thousands of people arrived each month. The main camp covered only about one square kilometer, and there was not enough room. So a tent camp, the Little Camp, was erected behind the last row of barracks. Nobody could deal with the conditions there. Bunks built for four hundred men had eighteen hundred or more pressed in. Prisoners on the upper bunks made holes to climb up on the roof in order to relieve themselves there because they had no way of leaving the barracks."

In addition to his verbal testimony, Kogon's *Buchenwald Report* provided vital evidence of the functioning of the camp. The report was originally published in a limited German edition in 1946 and was not commercially available in English until 1999. One of the many extremes of Nazi terror described in the report was the SS detail responsible for liquidating Russian prisoners of war. This detail was known as Commando 99.

35

Commando 99

Hitler never hesitated to break a promise if doing so furthered his plans for world domination. His pledge to Stalin that Germany would never invade Russia fell away in June 1941 when German soldiers marched on Moscow. By August the Germans had concentrated the biggest military force in the course of the Second World War on the Eastern Front. The invasion led to deportation of large numbers of Russians to concentration camps inside German-occupied territory.

"It was in the late fall," prosecution witness Paul Schilling described, "when the first Russian prisoners of war arrived. First three, then seven, and so on, continuously the number increased. Then I saw the first transports. They passed in front of my eyes, men chained two by two, going to the horse stable."

"Among these accused, whom do you recall seeing there?" Denson asked.

"There was Helbig, Otto, Zinecker, Schobert, Pleissner."

Another prosecution witness described the fate of those sent to the horse stable. "My name is Ludwig Gehm. I am forty-two years old, German. I worked in the locksmith's shop at Buchenwald and as a plumber in the horse stable, or Commando 99 as it was known. During the winter I helped to unfreeze water hoses and clean the drainage pipes in the stable."

"Tell the court, please," Denson said, "what you found cleaning out the pipes."

"My comrade and I found identification tags and blood."

"How do you know it was blood?"

"Up to our elbows we had to work in it, and it smelled sweetly."

"How many dog tags did you find?"

"Thirty to fifty. I couldn't draw any direct conclusions as far as nationality is concerned, but these were names used very often in Poland and Russia. SS Master Sgt. Helbig was pushing us, 'Hurry up, hurry up. You have to finish in half an hour. Our job is going to start.' We left perhaps twenty minutes later. We were curious about this job that was going to start, and on our way back we saw that Russians were being led in there."

Another witness, Kurt Titz, described what he had seen coming out of the horse stable on several occasions. "There was a van carrying naked dead bodies, with blood dripping from below. Later on a tin tub was built under that vehicle so that the blood would not run out in the street."

A defendant, one of the few Germans in the Buchenwald trial to offer candid details of his crimes, described what he had done and seen inside the horse stable. "My name is Horst Dittrich. I served at Buchenwald from June 1938 until December 1942."

"Were you ever a member of what was known as Commando 99?" Denson asked.

"I served on this commando four times."

A tripod was brought into the courtroom, and on it was placed a four-foot-square graphic rendering of the horse stable where Commando 99 operated. "Dittrich, I ask you to point out to the court where these prisoners of war came into the building."

"Here," the witness said, indicating a square on the chart. "This room was an ordinary stable. There was a loudspeaker in the frame in the wall. Whenever prisoners came into the horse stable, music came through very loudly. First, they had to undress completely in this room. One by one, they were led through these two doors to the room farther back. There was a table on this spot," indicating again, "with a list of names of the prisoners. This table over here was covered with a white tablecloth with two or three medical instruments on it. As far as I can remember, on this side of the wall there were two maps hanging, as are shown usually in a physician's office. One showed the muscles of the human body. The other was the kind of map used to check eye strength. A fake examination was made of the prisoner, telling him to lift his arms or open his mouth. After this, the prisoner was taken by an SS officer to this room here," he said, indicating a room on the map, "and turned with his back toward the wall. The SS officer gave a sign to another SS officer by stamping with his foot on the floor. Then this second officer through a slit in the wall shot his pistol at the back of the head of the prisoner. Two inmates dragged the body into this next room here. Then a man with a water hose cleaned the room."

"Dittrich, approximately how many Russian prisoners of war were shot in the horse stable the first time that you were there?"

"Twenty-eight to thirty. There might have been more the second time, but I do not remember that transports were ever larger than forty men."

"Was anything given to the men who participated in Commando 99?"

"Cigarettes, sandwiches, schnapps."

Lt. Col. John S. Dwinell was serving as Law Member for the court. "You testified that you assumed these Russian soldiers were correctly sentenced to death. Why, then, in your opinion, was it necessary to have this fake examination and all the other pantomime that went on?" Denson must have appreciated Dwinell's question. It was one he asked himself but for which he never found an answer. "I was never able to ascertain why the detail went to such trouble to bring about the deaths of about eight thousand in this fashion," he admitted years later.

"In my opinion," Dittrich said, "it wasn't necessary. I don't know why it was done."

"Why the bonus? I am referring to the cigarettes and schnapps that were given to the men on the detail."

"When I work day and night," Dittrich reasoned, "I have to eat something."

———

Later in the trial, Hermann Pister, who succeeded Karl Koch as commandant of Buchenwald, also testified concerning Commando 99. He argued that no prisoners of war had been executed, only partisans and commissars, and that the executions had been ordered by Berlin—perfectly legal as far as he was concerned.

"Let me refresh your memory," Denson offered on cross-examination. "You stated in Freising that the prisoners shot in the horse stable were 'Russian prisoners of war.' Now, before this court, you say they were partisans or political commissars."

"I have never denied calling these persons prisoners of war in Freising, but . . ."

". . . but that was before you had a chance to talk to defense counsel and prepare your case. Is that correct?"

"I have to object to this," Dr. Wacker said rising from the defense table, "on the ground that Mr. Denson refers to consultation with counsel. He has done so before, thereby implying that I have done something to change Pister's testimony. I object to that vigorously." Wacker had served as one of the defense lawyers in the Flossenburg trial, but the prior relationship did nothing to abate his anger over Denson's implication that he had prompted Pister to lie on the stand.

"The objection is overruled."

Pister was adamant. "I should like to state to this court now, under oath, that I was never advised by my defense counsel to make untrue statements. I think I know more about concentration camps than any lawyer defending us, and it was entirely immaterial to me or any of these other accused whether the Russians were prisoners of war or political commissars." The statement must have shocked Wacker: his client was denying an important argument in his own defense.

"We had our orders to carry out an execution," Pister continued, "and those orders are what we carried out. Any noncommissioned officer who participated in Commando 99 knew that it wasn't I who had issued these orders. They had come down from above. I don't see any generals here being accused of shooting hostages or prisoners of war, but they are the men responsible. The ones who issued the order in our case disappeared through cowardly suicide and left the responsibility on us. Furthermore, as you stated in your opening statement, Mr. Denson, it is all the same to you whether a man killed one, three, five, or more. The main thing for you is merely whether they were serving in a concentration camp. The highest-ranking legal officer in this theater, your own man Jackson, has stated that if a person was properly ordered to participate in an execution, it is not his duty to investigate whether it is a legal order."

The operative phrase in Pister's citing of Jackson was "properly ordered." Even German law recognized the difference between commands properly and improperly ordered, and such German laws remained in effect throughout the war. No less a Nazi luminary than Dr. Joseph Goebbels, minister of propaganda, published an article in May 1944 that asserted: "No international law of warfare is in existence which provides that a soldier who has committed a mean crime can escape punishment by pleading as his defense that he followed the commands of his superiors. This holds particularly true if those commands are contrary to all human ethics and opposed to the well-established usage of warfare." Nazi endorsements, however, did not appeal to Denson, who responded to Pister with an argument the tribunal was more likely to recognize.

"You are comparing these Russians executed in Commando 99 with your own lot. Yet is it not a fact that you are being given a trial and these Russian prisoners of war were not?"

"It wasn't up to me to investigate whether they had a trial," Pister said. "The Reich Security Main Office was the highest authority, not only for us but for all Germany. This was for us a legal and lawful act. Many of my comrades were also executed as war criminals without trial."

That riled Denson. He was proud of the war crimes program. Despite the summary execution of SS at the liberation of Dachau, despite other acts performed in the heat of the moment, despite all their shortcomings, the Allies to his mind had done a superb job before, during, and after the liberation. Pister's implication that U.S. army executions of war criminals were no better than Nazi executions of Russian POWs was to him the height of slander.

"Can you give this court the name of a single person who has been put in the category of a war criminal and who has been executed here in Dachau or anywhere else in this zone without a trial?"

"It would fill half an address book."

"Give us one, Pister."

"One? Waffen SS Lieutenant General Schmidt."

"Where was he executed?" Denson insisted.

"Near Mauthausen, with the reason as it was later given that he was one of those responsible for conditions in Mauthausen. This man never had anything to do with any concentration camp, and he was given no trial."

"Who executed him?"

"I don't know. Allied troops. At any rate, I wasn't there."

"You were not there. So you do not know anything about it of your own personal knowledge, do you?"

"When you sentence me to death and my wife isn't here, she will still find out about it later."

"Answer the question, Pister."

"I said I wasn't there. I wasn't there at Commando 99 either."

———

Throughout several days of testimony concerning Commando 99, the defense argued that their clients had committed no crime by executing Russians. Russia had never signed the Geneva Convention, they reasoned, and Russian soldiers could not claim its protection. Denson's outrage displayed itself most viscerally in these exchanges. Whatever energy remained he rallied here to disprove the defense's contentions.

"I think the cloak of sophistry should be removed and we should call a spade a spade," he told the tribunal. "The defense counsel has talked about not trying to argue the legality *vel nom* of Commando 99, but that's all he has done. I am perfectly ready, willing, and able to talk at this time of legality and of the law that is to be applied here.

"In Hall's *Treatise on International Law* we have the following quotation: 'More than necessary violence must not be used by a belligerent in all his relations with his enemy.' The fact that Russia was not a signatory to a convention did not give Germans the right to mistreat Russian prisoners of war. The Hague and Geneva Conventions were nothing more than a clarification of customs and usages already in practice among civilized nations.

"The next question is whether or not it would be murder without a trial. I think the court is aware of the answer to that question. It has been considered fundamental from the dawn of civilized justice that a man before he is condemned is entitled to a hearing. Defense witnesses in this case have testified that execution without a fair hearing was contrary to German law, and it is certainly contrary to principles of humanity and justice recognized by all civilized nations. Humanity and justice are broad terms, but they exist as guiding stars in the mind of every civilized man. It is only necessary to apply those concepts to determine what constitutes a custom or usage that is acceptable by the civilized nations of the world."

Wacker considered Denson's arguments, then stood to address the court. "I thoroughly agree with counsel for the prosecution when he says that The Hague and Geneva Conventions codified what civilized nations consider law. Now we have an exceptional fact, however, that Russia did not accept these laws as binding. We can imagine that, in the future, an institution of the standing and dignity of the United Nations will establish precepts of international law that will be law even for states that do not of their own free will consider them applicable. However, we are dealing with a case that lies in the past. You cannot fairly expect the German government to have acted in accordance with international law if a belligerent in opposition was not doing so.

"I will, of course, also agree with Mr. Denson that common standards of human behavior should always be valid. But as I view it, war is always inhumane, and it is uncertain whether in war both parties concerned will use the same standards. What is certain is this: There was no doubt concerning the legality of such orders for either the authorities who issued the orders, to wit the Reich government, or any persons who might have received such orders between the years 1933 and 1945.

"We now approach another difficult question: Where is the delineation between law and politics? America attempts to solve matters through law. Russia apparently attempts to complete its conflicts on political grounds. . . ."

"May it please the court," Denson interrupted. He had no patience for sophistry, and Wacker was vaulting clear-cut instances of murder into an abstract philosophical realm. "I object to any further argument of this nature."

Defense counsel Lewis had a different perspective and came to Wacker's aid. "Whether a nonsignatory nation has the right to demand that a signatory nation adhere to the Convention is a question that has never been decided, because we have had but one war since the Convention was signed. We contend that the question is a novel one, and it is for this court to decide whether Russia, a nonsignatory nation, could demand that Germany, which did sign, be bound by the Convention."

Denson disagreed. "That is not the question, may it please the court. The only question is whether or not shooting hostages or prisoners of war has, by custom and usage, become prohibited by international law. Now, counsel for the defense has not raised this question, but in fairness I think we should ask whether in fact Commando 99 was not a reprisal action. Here is the citation in Hall: 'Reprisal, or the punishment of one man for the acts of another, is a measure in itself repugnant to justice.' The only testimony that has leaped out of the cheeks of some of these witnesses is to the effect, 'Well, look what they did to our troops when we were in Russia.' This court should take notice of the fact that it was *Germany* that invaded *Russia*. The only testimony before this court is to the effect that 'they treated us badly, so that's what we did to them.'"

Lewis refused to back down. "If the prosecution insists on the equitable principle, we will throw it right back in his face and ask him why Russia never signed the Geneva Convention and never found itself bound to respect that Convention. We think that the language of the Convention is simple and clear. It binds only those nations who sign it as between themselves. It is not binding as between a signatory and a nation that has refused to join the family of nations. We have nothing further."

"Court will recess."

The confrontation over Commando 99 was never resolved, each side contenting itself with having offered strong arguments. Verdicts, they silently agreed, would determine who had argued more effectively. Meanwhile, Denson's superiors at JAG HQ grew restive. These debates over esoteric points of law were prolonging the trial. The paradox must have struck Denson as bizarre: his having to disobey superior orders to ensure due process for criminals who refused to disobey their own.

36

The Dachau
Death Train

The Buchenwald trial bounded back and forth between textbook crime
and unprecedented atrocity, between boring stretches of courtroom for-
mality and moments of dramatic outburst. Four months later, spring
had turned into summer. Former inmates hung wooden placards memori-
alizing sites around Dachau. This, visitors read, is the Hanging Tree. Here
is the Killing Wall. This Way to Crematory.

Inside courtroom A, Denson's appearance had begun drawing attention of its own. Neither his strength nor his weight had returned anywhere
near normal. "My shirt collar was so big, two could fit in it," he recalled.
Tribunal president Emil Kiel called a recess to allow him time to rest.
Denson would not stay down, and three days later he resumed work in
the courtroom.

When Rainbow and Thunderbird divisions arrived at camp Dachau,
they came upon a line of boxcars filled with dead and dying prisoners. The

history of that death train emerged during Denson's questioning of former Buchenwald inmates.

"My name is Martin Rosenfeld. I ask the court to consider my testimony in the name of the many thousands of Czech and other prisoners who died in the concentration camps by the force of the SS and who are buried in mass graves all over Austria and Czechoslovakia."

"Mr. Rosenfeld," Denson said, "when you returned to Buchenwald in 1945, did you ever meet a man by the name of Merbach?"

"Yes, I was on the transport from Buchenwald to Dachau on seventh April 1945. On our way from Buchenwald to the station at Weimar, approximately 350 prisoners were shot to death. I saw with my own eyes how Merbach shot ten of them. We were loaded ninety people to a boxcar—no place at all to sit down."

"Were you given food, Mr. Rosenfeld?"

"One hundred grams of bread and twenty grams of rotted sausage."

"When the transports headed off, what direction did they go?"

"In the direction of Pilsen. At Pilsen the population knew from the radio that concentration camp prisoners had arrived. They brought us great many foods. When Merbach saw, he took an automatic pistol and fired on these civilian people."

"What happened at the next station?"

"There it came our turn. He went from one boxcar to another. He shot people to death in my boxcar—twenty that I saw with my own eyes. There were three boxcars with French prisoners. Merbach ordered prisoners to push these boxcars onto a sidetrack. Then he ordered the French prisoners to leave the train—'Get out!' Then with the other SS murderers he shot them to death. I heard with my own ears his order to get out from the car. I saw him standing there with his pistol, with his other comrades. And he shot at them. The next morning, Merbach ordered prisoners from each boxcar to go down into a valley and dig a mass grave. The bodies were rolled down from the tracks. Weak people among us couldn't lift the bodies, so Merbach and his comrades stood there and shot these weak prisoners. Then we continued our trip, and between Pilsen and Munich we stopped because there was an air raid. The SS bandits went looking for shelter in the woods, but we were forced to stay there on the railroad tracks."

"Mr. Rosenfeld, where did this transport finally end?"

"Here in Dachau on 26 April 1945. From five thousand people, eleven hundred arrived. I weighed thirty-five kilos when I arrived."

"No further questions."

––––––––

On July 2, 1947, Hans Merbach took the stand.

"My name is Hans Merbach. I am thirty-seven years old, married, three children."

"Mr. Merbach, what was the reason that you entered the Allgemeine SS?" asked defense counsel Dr. Kopf.

"In 1928, I came to the Gotha Life Insurance Company, and there was a department chief who tried to get me to join the SS. Two years later I joined. My duties started in Buchenwald in December 1939."

"Mr. Merbach, what was your job as a deputy of the company commander?"

"I had to instruct guards about their attitude toward prisoners and about their duties, not to accept any gifts from prisoners, things like that."

"Mr. Merbach, a witness said he saw you shoot ten prisoners to death on the road from Buchenwald to Weimar. What do you have to say to that?"

"I would like to ask permission to tell the court what the situation was. I was never able to say this in any of my interrogations. As early as the second of April, there were already a large number of dead prisoners lying on the side of the road to Weimar—prisoners from out-details such as Ohrdruf who had been en route to Buchenwald. More than ten thousand prisoners came down that road from Weimar. Ahead of my transport, there was a big transport of Jews, more than three thousand men going to Flossenburg on foot. I, myself, saw at least fifteen dead prisoners lying on the road."

"Mr. Merbach, on this march did you shoot anybody?"

"No, just the opposite. I tried to get food for the prisoners. Bombs had destroyed several railroad ties, and it was clear the trip would take longer than expected. I called up Buchenwald and asked for additional rations. I was told that there was barely any bread left there and that I would have to get along on my own. The next stop was Dresden. I talked to a captain of the police there who told me that it was impossible to get a piece of bread because the city was overrun with refugees."

"What did you do to furnish drinking water to the prisoners?"

"At every stop I immediately ran to the local office of the National Socialist Welfare Association and demanded buckets and cans from them. Four prisoners would then go and get water in those buckets for the other prisoners. From Dresden the train continued first to Czechoslovakia, then to Pilsen."

"Mr. Merbach, a witness said that in Pilsen the population knew from the radio that concentration camp prisoners had arrived in the station and brought them food. This witness said you ordered the civilians to leave the prisoners alone. They refused, so you took a pistol and fired on them."

"That is not true. I was trying to get rations. I would never have refused aid from the Czech population. Furthermore, I consider it impossible that in such a short period of time the Czech radio would know that a train had arrived from Buchenwald."

"Where was the next stop of this transport?"

"Namering in Upper Bavaria. There we did receive rations. Still, a large number of prisoners were dead and others had escaped from the cars."

"When did you arrive in Dachau?"

"On the twenty-sixth of April. I was thinking about the fate of these men day and night. The war was not over yet, and I kept recalling the order I had been given: 'You are to deliver every one of these prisoners to Dachau.' I kept coming to the conclusion that by no means could I release them, because every time a prisoner escaped the most incredible things were happening among the civilian population."

"Could you tell at any time that your train would not arrive in Dachau quickly?"

"I kept counting on the Reich railroad authorities to get this train to Dachau in short order. I never thought that twenty-four hours, as was first estimated, would become three weeks."

———

Attorney Robert Kunzig conducted cross-examination for the prosecution. "At Freising on the eleventh of July, do you recall saying that when your train left Weimar 'there was not enough space for the prisoners to lie down. They could only remain in a sitting position'?"

"I might have said that, but I'd like to add the following. Here in Dachau I was interrogated by Mr. Rosenthal and by Mr. Westervail. The interrogation was unobjectionable and correct. In Freising, nothing was ever done correctly. Officers were beaten with a piece of cable in the face. And that, I suppose, is why the most incredible stories came out, particularly concerning this transport. That was the first interrogation I had ever been through in my life. I told this same thing to Mr. Rosenthal, and he told me that unfortunately nothing could be done about what had happened."

"In other words, you wish to change your sworn statement made in 1945, when your memory was undoubtedly fresher, is that correct?"

"Yes, my memory in Freising was better, but the methods of interrogation caused me to say crazy things. Among the accused here are other officers who were beaten at that time. May it please the court," Merbach said, addressing the tribunal, "I was raised by decent parents. In 1917 when I was only seven, my mother got very sick and a Jewish physician named Falkenstein treated her every day. I was very much grateful to him, although I knew he was Jewish. Even during my maneuvers with the Wehrmacht in 1936 and 1937 I didn't make any difference between Aryans and half-Jewish soldiers. I hated to participate in this fight of the government against religion. For me existed only one thing, love of my country and my people. It was not in me to participate in cruelties against unarmed people, to mistreat them or to kill them. I am horrified about the accusations that are made here in court against me. About the transport I have told you everything I know. I am imprisoned now for the past two years, and every day I search myself and weigh the good and the bad. I got food for prisoners, helped wherever I could and had deepest feelings for these poor people. If you members of the high court find me a criminal in this transport, I have confidence you will at least not put me on the same level with men who had bad intentions. Judge me as a man who tried to do his best. I had to obey crazy orders. Until the end I always tried the best. I await your judgment."

"Has the defense anything further?"

"Nothing further."

"Nothing further, sir," Denson said.

"Court will recess."

———

Investigations into alleged abuses at Freising did reveal transgressions by some American interrogators. Some of these reports were later discredited, some were confirmed. Among those reports that were confirmed, investigators found that often physical actions by interrogators had been prompted by belligerence on the part of German prisoners. However much truth there may have been to the reports, no American was ever prosecuted for abusing a German held for trial.

37

Tattoos, Lampshades, Shrunken Heads

Kurte Sitte was a thirty-six-year-old doctor of physics at Manchester University and had been a prisoner in Buchenwald from September 1939 until the liberation. "Dr. Sitte," Denson said, "to your knowledge was tattooed human skin processed in the pathology department?"

"Yes. The order was that the skin of bodies with colorful or interesting tattoos had to be stripped off and preserved. I may add that obscene tattoos in particular were considered interesting. Tattoos were often used to create lampshades, knife cases, and similar items for the SS."

"Dr. Sitte, do you know what relationship, if any, Frau Ilse Koch had with the practice of tattooed human skin?"

"I know that a lampshade had been delivered to Frau Koch. That was before my time in the pathology department. It was common knowledge also that tattooed prisoners were sent to the hospital from work details where Ilse Koch had passed by and seen them. These prisoners were killed in the hospital and the tattooing stripped off."

"Was that lampshade made of tattooed human skin?"

"Yes, sir, it was."

"I show you prosecution's exhibit fourteen and ask you to describe just what that is."

"That is a shrunken head of a prisoner, which I handed over to the American authorities after the liberation. It is the head of a Polish prisoner who escaped from the camp, was recaptured, executed, and then on the orders of SS doctor Mueller decapitated. This and one other head were among the main attractions when visitors came."

"The defense objects to the admission into evidence of the proposed exhibit," Lewis said. "The witness has testified that it was apparently ordered by Dr. Mueller, who is not one of the accused in this case. No connection whatsoever has been shown to any of the accused here today."

"Objection overruled. Prosecution's exhibit fourteen will be received in evidence."

————

"Is it not a fact," Lewis asked on cross-examination, "that skin was taken from habitual criminals and was part of scientific research conducted by Dr. Wagner into the connection between criminals and tattoos on their bodies?"

"In my time skin was taken off prisoners whether they were criminal or not. I don't think a responsible scientist would ever call this kind of work scientific."

"You would not call it scientific, but Dr. Wagner called it scientific, did he not?"

"The standards of some SS doctors were not the same as ours."

"You testified about a lampshade. Did you ever see a lampshade made out of human skin at Buchenwald—yes or no?"

"As I mentioned, I myself did not see a lampshade."

"Then you cannot definitely say to this court that any lampshade exhibited to the people of Weimar by American authorities was made of human skin, can you?"

"I cannot say."

"You testified also that you heard in camp that a lampshade had been delivered to Mrs. Koch. Would you say that the lampshade exhibited after the liberation was the same lampshade delivered to Mrs. Koch?"

"No, it was not. According to the description we got, the lampshade for Mrs. Koch had a base of human bones. One of the Jehovah's Witness prisoners told me he had seen it in the basement workshop of block eighteen. He was informed by his SS guard, 'The work should be done quickly. It is for Mrs. Koch.'" Jehovah's Witnesses were sent to concentration camps for refusing to work in war industries or carry arms. The SS would periodically try to make them sign statements swearing they would abandon their beliefs and become decent German subjects. Few if any ever agreed.

"The point is, you never heard directly with your own ears from anybody who had been in Mrs. Koch's house that they saw such a lampshade there, did you?"

"No."

"Did you ever see any book covers made out of human skin?"

"No."

"Then the only thing you know about human skin was the knife sheath and lampshades, is that correct?"

"I was told of several other objects. I do not remember exactly what any more."

"You testified also that Mrs. Koch took down the numbers of prisoners and reported them, did you not?"

"Prisoners knew about such things, the same way they knew of other misbehavior by Mrs. Koch which will no doubt be called to the notice of the court. . . ."

"Dr. Sitte, I would like you to talk only for yourself. Do you know of any instance, either from your own knowledge or from what you learned at camp, where a prisoner was reported by Mrs. Koch and killed and his skin made into a lampshade for her?"

"That was the talk in camp. I never personally met anyone who was present at that time."

"No further questions."

Solomon Surowitz rose from his chair and announced, "Prosecution calls as the next witness Josef Loewenstein." Loewenstein, a forty-four-year-old German, had been a prisoner in Buchenwald from 1939 until

1941, then again from January 1945 until the liberation. During his incarceration he worked in the gardening detail.

"Mr. Loewenstein," Surowitz asked, "did you know Ilse Koch?"

"I knew Commandeuse Koch very well. I was finishing some work in the Koch garden. A comrade was present, an elderly gentleman from Vienna. He could not work at the same clip as a younger person, and Mrs. Koch, who was standing at a window, called down to her husband who happened to be walking through the garden, 'Look at that dirty Jewish swine over there, too lazy to work. I don't want to see him anymore. All he does is stare at me, anyway.' I pulled him up from the ground and walked out with him to prevent his number from being taken down."

On cross-examination Captain Lewis asked, "When this incident occurred near the home of Mrs. Koch, did she tell her husband to beat this man?"

"No," Loewenstein admitted. "She told him he should see to it that this man 'disappeared.' In Buchenwald, that was sufficient."

––––––––

One by one, ten witnesses were introduced who provided evidence of Ilse's criminal behavior. Another former inmate, Josef Broz, spoke of his experiences while working at the Koch villa. "In the summer of 1942 eleven prisoners worked at Ilse Koch's house under the supervision of a foreman. Ilse Koch came out of the house and saw berries on the road. She scolded the foreman and asked him which prisoners had been working near the berries. She told him to report the numbers of these prisoners within ten minutes, otherwise he would find out what would happen to him. The foreman told her that her children had picked these berries and had spilled them over the road. After work on our way back to camp, we were stopped at the gate. Ilse Koch had phoned to the gate and reported the foreman as well as the eleven other prisoners who had worked with him. We received five blows on the nude body."

Another former inmate, Kurt Froboess, had been put to work digging ditches for laying cables. "I was working together with a Czech chaplain," he explained. "This chaplain loosened the soil and I would throw it up with the shovel. Suddenly somebody was standing on the top of the ditch, yelling, 'Prisoner, what are you doing down there?' We looked up to see who it was and recognized Mrs. Koch. She was wearing a short skirt, standing with her legs straddled over the ditch without any underwear. She said, 'What are you doing looking up here?' And with her riding crop she beat us, particularly my comrade across the face, so that he started bleeding."

"Did you ever see Ilse Koch with any tattooed skin in her possession?" Denson asked.

"Yes. I saw a photo album. The cover had a tattoo on it. And on one occasion she was wearing gloves. They were a whitish-yellow color, and a star was tattooed on the back side of the left glove."

"Mr. Froboess, did you ever work in any detail where people had tattooed skin?"

"Yes. A lot of comrades had tattoos, former sailors, and so forth."

"Were you ever present when Ilse Koch came in contact with such a man?"

"Yes. That was in the area where the railroad station is now located. An SS stadium was to be built there, and the prisoners were to level the ground. It was a hot day, and some of them were working without a shirt. Mrs. Koch arrived on a horse. There was a comrade there—his first name was Jean, he was either French or Belgian—and he was known throughout camp for his excellent tattoos from head to toe. I particularly recall a colored cobra on his left arm, winding all the way up to the top. On his chest he had an exceptionally well-tattooed sailboat with four masts. Even today I can see it before my eyes very clearly. Mrs. Koch rode over until she came pretty close and had a look at him. Then she told him, 'Let's work faster, faster.' He looked at her in surprise, and she took his number down. He was called to the gate at evening formation."

"Did you ever see him again, Mr. Froboess?"

"It might have been a half year later, I visited a friend who was working in the pathology department, and he showed me some of the unusual things there. The doctors had made gypsum casts of peculiar faces or skulls. There were specimens kept in alcohol, and there were skins. To my horror, I noted this same sailboat that I had seen on Jean."

"Did you ever see this skin again after this time, Mr. Froboess?"

"That was the skin that was on the photo album."

———

Cross-examination was conducted by Captain Lewis. "You testified about Mrs. Koch that she was riding a horse," he said. "When did this occur?"

"The beginning of 1940."

"Isn't it a fact that Mrs. Koch gave birth to a child in 1940 and was unable to ride horseback all during that year?"

"I know that she gave birth to a child. I don't know the exact time anymore, but at that time she was on horseback. There is no error."

"You testified about a pair of gloves that you saw the accused wearing. Did you ever feel these gloves?"

"No."

"Upon what do you base your opinion that these were made of human skin?"

"Because of the tattooed star on the left glove which she was wearing. That was a very common tattoo on very many persons I saw."

"For all you know, your friend Jean may have died a natural death, isn't that so?"

"I don't believe so at all. He was a strong, healthy fellow."

————

"My name is Kurt Wilhelm Leeser. I am a merchant. I was in Buchenwald until the liberation. I worked in the pathology department."

"Did you ever know any prisoner whose skin you later saw there?" Solomon Surowitz asked for the prosecution.

"Yes, Josef Collinette. He had a tattoo of a big boat on his back. His legs and arms and chest were tattooed as well."

"When was the last time you saw Josef Collinette alive?"

"I saw him on a Friday, and the following Thursday I saw the skin in the pathology department."

"Do you know what disposition was made of the skin of Josef Collinette?"

"That was used for the lampshade on a lamp. The stand of that lamp was a human leg."

"No further questions."

————

"Do you remember on the lampshade how many masts the ship had?" Captain Lewis asked on cross-examination.

"I only saw the ship on the back of Josef Collinette, not on the lamp."

"Didn't you just testify that you saw a lampshade with the same ship on it?"

"No. I said that I saw Josef's skin, but it was his arm tattoos that I saw on the lampshade."

"So you never did see a lampshade with a ship on it, is that right?"

"Not a ship, only arm tattoos."

"No further questions."

On June 11 the defense called Dr. Konrad Morgen to the stand. His reputation for having successfully convicted Karl Koch preceded him, and both defense and prosecution expected he would help their respective cases.

"What is your profession?" Dr. Aheimer asked for the defense.

"I was a judge at the state court in Stettin."

"Were you ever demoted in the SS in any way?" Aheimer asked, seeking to establish Morgen's objectivity.

"Yes. I was presiding judge in a trial that concerned race. When I acquitted the defendant, whom I believed had been coerced into pleading guilty, Himmler accused me of sabotage. Then until May 1943, I was appointed by Prince zu Waldeck to investigate Commandant Koch on charges of corruption. The investigation began as a result of reports that a certain prisoner had been shot attempting to escape. In fact, this prisoner had been told to get water from a well some distance from the camp, and he was shot from behind. My office was called to investigate this charade. It turned out this prisoner had treated Koch for syphilis, and in order to keep his disease a secret Koch had this man eliminated. Koch was a born criminal. In his youth he started with thefts of postal banks. Then he and his brother were stool pigeons for the police. The whole family was criminal. One of his sons had to be punished in musical school for stealing radios. His second son was in an insane asylum. I think the human language is not capable of describing the horror of Koch's crimes. He was mad for power and took every occasion to get rich off of the prisoners. I am convinced he stole millions of marks from the camp."

"Were your investigations in Buchenwald also directed against Pister?" Hermann Pister had succeeded Koch as commandant after Koch's arrest.

"No. At first, of course, I mistrusted Koch's successor. But it is impossible to compare these two commanders. There were many prisoners who told me that after Pister became commandant they again had hope to live."

"In connection with your investigation," Lewis said, "did you have occasion to search the Koch home?"

"Yes, very thoroughly. There wasn't a desk drawer left unopened."

"Did you find any lampshades of human skin on the premises?"

"No, not a one."

"Did you find any gloves of human skin?"

"No."

"Any photo albums made of human skin?"

"No."

"No further questions."

————

Lampshades of human skin may grab headlines, Denson calculated, but more verifiable offenses—the gravamen, or essence of the charges, against her, namely her role in the common design—would get Ilse convicted. "In the course of your investigation," he began, "did you not ascertain that Mrs. Koch was responsible for having prisoners beaten?"

"Yes."

"And that she made obscene remarks to the prisoners, such as, 'Just look in this direction if your ass is worth twenty-five to you'?"

"Mrs. Koch loved to make remarks of this type," Morgen replied. "Her behavior was scandalous. She wore clothes deliberately chosen to incite the prisoners, and whenever a prisoner looked at her, her pleasure was to see him severely punished. It is my opinion, although I have no proof, that prisoners also died from these beatings."

"Doctor, did you ascertain what connection Mrs. Koch had with the valuables that her husband stole from prisoners?"

"Mrs. Koch's personal worth before the war was 121 Reichsmarks and ten pfennigs. After the persecution of the Jews and the first few years of the war, this increased to eighty thousand marks, deposited in several bank accounts in the name of Mrs. Koch and her children. The first time her husband was arrested, she distanced herself from him so as not to be implicated. She called him a criminal and a murderer and said he belonged behind barbed wire and tried to give the impression she had been tyrannized by him and was suffering very much as a result. When her husband was released a few days later, she realized he was protected by the highest authorities and changed her attitude, saying she had had a nervous breakdown and was not responsible for what she said at that time."

"Now, you found that Buchenwald was nothing more than a cesspool of corruption, is that not correct?" Denson asked. The question was unusual, vague, the first of several that were out of character for the usually precise but now exhausted chief prosecutor.

"I don't understand the question," Morgen said.

"The whole concentration camp system that existed in the German Reich," Denson elaborated, "was nothing more than a cesspool of corruption, is that not correct?"

"I can't answer in a general way like that. However, it is true that I did find a large number of abuses."

"And you further found that Buchenwald was making criminals rather than correcting them, is that not correct?"

"These were already the worst type of criminals," Morgen scoffed. "It was not possible to make these persons any worse."

"It was rather easy to fool this man Pister, was it not?"

"Considering the devious methods used by Koch's former officers, any commandant would have been fooled."

"Isn't it a fact that you told him you thought it strange that he had been in office so long and had done nothing to correct the situation there, that it was unfortunate they had to wait until you came to do anything about the conditions?"

"The prosecutor is confusing things here. . . ."

"Just answer the question, please. There is nothing confusing."

"Pister, on his own initiative, very fundamentally changed conditions existing in Buchenwald."

That Morgen, an investigator capable of identifying Koch as "the worst type of criminal," could also laud Pister for improving conditions in Buchenwald revealed the workings of a Teutonic mind. From Morgen's perspective—that of a German who had never known life inside a camp as inmates knew it—a commandant such as Pister was relatively "decent" and "correct," the distinction between a model SS officer and a model human being having blurred beyond recognition. Denson, however, was not about to allow that misimpression to go uncorrected.

"Dr. Morgen, you testified that the number of killings in Buchenwald decreased during Pister's time, is that correct?"

"Decreased is an understatement. The number became very small, and any violations were either against his will or else conducted in secret."

"Starvation is a violation, is it not? Do you know that prisoners starved to death in Buchenwald in '43 or '44?"

"I considered it impossible for any prisoner to starve on the rations they were issued at that time. I saw the food being prepared in the kitchen and issued. I am not a nutritionist, but the soup was always thick and bread and meat and fat were issued every day. I might also add that during the time I was interned in American camps I met many former prisoners who wished they were back in German camps."

Denson had studied the diet of camp inmates and knew that the calorie count hardly ever rose above one thousand in a day. "You are telling this court that food issued to concentration camp prisoners was better than the food prisoners get here today, is that correct?"

"I merely repeat to you the opinion of former prisoners with whom I spoke. I do not consider myself qualified to pass judgment on it."

"These prisoners, after having worked twelve hours a day, came back to barracks that were freezing cold, did they not?"

"As far as I know, the barracks were heated. And there were wood chopping details that worked all year long to provide for the winter."

"You never heard of a prisoner suffering from frostbite or frozen limbs?"

"Yes, if it was winter and the prisoner had been on a transport that was bombed and therefore under way longer than planned."

On that inconclusive note, court adjourned for the day.

———

The final witness for the prosecution, Max Kronfeldner, related the time in 1940 when he was walking to the hospital for treatment with two other prisoners. "Ilse Koch was riding horseback with Adjutant Florstedt, and she came toward us and beat us with her riding crop."

"What was the reason?" Denson asked.

"Because we were looking at her. We saw a woman riding a horse, and we looked."

"No further questions."

"How did you find out she was the wife of the commandant?" Captain Lewis asked on cross-examination.

"Some comrades saw I had a red streak across my face and asked what happened. I told them that this redheaded woman polished my face, and they said, 'Guess what. That was the commandant's wife.' So I said, 'No kidding! Well, she can kiss my ass!' And that's all."

Denson turned to the tribunal. "The prosecution rests."

————

Two American lawyers served with Denson on the Buchenwald case: Robert Kunzig and Solomon Surowitz. Kunzig shared Denson's unflagging conviction that everyone who had taken part in the camp administration was guilty of participation in a common design. Surowitz, however, doubted the reliability of some witnesses and felt offended by the press's vilification of Ilse Koch. He had continued to play his part but with waning enthusiasm.

That evening, Surowitz approached Denson and tendered his resignation. "I can't stand it," he said. "I don't believe our own witnesses—it's all hearsay. Bill, you know we didn't get the real guys who were running the camp. And these witnesses would swear to anything if it gets the Germans killed."

Denson listened, reflected. "We're going to proceed on the basis of what we have," he said.

"There was a difference of opinion about the law," Surowitz recalled more than a half century later. "But that didn't affect my believing that Bill was a very good lawyer. I was fond of him, and he did quite a good job. But I felt the outcome was a fait accompli. There were so many times when the judges accepted testimony you couldn't accept in a court of law."

Surowitz may have felt differently about hearsay evidence had he spoken with Dr. Kurte Sitte, a former Buchenwald prisoner who testified at Senate subcommittee hearings in 1949 investigating the outcome of the trial. Sitte, then a professor of physics at Syracuse University, provided revealing details of how inmates gathered information in Buchenwald.

"This is a point I feel very strongly about," he told the committee. "So much of our evidence is called hearsay and is therefore dismissed lightly. We hear it called camp gossip—we could not listen to gossip. That would have been disastrous. We had to know exactly how the situation was, what the other side, the enemies, the SS, were doing. And therefore when I say, for instance, that I know from hearsay that people have seen that lamp-shade—I am as sure as if I had seen it myself that it did exist."

38

The Bitch

"May it please the court," Captain Emmanuel Lewis began for the defense, "the newspapers have been filled with inflammatory stories concerning camp Buchenwald, and these accused have been waiting patiently for two years to present their side of the story. Now they have the opportunity to present the full truth concerning exactly what did happen in Buchenwald, and they welcome this opportunity to show the court that what has appeared in the newspapers concerning their activities is not true. Defense calls Ilse Koch."

Ilse Koch was visibly pregnant when she walked up to the witness chair. German defendants snickered, photographers snapped away, and former inmates—who knew her as *Commandeuse*, or more frequently "the Bitch"—remembered the suffering they and others had endured because of her. Among them was Dr. Paul Heller, who later became a physician in Washington, D.C. At the Senate subcommittee hearings on the Buchenwald trial in 1949 he testified, "It was my policy to keep a little bit distant from her because I knew what she did. I recall one day very distinctly, the fourteenth of April 1940. This day, I think, was the fifth day after the occupation of Denmark and Norway. When the Nazis were successful against their enemies we had a very hard time—they celebrated at our expense—it was probably fear of revenge that led the Nazis to this treatment of their prisoners. When they defeated Denmark and Norway—I did not think I should survive it. The fourteenth was a Sunday. Sunday was usually a day off for Aryan prisoners, but the Jews had to work. A group of about sixty Jews were selected on that day and led outside the camp. They had to dig in the ground and carry the dirt about three hundred yards away, and always running."

"How much weight?" subcommittee chairman Sen. Homer Ferguson asked.

"I guess forty or fifty pounds, running back and forth. That went on for about two hours. Mrs. Koch appeared, and she stood there with her dogs. I do not know what kind of dogs, but they were fear-inspiring. She stood there for two or three hours. At that time it was absolutely horrible what happened to us. Several SS came out—about one hundred SS to about sixty of us prisoners. You may imagine what that means. I was beaten and had big gashes on my back. She only stood there, but her appearance was the signal for every SS man to increase the tempo and to rage more than usual. She never wore SS uniforms. She always had on a fur coat, always dressed as if she were going to a ball or to some kind of celebration. Several prisoners had to be carried back to camp. I know of two who died within the next twenty-four hours. She stood there fascinated and apparently liked it. As soon as she disappeared, the tempo subsided. It was personally the most horrible experience that I had in the camp."

———

The woman who took the stand only vaguely resembled the redheaded beauty she once had been. Looking at her swollen belly, unbrushed hair, and frumpy clothes, one might have guessed Ilse Koch to be a careless housewife, not the temptress who had once ruled Buchenwald. Spectators watched her approach the witness chair, whispering to their neighbors. Defense counsel Lewis was all business.

"Mrs. Koch, you have occasionally been branded as the *Commandeuse* of Buchenwald. What do you want to say about that?"

"I only heard about this here in court," she said, "and I read it in the press. Before now I never knew that was my title. I should like to add that in the SS it was prohibited for the wife of an officer to be addressed by her husband's title."

"Mrs. Koch, are you familiar with the term 'Bitch of Buchenwald'?"

"I read it in the newspapers."

"Mrs. Koch, have you anything to say about the charges that have been leveled against you in the press?"

"Yes. For the last two years I do not think there is any vulgar expression in the German language that has not been used against me. I have succeeded in keeping some distance from these things in order not to suffer mentally. But as a mother I cannot stand by while my children are in such a state that they cannot even go to school. In the papers I am described as the pinnacle of sadism and perversion and corruption. I am said to have a whole collection of objects made out of human skin in my house, and the worst things are being told about my private life. I have no idea who is spreading such stories. These reports in the newspapers are of the most vulgar type, and the way they are stated is not that I am under suspicion but that it is a fact that I own lampshades made out of human skin. During sixteen months that I was being investigated, it would have been easy for me to obtain false papers and live somewhere under a false name. But I was acquitted at my husband's trial. I had no reason whatever to disappear. Even after being interrogated by the Americans I still did not attempt to disappear, because I never even conceived of being put on trial. I never did any of the things that have been presented against me."

"Your witness."

————

Denson was approaching the end of his time in Germany, and the end of his patience with the obfuscations of the accused. The trial transcripts reveal his emotions surfacing with greater frequency, feelings of revulsion lurking just below the surface of his controlled cross-examination. "Mrs. Koch," he began, "did you ever hear of human skin being collected at Buchenwald?"

"In the courtroom here, I heard."

"I show you prosecution exhibit P-14, the shrunken head of a prisoner, and ask whether or not you ever saw this exhibit or one similar to it in your husband's office in Buchenwald."

"No, never. The first time was here."

"Did you ever hear of a prisoner at Buchenwald being mistreated in any form or fashion?"

"No. My husband never told me about such things, and I didn't come in contact with anybody else."

"There was a garden located around your house and sometimes Jewish prisoners would work there, would they not?"

"Jewish prisoners never worked in the garden. There always was a regular detail of German prisoners in my garden."

"Why was it that Jewish prisoners were excluded from your garden? Did you give instructions that Jewish prisoners were not to be used in your garden?"

"I didn't care a bit who was working in my garden. And you also overestimate my prerogatives. As the wife of the commandant I did not have any authority to get involved in any kind of camp affairs. In the SS it was not common practice for the wives of officers to take part in their husbands' business. I think men would have objected very strenuously to that. I had three children, and my time was fully occupied taking care of them."

Sitting smugly in the witness chair, denying the least shred of wrongdoing, Ilse Koch epitomized for Denson the arrogance of the Third Reich. She was to his mind "indeed a bitch" who had played at being a camp *commandeuse* and now was again a mere bitch, only pregnant. It was, he admitted, a clever way to avoid the death penalty. The most he could hope to achieve against a woman carrying a child was life, and that would be sufficient. But something should be said to draw attention to her foulness.

"You have maintained the same standard of conduct since your confinement that you maintained while you were living in Buchenwald, is that not correct?"

Lewis was on his feet, incensed. "If the court please, we will object to that question as being immaterial."

"May it please the court," Denson said, attempting to justify the slight, "this accused has tried to give this court the impression that she is an adoring, loving mother, whose interest was in her home. I think her conduct here is just as material as it was in Buchenwald. A raven doesn't change its colors overnight."

"This woman's morals are of no concern to this court or anybody else under the sun but herself," Lewis shot back. "She is not being charged with immorality but with having conspired in a common design to kill and mistreat prisoners. If the prosecution intends to prove by this woman's 'subsequent conduct' that she killed and mistreated prisoners in Buchenwald, and if this court is willing to entertain such testimony, then—I have nothing further to say."

"The objection of the defense is sustained."

Years later he would admit regretting the question. In his anger he had stepped over a line. "Let us go back to the description of your house in Buchenwald, Mrs. Koch. Please tell the court whether you could see through the fence near your house that surrounded the prison compound."

"I don't know. I didn't pay any attention."

"You lived at Buchenwald for six years and you cannot tell the court whether or not you could see through the fence which surrounded the prison compound?"

"I never went there."

"The zoological park was just across from your house. Did you ever go there?"

"Yes."

Denson walked over to a large map of the camp that had often served in the course of the trial. "Tell the court how far it is from the zoological park to this bunker."

"It is hard for me to estimate. Ask somebody who observed it more closely. My children were very young. I didn't take them there that often. Construction was still going on everywhere and there weren't any roads yet."

"So you want this court to believe you were a prisoner in your house from 1937 until 1940, is that right?"

"I never said I was a prisoner in my house. I was quite comfortable. I had no desire or interest to be running around the outside area."

"You were something of a sportswoman, were you not? You liked to ride?"

"I was giving birth to a child every year. I wasn't in a position to do much riding between 1938 and 1941."

"You were a frequent visitor to the riding hall, were you not?"

"No, four or five times at most."

"You didn't have a band playing for you while you rode around inside?"

"No. That is one of the stories they tell about me."

"And you also had a big mirror installed so you could observe your manner of riding, did you not?"

"There was a mirror in every riding hall in every city."

"I don't suppose you ever heard of a crematory at Buchenwald, did you?"

"Here I heard about that—also that it wasn't built until 1941."

"You were there until August 1943, were you not?"

"But never in the camp."

"Ever hear of any killings, mistreatments, or corruption in Buchenwald?"

"No."

"Then can you explain to the court why during your husband's trial you called him a murderer and a sadist?"

"Objection," Captain Lewis said. "There is no proof from her mouth that she ever called her husband a murderer and a sadist, and until the predicate is laid the question is improper."

"May it please the court," Denson replied, "I am not bound by the statements of this witness. That testimony has already been put in evidence by the defense's own witness, Dr. Morgen."

"Objection is overruled. Answer the question, please."

"I don't remember ever calling my husband that. During a nervous breakdown I am supposed to have said these things, but those were stories then and they are stories now."

"Prisoners working in Buchenwald looked emaciated, did they not?"

"I can't say. I didn't particularly search out prisoners to observe them."

"Did you never, at any time, see a transport of prisoners brought to Buchenwald?"

"No."

"And you were there for six years?"

"I have already explained to you that I wasn't in the camp area. I had no way of seeing a transport from my house."

"I suppose you never heard of Commando 99, did you?"

"No."

"I'll ask you this. Did you know anything about the execution grounds that existed less than four hundred meters from your home?"

"No. There was a patch of woods there. There were woods all over. I never saw any execution grounds."

This was fruitless. Denson was exhausted and he had had enough. "No further questions."

"Take your place in the dock," Kiel instructed.

———

Tribunal president Emil Kiel pulled Denson aside after the day's proceedings and urged him to take time off. He followed up his offer with a letter. "This is to certify that Mr. William D. Denson has worked overtime on holidays, weekends, and nights for an approximate three hundred hours. For matter of record, the undersigned advised Mr. Denson that this excessive overtime would have to be limited because of the possibility of injury to Mr. Denson's health."

Denson politely refused and continued preparing to meet the defense's case.

39

The Commandant

"The defense of Hermann Pister concerns itself exclusively with the innocence of this accused, not with the defense of concentration camps," Dr. Wacker announced. "The defense will prove that the accused Pister was responsible neither for the existence of Buchenwald nor the orders he received there, and is therefore not guilty. The defense will give the accused Pister an opportunity to express his point of view and show for what reasons he did not look upon those orders as criminal, but carried them out, believing in good faith in their legality."

"You are advised," tribunal president Kiel said addressing the witness, "that the court may draw such inference as the circumstances justify from your refusal to answer or from your failure to take the stand in your own behalf. Are you now willing to testify?"

"Yes. My name is Hermann Pister. I am sixty-two years old, married, three children, twenty-two, eighteen, and four years."

"Where is your family at the present?" Wacker asked.

"Since 1946 my wife is under arrest. She is in an internment camp in the French Zone in Landau. Our youngest child is with my parents-in-law."

"Do you know why she was arrested?"

"No."

"Herr Pister, what was your profession?"

"I was a professional soldier since the age of sixteen in 1901. I served with the then Imperial Navy as a signal master. After the war I went into the automobile business as an engineer, then started in auto repairs and sales. During all these years I had a great interest in automotive sports. I was in charge of all motorized sports of the Allgemeine SS as well as of the Waffen SS. In 1938 I participated in my last large motorsports event with the SS crew in England."

"What were your duties during the war?"

"In 1939, I was put at the disposal of Road Construction Minister Todt. He told me that disobedience and laziness were very high in his labor force. As a result, there was a labor shortage and I should make suggestions to him in this respect. I suggested that instead of sentencing these laborers they should be assembled for educational training. I want to stress that at that time I had never heard of concentration camps. My recommendation to the minister was to educate these men for their jobs, billet them correctly, and keep them away from alcohol. They were not to be called prisoners and should be paid full wages, as any other workman. This money was transferred to their families every two weeks so these families no longer needed to depend on welfare. The ministry put a small camp at my disposal, with billeting and equipment for six hundred men. Then a second and a third camp were erected with a capacity of two hundred. The guards and the administrative personnel of this camp were not soldiers but volunteer veterans of the First World War. I was made commandant of these labor education camps. I can state here, under oath, that not a single inmate ever became criminal again, not because they were ever mistreated but because they got accustomed to a clean, orderly life. In December 1941, I received a telex saying the *Reichsführer* had appointed me commandant of Buchenwald."

"At that time, didn't you have any objection to taking an assignment in a concentration camp?"

"Not in the least. It was explained to me that the camps were for certain classes of prisoners: political enemies, Jehovah's Witnesses—not for their religious convictions, but for their Communist tendencies—professional criminals, that is, those who had been sentenced for crimes at least three times, and antisocial elements such as habitual drunkards and vagrants. I had no hesitation taking over such a camp in order to protect the general population against crimes by such people."

"Did the type of prisoners remain the same during the years to come?"

"No. The increase in labor needs led to drafting large numbers of workers, especially from the Eastern states. Along with them came a great number of criminal elements who were transferred to the concentration camps."

"Herr Pister," defense counsel Wacker asked, "what authority did you as commandant have concerning punishment?"

"Corporal punishment was laid down by law. For such a request, three forms in different colors were sent to office group D in Berlin, and two copies returned after approval or disapproval. At the time I took my job, there were at least fifty applications that had not been processed. I had those destroyed. Furthermore, I frequently changed applications to lighter punishment."

"Will you please explain to the court why you did not stop the abuses?"

"First, you must understand that when I came in I found mechanics doing appendectomies and other such conditions, and there wasn't anybody who had tried to change any of this. Second, on my arrival it was not possible to instantly determine what all the abuses were in such a big camp. Gradually I stopped what I personally could take responsibility for, by repeated urging. To my knowledge no mistreatments took place as long as I was in charge, and there was no need for me to issue any reminders."

"Describe to the court the conditions in Buchenwald when you took over in 1942."

"I was surprised by the good installations in the camp. There was a bed for every prisoner, covered with a sheet and two woolen blankets. The capacity was, under normal circumstances, about fifteen thousand. At that time there were eight thousand. Each house consisted of two bedrooms, two dormitories, two dayrooms, and toilets. There was a huge sewer system, an excellent steam kitchen which could prepare food for ten thousand at a time, a cold storage room underneath the kitchen in which five million pounds of potatoes could be stored, a modern laundry, electrical pressing equipment, and a large clothing warehouse where the prisoners' clothing and valuables were hung up in a sack with a number on it. The prisoner hospital had two large operating rooms, a TB station, X-ray stations, and heated bath. There was a barber in each block and cleanliness was excellent. Seeing such facilities, I believed I could create the same results as I had achieved on a smaller scale at the labor education camp."

"What did you find out about the management of the camp by your predecessor?"

"I heard the worst things concerning the treatment of prisoners. Commandant Koch seemed to have been under the impression that he had the right to carry out mistreatments on his own initiative, perhaps to save himself the trouble of making a report to the higher authorities. I immediately issued an order that mistreatment would be punished most severely. I referred to an order issued personally by the Führer that read, 'I am the one who decides about the life or death of a prisoner or also my representative appointed by myself.' Of course, I couldn't do away with all mistreatments overnight, but witnesses can testify that any mistreatment of which I heard was punished by me immediately."

"Herr Pister, what other measures did you take contrary to those of the former commandant?"

"There was a tremendous lack of water in Buchenwald. I had my administrative chief, Major Barnewald, one of my fellow accused, contact the ministries in Weimar. Shortly thereafter, water was supplied for the hospital and bathing installations."

"Any other orders?" Wacker asked.

"There were prisoners serving in the officers' houses as cooks and maids. I abolished that and was told that as a result some of the SS wives even bought themselves cookbooks."

"Did anything change in the stone quarry?"

"It was the job of prisoners to pull carts up a 40 percent incline. At my request an electrical winding apparatus was installed, after which these carts were pulled up electrically."

Pister paused, then added, "I wish to speak about the prosecution witness who claimed I did nothing to get the many sick people transported from the railroad station to the camp hospital."

Pister was referring to accusations made by prosecution witness Jean Rousset, a physician and former prisoner who had seen the arrival of a transport train from Auschwitz in January 1945. "German inmates working in the hospital were so disgusted at the sight of what was going on," he told Denson on the stand, "that they obtained permission to volunteer. There were ten of us. Two Frenchmen, some Russians, some Poles."

"Where was Commandant Pister at the time this transport came into the camp?" Denson asked.

"On the station platform. He saw the whole scene. He saw everything. It was something terrible, the worst thing I ever saw in my life. There were open boxcars full of bodies. The only closed boxcar was reserved for the SS of the transport, who had brought along two women prisoners for their own pleasure. It was approximately twenty below, maybe colder, snowing. The prisoners had been traveling for nine days. In every car they were either dead or dying or they had frozen limbs."

"What did Pister do when he saw the condition of these prisoners?"

"I think his conscience must have bothered him. He telephoned Berlin not to send any more prisoners, that the camp was full. But he didn't do anything to take care of the dying. And we couldn't do anything because we didn't have any way of transporting them to camp. Finally some Polish or Russian prisoners got small sleighs that could carry about two men."

"How many of these prisoners died there after they got to Buchenwald, doctor?"

"That is difficult to say, but certainly five hundred. Even people who had not died yet were carried directly to the crematorium. We heard them hollering in the yard of the crematory during the whole night. They were hollering in all languages that they should be taken out of there. Under their weight the floor of barrack twelve broke, and they fell down into a cellar about twelve meters deep. The whole scene was like a battlefield. There were bodies and clothes everywhere. We went back to the hospital and I told the Frenchmen, 'Go out there if you want an idea of what the retreat from Russia must have been like in 1812.'"

"Doctor, based on your experience as a physician, how many could have been saved if they had been given proper treatment by Pister?"

"I did not examine everyone. But if they had been given a hot tonic or rubbed with snow, certainly many could have been saved."

––––––––––

"All right, Herr Pister," Wacker said. "Please tell us how you first heard about the arrival of this transport."

"That transport arrived in January with not a word of prior notification. I learned about it accidentally the morning I came to the railroad station. The stationmaster informed me that in this transport were many sick people and many dead. This transport was supposed to be sent somewhere else, but in spite of the overcrowded conditions in camp, I ordered that it remain in Buchenwald."

"Why did you order that?"

"It was obvious that if we sent the transport on, those prisoners whom we might save through medical treatment in Buchenwald would perish, too. That transport was out from Gross-Rosen already for nine days during a cold winter when the mornings were twenty to twenty-eight degrees below zero."

"What food had the prisoners been supplied when you saw the transport?"

"No food at all. The prosecution witness forgot to tell the court that immediately I gave orders to the administrative leader to have hot food and drink given to these new arrivals. I would like to mention that the dead men who came in these transports were debited against Buchenwald."

"Herr Pister, when you saw this transport arrive in such condition, did you take any steps?"

"I ordered that prisoners unable to walk be transported to camp on trucks. Our motor pool at that time was very small. The available trucks were on the road day and night to get necessary foodstuff. But we had some vehicles that could be drawn by hand. Even if the transport of these prisoners took four hours, that was still better than keeping them on the train for another nine days. I used all available means of transportation to do what really was the job of physicians and the motor pool—but of course, who will care to attribute such human feelings to the commandant of the infamous camp Buchenwald?"

"Herr Pister, you testified that you ordered the post physician to give you constant reports in regard to the health of these new arrivals," Wacker continued. "What were these reports?"

"Catastrophic. In spite of hot baths and all medical treatment, out of eight hundred prisoners only three hundred were still alive three weeks later. These people, too, would have died if the transport had continued."

"Were transports directed to camps other than Buchenwald?"

"Most transports from the East, from Auschwitz, Lublin, Gross-Rosen, Warsaw, and Czonstochow, were sent as a rule to Buchenwald—as I said before, usually without any advance notice."

"Did you know about so-called death transports?"

"I knew as little about so-called death transports as I did about so-called extermination camps. When camp X or Y needed additional workers, I was requested by Berlin to transfer a number of prisoners to that camp, in accordance with the skill requirements."

"Weren't there also transports not to be used for work, for instance transports of Jews?"

"Later on orders came from Berlin that prisoners who were not fit for work were to be transferred to Bergen-Belsen. I state here, under oath, that Bergen-Belsen was never known to us as an extermination camp. Neither was Auschwitz."

"In the orders for such transports, was there anything about why Jews were to be transferred to those other camps?"

"No, but one can say this much, that from one such so-called extermination transport so far five Jews have taken the witness chair in this courtroom."

Wacker asked, "Is there anything else you wish to say about transports?"

"Yes, I recall in 1945 three thousand prisoners unfit for work were to be transferred to Bergen-Belsen. Pohl said to me, 'It is impossible to send these men. The camp is overcrowded.' My question is this. If Bergen-Belsen was an extermination camp, how could it have been overcrowded?"

"Herr Pister," defense council Wacker said, "I want to talk now about Commando 99."

"I ask my defense counsel to spare me this question. Six prosecution witnesses have testified about this already in detail."

"Who was executed through Commando 99?"

"We heard here in court that they were Russian prisoners of war," Pister said, resigned to exploring a topic he wished would go away. "That is not correct. These men were exclusively Russian political party organizers, men who had been denounced to officers of Reich Security Main Office, men who furthermore were members of a nation that was not a signatory to either The Hague or the Geneva Convention."

"What orders did you receive when they were handed over to you?"

"They were not handed over to me. When I took over the camp, this whole business was already in progress and was already dying out. Therefore I cannot say anything about it because I wasn't present, and enough testimony has been given about this question already."

"Did you consider the execution of these Russians to be legal?"

"I was a soldier. This was the law. There is one further point I will say. During the German-Russian war such terrifying news was published about the treatment of German soldiers by just such Russian commissars that an order had been given: no German soldier should allow himself to be taken prisoner. Those Russian party organizers who were legally executed in Commando 99 got off easy."

Wacker asked, "Did you know that guards in Commando 99 received schnapps and cigarettes?"

"I had 125,000 prisoners, 47 guard companies, 380 headquarters staff, 800 female supervisors, and 80 out-details all over central Germany. Officers getting five cigarettes was of no importance to me, and frankly I can't imagine any officer participating in an execution just to obtain a few cigarettes or a little glass of schnapps. I have nothing more to say about this."

"Herr Pister, I am talking now about the evacuation of the camp. When was the evacuation of the camp talked about for the first time?"

"At first, there was to be no evacuation. Everyone both inside and around the camp area had expressed their fear of rioting. My suggestion therefore was to personally hand Buchenwald over to the enemy, and that was a comfort to all involved. But I couldn't keep my intentions. On the sixth of April, a telephone call came from the commander of the security police with the message, 'The *Reichsführer* SS has ordered the Higher SS and Police Leader to reduce camp Buchenwald to the minimum.' I immediately contacted the railroad department and told them that approximately thirty thousand inmates had to be transported from Buchenwald to Flossenburg or Dachau. I was personally acquainted with the president of the railroad administration, and he told me he would do everything in his power to get empty railroad cars to Buchenwald. But since no definite time could be given, I had the first transport leave on foot on the morning of April seventh. I have to stress that men on this transport had been picked after medical examination and found fit to march."

"Herr Pister, regarding the movie that was shown here on the first day of the trial, in what condition did you leave the camp? I mean, is it accurate what was shown in this movie—corpses lying around, things like that?"

"People died daily. On account of the scarcity of coal and oil, cremation was not possible anymore. We buried as many as we could, right up to the day before my departure."

"How many corpses did you leave lying around?"

"No one was left 'lying around.' That movie was shot ten to twelve days later, so of course a number of corpses had again accumulated. One prisoner here in Dachau told me that the bodies of prisoners who died in the hospital after evacuation were added to the yard of the crematory, and after that pictures were taken."

"Herr Pister, do you have anything else to say about the evacuation?"

"I would like to testify about my own feelings. As commandant I knew my camp had a maximum capacity. Yet I was forced to crowd in so many people that terrible conditions were created. On the other hand, I knew that through an evacuation I could move the surplus of camp inmates in eighteen hours. I was satisfied that in this way conditions in camp could be improved. If the transports took so much longer, blame the events of war—not me."

———

Stacked in front of Denson at the prosecution table were photographs of Pister's "improvements," along with orders he had signed to transport Jews and others to their death. "You were acquainted with extermination camps, is that not correct?" he asked on cross-examination.

"No. I didn't even know there were extermination camps."

"You never heard of prisoners whom you sent to Auschwitz or Bergen-Belsen tending gardens, did you?"

"If prisoners were sent there only for extermination, then who would work in the rubber factories and other industries near Auschwitz? Right now in Nuremberg, the I. G. Farben Industry is being charged with having used hundreds of thousands of prisoners for labor in the vicinity of Auschwitz. . . ."

"That does not account for the two and one-half million who were sent there, does it?"

"They didn't all come from Buchenwald."

"A good percentage came from Buchenwald, did they not? How many did you send to Auschwitz?"

"I can't even give you an approximate figure. Thousands of transports left Buchenwald. But the fact is that from this one transport that was discussed so very much here, six men have sat on this witness chair—Jews all of them—and every single one testified under oath that he was sent to Auschwitz for extermination."

"And the other 994 you sent out on that transport—of what did they die, Pister?"

"They arrived in Buchenwald in such a state of emaciation that it was impossible to keep them alive, in spite of good rations and medical care."

Denson rose from his chair. "I saw those half-dead corpses who came into Buchenwald, Pister. You put them in the Little Camp where there wasn't even space to lie down, didn't you?"

————

The Little Camp was constructed in 1942, composed of primitive wooden barracks that resembled horse stables, consisting of one room without beds, windows, ventilation, drains, or toilets. One privy and one lavatory serviced the entire Little Camp population. The camp began to fill up when huge transports from Russia reached Buchenwald during the Germans' retreat from their defeat in Stalingrad. Transports from France added to these numbers, and later on others from Eastern camps including Auschwitz, Oranienburg, and Gross-Rosen. For some time, the Little Camp became a quarantine center, separated from the main camp by guards and barbed wire. The initial population of five thousand prisoners swelled to more than twice that number. Vermin, filth, and disease grew beyond control. "When the American army took over Buchenwald," wrote former prisoner and obstetrician Miloslav Matousek, "it was the Little Camp which horrified them beyond conception."

"I couldn't throw them out in the street, could I?" Pister replied.

"That would have been far better than to keep them in there with insufficient food," Denson shot back.

"Where would they have gotten the food? The population didn't have any food. I suppose it would have been better to let them escape so that they could kill and steal?"

"You knew prisoners at Buchenwald were not properly clothed, did you not?"

"Yes, I knew. And I took every step possible—in writing, verbally, by telephone—but no deliveries were made. The persons who failed to deliver and were responsible for such conditions are now on trial in Nuremberg."

"What did you do with all the clothes that were held in the storehouses?"

"What clothes? If two thousand men arrive naked, how do I obtain any clothes from them? When laborers from the East came in rags, they remained in rags."

"You knew a system that tolerated mistreatment was wrong, did you not, Pister?"

"And what was I to do about it?"

"You answer my question!"

"Shall I answer that I was responsible? The system came into being long before I became commandant."

"And you continued to aid, abet, and participate in this system as long as you were commandant, did you not?"

"Yes—in order to improve the prisoners' condition as far as possible."

"Did you ever tell Pohl or Himmler that the system was wrong?"

"I reported all deficiencies to these gentlemen, and if the big boss Himmler shirked responsibility by committing suicide, then I guess I am responsible, is that it? And if Speer, who was sentenced to twenty years' imprisonment for so-called slave labor, is no longer available for comment, then I suppose I am to take upon myself the burden of his crimes as well? They knew. They passed the sentences. They issued the orders."

"How frequently were you in the crematory?"

Pister's self-righteousness fell away. "I was paying more attention to other conditions in Buchenwald."

"Never saw the hooks hanging on the wall?"

"No."

"Never saw prisoners hanging on those hooks, strangling to death?"

"No."

"How many men were killed there in Buchenwald during your time?"

"I don't know."

"Don't know, or was it so many that you cannot recall?"

"Only individuals. Things like that didn't go on all the time. Furthermore, the mistreatments that were described here took place before the time that I took office."

"You were responsible for the construction of the railroad from Buchenwald to Weimar, were you not?"

"I was responsible for everything." Pister's startling response may have been prompted by exasperation over Denson's relentless questions—or by a dizziness of which Pister had been complaining since the trial began.

Denson stopped. "Will you read that answer back to me please, Mr. Reporter?" Even if Pister's admission was prompted by his dizziness, Denson wanted it clearly noted by the tribunal. Within the sober objectives of his mandate as chief prosecutor, a vulnerable witness served his purposes.

Dr. Wacker intervened. "I would like to ask the court to put a stop to this at this time. I don't think Herr Pister's health is allowing him to follow the trial."

"The court will recess until Monday morning at nine o'clock."

———

The weekend interlude provided Denson time to review Pister's signed confession and prepare for a final round of cross-examination.

"Did you see Russian prisoners of war killed at Commando 99?" Denson asked Pister as the trial resumed Monday morning.

"In Buchenwald no Russian prisoners of war were ever executed, only the political organizers."

"Do you recall making a sworn statement on the twentieth of July in Freising that, 'During the first days, a transport of Russian prisoners of war arrived'?"

"If I called them prisoners of war at that time, I used the wrong expression. Anyway, it doesn't matter. For me as for every man, orders were sacred and had to be carried out."

"Even though you knew they were wrong, is that correct?"

"How should I know if an order given from the highest headquarters is illegal? Every one of us took an oath that we would follow the orders of the Führer without hesitation. Anyway, on my own I did not give any orders."

"Otto took orders from you, did he not? Helbig took orders from you, did he not? If you had ordered Helbig not to carry out an execution, he would not have carried out the execution. Is that not correct?"

"That is correct."

"And the same thing is true with respect to all the other SS men at Buchenwald, is that not so?"

"Yes."

"So you permitted prisoners to be killed when you could have stopped them from being killed. All you had to do was say, 'Helbig, don't do it. Otto, don't do it,' and they would not have done it. Is that not correct?"

"And then? Somebody else would have done it."

"So you preferred to be commandant and let these prisoners be killed."

"I didn't prefer anything. I was a soldier. I let orders from above be carried out as they were ordered."

"You knew that according to The Hague Convention an occupying power must respect the rights and lives and religious convictions of persons living in the occupied zone, did you not?"

"First of all, I did not know The Hague Convention. Furthermore, I did not bring these people to Buchenwald."

"You mistreated them after you got them."

"I didn't mistreat anyone. Not me. Nor did I permit others to mistreat."

"Can you tell this court that until the time you left in 1945 no prisoner was mistreated or beaten or killed or tortured?"

"Not on my order. Not with my consent."

"To what did you attribute the high death rate?"

Pister started to fade. He rubbed his forehead as if in a daze. "The majority of prisoners coming in from the East arrived three-quarters dead. And those who died were added on as dead from Buchenwald."

"Is your memory all right today, Pister?"

"As far as my health will permit."

"You knew that lampshades of human skin were made at Buchenwald?"

"I never saw a lampshade made of human skin."

"Did you have a shrunken head sitting on your desk?"

"No. There was one from my predecessor in a cabinet by the wall, standing there with other utensils gathering dust."

"No further questions."

40

An American Collaborator

"Edwin Marie Katzen-Ellenbogen was born in 1882," Denson told an audience in 1991. "He was sixty-five when I prosecuted him. He became a U.S. citizen and married the daughter of a Massachusetts Supreme Court judge. The couple had one child that died in a fall from a window. Katzen-Ellenbogen then went back to Europe alone and never returned to the U.S. He practiced in Marienbad, Czechoslovakia, and when Hitler took over the country in 1937, Dr. E. escaped and went to Paris where he continued to practice until he was picked up by the Gestapo and put in 'protective custody' in Buchenwald. Because of his misconduct there, he was hated by the prisoners. The evidence showed him to be devoid of any of those benign traits that are usually associated with those who take the Hippocratic Oath."

Katzen-Ellenbogen may not have been a brownshirted Nazi fanatic, but Teutonic blood ran just as swiftly through his veins. As a prosecutor Denson divorced himself from the concept of revenge—justice, not punishment, was his ideal—but this was different. Katzen-Ellenbogen stood out from the others in the dock. Most of the German prisoners held at Dachau were uneducated, unemployed victims of their time, waiting to pay for their crimes. This man was an intellectual devil needing to be exorcised. Several witnesses had offered testimony against him, including one of the few Americans to be called to the stand.

———

"My name is Karl Berthold. I am fifty-four, born in Aurora, Illinois. I arrived in Buchenwald in January 1944 in a boxcar. We had been traveling for three days. We were sick, sore, tired, thirsty. There was an American in the camp named Burnham Robinson, born in New Haven, Connecticut. He was about six-foot-four, and they had outfitted him in green trousers that came just below his knees and sleeves just below his elbows. He looked like a scarecrow. He worked the night shift on the railroad tracks and had become weak from overwork and malnutrition and like all of us was getting abscesses all over his body. I went to Dr. Katzen-Ellenbogen and asked, 'Isn't there something we can do for a fellow American?' He said, 'Oh, he will have to be taken care of in the regular way.' He wasn't the least bit helpful. When I returned, Burnham had already gone to the hospital. That was the last I saw of him alive."

"Was Dr. Katzen-Ellenbogen a prisoner just like yourself?" Captain Lewis asked on cross-examination.

"He was a prisoner, but not in the ordinary sense. He was a privileged prisoner."

"You spoke about the transport that took you to Buchenwald," Lewis said. "Was the camp responsible for the number of days you were en route?"

"That's not for me to decide. Only God knows."

"Do you know that the prosecution has brought so far seven witnesses who managed to survive for six years in Buchenwald?"

"Yes. But they couldn't bring back Robinson."

———

Dr. Jean Rousset testified against Katzen-Ellenbogen. "He was chief doctor of the Little Camp. He was a prisoner, but I knew he had been an SS agent in France."

"In what manner did Katzen-Ellenbogen discharge his duties?" Denson asked.

"Very badly. As a matter of fact, he didn't discharge them at all. He beat the prisoners and was completely indifferent to seeing them die. If a prisoner did not have cigarettes or food or something to give him, he would not take care."

———

"You say that Katzen-Ellenbogen beat prisoners," Lewis asked Rousset on cross-examination. "When was that?"

"All the time. Every day. It was as sure a ritual as morning and evening roll call."

"You went through the barracks every day, did you?"

"I couldn't say I went through every day. . . ."

"You just said you saw Katzen-Ellenbogen beat prisoners every day. Do you want to change your testimony?"

"I did not say that I saw him do it every day. I said he did it every day."

"Did he ever use a stick or a weapon to these prisoners?"

"Personally, I never saw that."

"All you saw were slaps and fist-blows, is that correct?"

"I think that is sufficient. I belong to a country where people are not in the habit of beating inferiors."

"If the court please, I ask that this answer be stricken from the record."

"May it please the court," Denson said, "I think he has answered the question fully and properly. He asked for it," nodding toward Lewis, "and he got it."

"Request is denied."

———

"My name is Joseph Rous. I am thirty-five years old, a resident of Perpignan in France. I am a reserve captain. We arrived from Auschwitz in a complete state of exhaustion. We had undergone all kinds of tortures. Katzen-Ellenbogen came in the morning to visit the place. There was one comrade who was sleeping on the third tier of his bunk, maybe two meters from the floor of the barracks. We told Katzen-Ellenbogen that this comrade was sick and unable to come down from his bed. Then he got mad and pushed some prisoners away. He climbed onto the bed and pulled this comrade by the feet, and he fell to the ground. When he fell, he cracked his skull. There was blood running down his shirt. Katzen-Ellenbogen said, 'You Frenchmen, you can all croak,' and then he left. We took our comrade and put him in the lower bunk. The next evening he died."

When Katzen-Ellenbogen took the witness chair, he startled the courtroom with a deep baritone voice. "I studied with the father of modern psychology, Wilhelm Wundt," he said. "In the course of my studies, I became enormously interested in abnormal and forensic psychology, so I took a second study subject, medicine, and graduated first in philosophy and then in medicine from the University of Leipzig."

"Dr. Ellenbogen," Captain Lewis said, "were you ever in the United States?"

"My father was adviser for European firms operating in the United States and also for certain banks, for instance Chase National and Knickerbocker Trust. As my mother was a chronic invalid and I the only child, he often took me on voyages he made, so as a child I was off and on in the States. In 1904 I became engaged to an American girl, the daughter of a judge of the Superior and Supreme Court. I arrived for permanent residence in 1905. I do not desire to drag in the names of my relatives either on my father's side or my wife's side. They are prominent men. One is a corporation director, another is a university professor."

"After your marriage, doctor, did you return to Europe?"

"With introduction letters to different U.S. ambassadors that had been furnished to me by Sen. Elihu Root, I returned to continue my postgraduate studies. The following two years I spent perfecting my studies of abnormal psychology, hypnotism, and psychotherapeutics. Being married and also having ample private means, I was able to study in France and in other countries with the leading names known on the scientific horizon of this branch of science."

"After your studies in Europe, did you again return to the United States?"

"I returned in 1907 and stayed in New York, volunteering at Bellevue and at Post Graduate Medical, then took a position in the Children's Mental Hospital on Randall's Island. In 1909, I was appointed lecturer of abnormal psychology at Harvard University. In 1911, I became scientific director in the State Village for Epileptics at Skillman, New Jersey. While there I drafted a law for sterilization of epileptics, criminals, and the incurably insane for the State of New Jersey. That law passed, but the State Supreme Court declared it unconstitutional."

"After you became a U.S. citizen, did you return to Europe?"

"I returned in 1914."

"Can you tell us why you were incarcerated in Buchenwald?" Lewis asked.

"While I resided in Germany, Hitler came to power. Not being able to stand Nazism, I went to Prague and occupied myself with physicians who wanted to emigrate to the States, to help prepare them in English as well as for the state examinations. I do not wish to, but I could furnish names of men residing now in the States and England whom I helped get out, furnished them with papers—but that has nothing to do with Buchenwald. And I know enough of the proceedings in United States courts of justice," he added, "to know it is forbidden to discuss the previous life of the defendants, not to prejudice the jury, no matter how good I have been before Buchenwald. Well, I got notice that the Gestapo were wise to my helping. Preferring not to wait for arrest, I went to Italy."

Patiently waiting out the verbiage, Lewis repeated, "The question was, why were you sent to Buchenwald?"

"I was arrested in 1941 in Paris by the AST, the *Abwehrleitstelle*, an army organization related perhaps to the counterintelligence corps. I was kept five months in the German military prison in Fresnes and then discharged. I was told that the charges, which were along the lines of spying and helping the Allies, had been dismissed. In February 1943, I was rearrested. A Gestapo gentleman arrived and informed me that he was sorry to disappoint me but the SD is against my freedom in Germany. Although they have nothing particular against me, they can't trust me. I was told I am going to be a physician in a camp for civilians. I, of course, did not know that camp meant concentration camp. On third September, with about one thousand mostly French reserve officers, I was sent to Buchenwald."

"When you arrived, what were the conditions that you found there?"

"I was really amazed by the efficiency and by the sanitary arrangements. The bathroom was all right, and everything was very clean, practically an assembly line. All my hair, mustache and everything else was shaved off, all belongings were taken away. We were marched to the quarantine station. There I stayed fourteen days. My dressing was not zebra dressing, but some civilian clothes. You can imagine, the shirt was meant for a child of ten years. I got those wooden shoes, both left ones. I limped about until a noncommissioned German looked at my legs and said, 'For God's sake, you can't work in that condition,' and sent me to the big hospital."

"Now tell us what happened in the hospital," Lewis asked.

"I developed phlegmons due to the infection. The prisoner doctor Matousek, at the present time minister of Czechoslovakia, made a visit. We had mutual friends in Prague whom I had helped escape to London. He told me, 'I must see that you find some occupation in the hospital.' Finally I was sent to the Little Camp. My duty was to go through the blocks and find out who was sick. I was not given any medicine or even a thermometer."

"At some later period did your duties increase in the Little Camp?"

"Yes. By February, Obenauer became *kapo* of the hospital. In spite of the fact that we were not on friendly terms, he told me that I can now examine the patients myself. So I arranged first with Chief Medical Officer Busse to have medicines. At the time medicine was still in sufficient supply in the pharmacy. I must say, sitting here, that I am surprised that the real culprits for so many deaths, tuberculosis and so on, are not in this room as accused. Those barracks were absolutely not fit for human beings, with no doors or windows that could be opened, and thousands packed together. Once I found that half of the Frenchmen in block fifty-nine had scarlet fever, I persuaded Schiedlowsky and Reschke, the *lager* eldests, to make a quarantine station for them. In this way I squashed the possibility of scarlet fever spreading all over the camp."

"Were you ever removed from the Little Camp at any time?"

"In February 1944, I was accused of selling drugs. Eventually it was publicly declared that the charges were untrue, and I continued my duties."

"Doctor," Lewis continued, "do you recall the testimony of the witness Blackhan concerning the presence of Allied fliers in Buchenwald?"

"I do. In August those men were brought to the Little Camp and left in the open. They were treated like all the prisoners who arrived, and when I visited I saw they were lying on stones and in mud. I went to Schiedlowsky and told him, 'American and English prisoners of war are illegally kept here in the concentration camp, against the Geneva Convention. The luck of war is changeable. Germany may lose the war, and then everybody who is responsible would be shot for his deeds.' For his own sake I wanted him to do something about it, that they should be transferred to an officers' camp. He answered that as a doctor he had nothing to do with that. I told him that he is also an SS officer. So in my presence he called up Schmidt, the adjutant, who is one of the accused, and ordered that those prisoners of war should be transferred to block forty-eight, where they were not taken into any work. Every day I had one or two of them to vegetable dinners that I was able to procure from the gardening detail."

"Doctor, there has been some testimony here concerning the parcels which the Danish prisoners received."

"Those parcels were the nicest parcels. For the general inmate it was a wish-dream package. They were brought into camp by the Danish Red Cross and distributed by a prisoner who was their man of confidence, a Mr. Rasmussen, who was also a prisoner there. One day Rasmussen brought me twenty-one packages. I opened those parcels in the presence of the address-ees. Four of them contained a large quantity of morphine. I told their owners I would retain that medicine in my medicine closet, because it was too dangerous to give out. The quantity was sufficient to poison a man if taken at once. A few days later, as I said before, I was asked to go to the work detail, and I was removed from the hospital work. Nobody told me why. In the evening when I returned, all my belongings had been removed from my room and I was sent to block forty-two. That's where I learned this rumor that I had stolen large quantities of Danish medicine and was selling one aspirin tablet for seven marks."

Lewis continued. "Do you recall the testimony of the witness Rous that in May 1944 there was a sick French prisoner from Auschwitz on the third tier of bunks, and that you allegedly pulled this prisoner down by his legs and he cracked his skull and died?"

"If I have done that, then I should be examined by an analyst. Why should I suddenly come in there to pull that man out of bed? But if the court would order an experiment by placing here one of the beds from the bunker and show how I or anybody could do it as described, then I would have nothing to say about it anymore. The man was lying on the third tier—that means about ten feet over me. I approach, according to the testimony, between two tiers and pulled him by the legs. I would have to be standing on the tips of my feet. Otherwise, I couldn't reach. Then I would have to turn, lift him—because there was an edge—and pull him down. At the time, I was sixty-three years old, not a young strong athlete. Even then, standing in the middle of this row when he fell, I would have broken his fall. Break his skull? Make your own inferences."

"Doctor, what was your first employment after you were liberated from Buchenwald?"

"On the suggestion of the international committee, I was given the distribution of goods brought by the American Red Cross—foods, clothing, shoes, and so on."

"Doctor, when were you first arrested and charged with a war crime?"

"I was told by a special agent of the American Criminal Investigation Committee that there is against me an accusation that I was giving euthanasia injections to thousands of prisoners in Buchenwald. On the first of November 1945, I was brought to Dachau. The special agent told me it would take five or six weeks before I was cleared. It has taken a little longer."

———

Denson had reached the end of his patience. "May it please the court, a little of this is all right, but I think it is going too far. I object on the ground that it is immaterial and irrelevant to the issues in this case."

"He made a statement," Lewis said. "I am leading up to the circumstances."

"Objection overruled. Make it snappy."

"I was put in bunker one that evening, and an American—Lieutenant Guth, G-U-T-H—came to see me. I told him I don't know why I am here, and he promised to look into the case. Six weeks elapsed and nothing happened. Then he told me that I will be requested to be a witness in the Buchenwald trial which probably will start in February or late March 1946. Then he utilized me in this court hall to interrogate Slavic witnesses and translate into English. Then I interrogated also some of my co-accused."

"No further questions."

———

Beyond the available testimony, Denson had no idea how often Katzen-Ellenbogen had personally taken part in the murder of Buchenwald prisoners, but the doctor had shown himself on direct to be an arrogant man who had rarely been thwarted in his desires. Denson could easily envision a situation in which Katzen-Ellenbogen let his temper get the best of him: intelligence was no prophylactic against violent impulses. The job now, on cross-examination, was to bring out that nature before the tribunal.

"You were working in the big hospital as of January 1945. Do you recall transports coming into Buchenwald during those months?"

"I do. Anybody who lived through January will never forget that."

"Isn't it a fact that the physical condition of many persons on those transports was such as to require immediate medical attention?"

"Half of them required undertaker's services rather than a doctor's. Many of them died within a day or two. You have to consider that they were for ten or twelve days without food or water, and I know of a Russian transport where they were drinking finally their urine. But that, naturally, is not the fault of any of the accused in Buchenwald but of the transportation personnel."

"Isn't it a fact, though, doctor, that many of those prisoners who came in the condition you described would have been saved if they had been given immediate medical attention?"

"Some of them, yes."

"Doctor, approximately how many prisoners did you see attempting to get into the surgical department each day?"

"At the end about two hundred or so, but they were not all injuries. There were as well phlegmons, furuncles, skin diseases."

"Well, approximately how many of those two hundred or so were suffering from injuries?"

"I couldn't tell you."

"What is your best judgment about it?"

"It would be really useless to guess. I had absolutely nothing to do with it."

"While you were there, did you see men who had their heads split open?"

"I saw men lying on stretchers, but I didn't know the cause."

"Well, isn't it a fact also, doctor, that prisoners would have to line up outside that dispensary and wait their turn from morning until evening, and that many a prisoner died while waiting his turn to be examined?"

"Well, Bukowski was the chief of that dispensary, and when patients arrived he went always outside and looked who needed immediate attention."

"Just answer the question please."

"Mr. Denson, if you want me to answer the question yes or no, then I will have to answer no."

"Then your answer is that at no time did a prisoner die while waiting his turn to be examined in the dispensary?"

"You say those questions with a revolver, with 'Hands up!' It is impossible to answer yes or no."

"You were there, were you not? You know whether a man is living or dead, don't you? Did any man die while he was waiting his turn in that line?"

"Sure he did."

"I thought you said a moment ago that he didn't."

"Yes—not because of waiting, but because he was in such a condition that a few minutes later he was dead."

"Just listen to my questions please, doctor. I did not say, 'because he was waiting in that line.'"

"I know you won't want to listen anymore."

"You just answer my questions. You testified that no inmates of the invalid blocks were permitted to go to the hospital. Who issued that order? Did Bender know about that order?"

"Bender had nothing to do with the treatment of patients."

"What was he doing there in the Little Camp?"

"In some of the blocks he was selecting—rather, he was *examining* inmates for their ability to work. I think it was not mentioned, but after quarantine all men who came with a transport were examined by one of the SS doctors about their working capacity. So Bender surely saw the terrible conditions. He often told me, 'Something should be done. I don't know what, but these conditions are horrible.'"

———

Every man in the dock was to Denson repugnant for having taken part in, or supporting, cruelty beyond anything ever recorded. The majority of defendants at least had their own stupidity to blame. Katzen-Ellenbogen's crimes were the greater for the malevolence they represented: the haughtiness of a squat, bitter man who took his God-given intelligence and wove a twisted philosophy of racial superiority—proudly announcing his authorship of a proposal to establish euthanasia in the State of New Jersey—then turning his disdain for "lesser beings" on helpless inmates at Buchenwald. His crimes were all the greater for his attempt to dress them in robes of dubious respectability. Here was a man who had immigrated to America, insinuated himself into an established Boston family and into respected institutions of learning, and had returned to exploit those credentials in Nazi Europe. Then, when even the Germans could no longer bear his conniving and demagoguery and had thrown him into the camps, he used his knowledge of human behavior to establish himself as a diplomat among thieves, a nobleman among killers, and had abused that position to the point of murder. Katzen-Ellenbogen shifted his corpulent frame in the chair.

"How much did you weigh when you got to Buchenwald, doctor?" Denson asked.

"I don't know exactly, but I am a very funny man. I don't change. I will look in good and bad nourishment exactly the same. I was twenty-three days in the bunker and hardly ate anything, yet I lost only one pound exactly."

"What position did you hold in the German ministry?" Denson asked, in effect accusing him of having been an SS informer.

"In the German ministry? Will you please . . ."

"Just answer my question."

"If you will be my witness, Mr. Denson, then when I call you, you can tell me where you get your information."

"You talked about vegetables. How many other prisoners in Buchenwald had vegetables to eat besides you?"

"All the prominent *kapos* and block eldests. They were getting it in an organizing way, and I got it legally."

"Then you were one of the favorite few there at Buchenwald who were able to get enough vegetables each day, is that not correct?"

"Relative to percentage of inmates, one of the very, very few."

"Doctor, do you remember a case in February 1944, in which a prisoner in block fifty-seven or fifty-eight had gone insane?"

"To tell the truth, I don't recollect any details about such a case."

"As a matter of fact, do you not recall that you had him stretched spread-eagle out on one of those bunks?"

"That what? Are you testifying again yourself, or are you . . ."

"You answer my question, doctor."

"Nobody ever until now brought that point out. If you are asking that, then you are testifying."

"Will you answer my question, doctor?"

"I don't remember doing anything like that. If I don't know anything about the case . . ."

"Is it not a fact that you let him lie there for approximately three days without any food or water or any treatment at all?"

"This is a purely hypothetical case that you are testifying about, Mr. Denson, I can't answer you regarding food and drink and so on."

"Answer my questions. Is it or is it not a fact?"

"No. If you want a case like that, I answer you no."

"Is it not a fact, doctor, that that prisoner died?"

"We have here a prisoner—"

"Just the question yes or no, whether it is or is not a fact."

"Your hypothetical patient out of fiction could have died."

"Is your answer yes or no?"

"Mr. Denson, you are the author of this fiction. You know whether you killed that patient or not. I don't know."

"At that time, doctor, is it not a fact that you were charged with the medical treatment of the prisoners there?"

"Yes. Now we are on factual grounds."

"During that time was it not a part of your duties to see that prisoners who were unable to get the food themselves, because of their physical condition, got their food?"

"Not at all."

"In other words, if a prisoner was so ill he was unable to go and get his food, then he died because no one there was willing to get it for him."

"I will not help you anymore."

"You did not help anyone, did you, under these circumstances?"

"How could I help six thousand persons, to see whether they had food—may I make a statement?"

"Subject to cross-examination," Kiel said.

"Yes, first I want to make a statement in the direction of the prosecution. When I was examined by Mr. Wolf he emphatically told me that nobody thinks of indicting me, that he talked with persons in high positions and they all told him I would not be indicted, that I am here only as an expert witness for conditions in Buchenwald, that nobody wants to blame me for block sixty-one. And when I was indicted, I was so cut up that I told the counsel of the defense, 'I don't want to defend myself. I don't want to say anything. I would plead guilty in order to get out of that thing. I am disgusted with life.' When the testimony of the two doctors Rousset and Denis came, then I understood why I was indicted. I must say in all justice to the prosecution that even if I would be Mr. Denson's brother, still his duty was to indict me. What could he do with the statement of two Frenchmen of high professional standing? So I was rather glad that I was indicted because this way I was at least in a position to clear myself. Only here I was able to find the missing link to this hostile attitude against me in the camp, and now I can see now rather clearly how it happened.

"I told Chief Medical Officer Busse that while I was imprisoned by AST in Paris, I was used as a physician. The word 'AST' was overheard and reported to the secret government of the camp. You have to understand, we were surrounded by spies. The life and liberty of hundreds of us were saved only by that secret system of supervision by certain persons. Now, those men, Rousset and Denis, are French patriots, true patriots. And right here I say I am perfectly willing to go before the French court and answer any charges that I harmed any Frenchmen or any French organizations. Out of patriotic reasons, Rousset and Denis testified here falsely in order to punish me for some crimes against the nation that they thought I had committed. In the French nature, we know it from history, that if a Frenchman for the glory of his country would have to make a false statement, he will do so. I recall that the members of the court in the case of *Dreyfus*, gentlemen of high standing, perjured themselves in order to capture the real culprit, Major Esterhazy. The only personal motive that governed those men was love of their country.

"I further state that I had nothing to do with the ministry of Germany. That was the only highly improper statement that Mr. Denson said, what he charged. If this would be America, my learned judges, you would give instructions to the jury to disregard that statement because it was not proved in any proceeding of the court.

"I will now make a very peculiar statement. It is a legal principle of all courts of all nations, *in dubio pro vero*—give the benefit of the doubt. If you are in doubt about my guilt, you have to acquit me. But I reverse that. If you are in any doubt that I am *not* guilty, then convict me so that I will have a chance in higher courts to defend myself in a way that perhaps I can't do here. Think about the articles that have appeared about me in the newspapers, first that I was responsible for thousands of injections, for killing thousands, and further that I was hypnotizing prisoners in order to extort confessions and deliver them to the Gestapo. That slander was also repeated on the radio. Acquitted or not, that did me so much harm that my age, sixty-five, will not allow me to live under that strain too long.

"I recognize you as my high court of justice. But the greatest speech of defense was made by Socrates: 'While I respect you as my judges, the only judge whom I recognize is my conscience.' My conscience doesn't bother me in this respect. Probably I did many things there that were mistakes. But the one that didn't do any mistakes should throw the first stone. That is so much I have to address the court."

———

"Have the prosecution and the defense rested?" tribunal president Kiel asked on August 11, 1947.

"The prosecution has rested, sir," Denson said.

"The defense has rested," Maj. Carl E. Whitney said. While he had taken only an occasionally active role inside the courtroom, Whitney was Denson's counterpart, chief defense counsel.

"The defense, the accused, and the prosecution have waived final argument," Kiel announced. "There being nothing further to be offered, the court will be closed."

Why had Denson agreed to waive final argument? Did Whitney tell him there was no need for one? Had Kiel or some other member of the tribunal told him that he had proved his case and that final argument was extraneous? Perhaps Denson felt that members of the tribunal had already made up their minds as to verdicts and sentences. Perhaps his weakened condition was to blame. In his three previous trials he had offered eloquent closing remarks, but for reasons that remain unclear he agreed to forgo doing so now. There were no closing remarks at the Buchenwald trial.

41

The Verdicts

On August 12, 1947, the court reconvened at ten o'clock.

"Court will come to order," court president Kiel announced. "As I read the following names, I want the accused to rise." The thirty-one accused rose as their names were called.

"The court in closed session, at least two-thirds of the members concurring in each finding of guilty, finds each one of you guilty of all of the particulars and the charge. The accused may be seated."

"May it please the court," Dr. Renner said, "some of the accused desire to take the stand and make a statement concerning extenuating circumstances or in mitigation."

Such statements carried weight. During the Dachau program, a total of 3,887 cases were opened as a result of army investigations. Of these, 1,672 actually went to trial. Because of this large number of cases, sentences for similar crimes often varied. To equalize things, the War Crimes Branch decided that reviews should also consider sentence reduction based on the defendant's prewar record, his age, physical condition, behavior in prison, family situation, and willingness to learn a worthwhile trade while in prison.

Review committee decisions fell under the jurisdiction of Lt. Col. Lucius D. Clay, who in March 1947 had succeeded Eisenhower as military governor of Germany. During those postwar months, Clay was responsible for rebuilding U.S.-occupied Germany. He confronted enormous problems and relied on succinct reports to make quick, firm decisions. For his review of war crimes sentences, the military authorities provided him with trial summaries that recapitulated in short, cursory fashion thousands of pages of transcripts. With tens of millions of people to look after, Clay can be excused for not having read the original transcripts, but without seeing the Nazis on trial or knowing the details of their trials, his review of their sentences took on a mechanical quality. In his book *Decision in Germany*, Clay explains that he could make decisions based only on the record he was presented, and on that basis hundreds of sentences were commuted. Encumbered by their own enormity, the trials of those who ran Hitler's concentration camps became little more than parole hearings.

––––––

The Nazis who ran Buchenwald took the stand and offered reasons why their sentences should be mitigated. Arthur Dietzsch had been chief *kapo* of the medical experiment block and had indulged in acts of sadism against his fellow inmates. He told the tribunal he had been an active opponent of the Nazi regime who had never harmed a non-German and claimed to have saved the lives of innumerable prisoners at the risk of his own life.

Hubert Krautwurst, who had killed prisoners working in the camp's gardening detail, took the stand. "May it please the court," he said. "I ask that you take into consideration that when I was transferred to Buchenwald, I was only seventeen years old. That is all."

Peter Merker took the stand. Merker had been commando leader of the Gustloff works, an out-command of Buchenwald where hundreds of slave laborers died. "I did not commit any crimes," he told the tribunal. "Only two persons died during the sixteen months that I was detail leader at Gustloff. I did beat certain prisoners maybe a dozen strokes—but that was because they themselves asked me for it so they would not be punished more severely. I ask the high court for a just sentence."

Hermann Helbig took the stand. He had been crematory chief and executioner at Buchenwald. "May it please the court, I stand up for all of my actions. I did participate in executions upon orders of my superior officers, and those executions were under the supervision of SS officers and doctors. For that reason I never doubted the legality of the sentences being carried out. Just like any American soldier, I carried out the orders of my superior officers. As soldiers of the American army, you have probably received orders to which you objected but were forced to carry out. I was a soldier for twenty-five years and knew nothing except my country and my orders."

Dr. Katzen-Ellenbogen took the stand. "If it please the court, you have placed the stigma of Cain on my forehead," he said, his deep voice echoing across the courtroom. "I shall not plead any extenuating circumstances. If in your opinion I am guilty, then I am more guilty than any of these other accused. They at least had an excuse: they were Germans and soldiers and had orders that they had to comply with. I can make no such claim. I was not a German, I was not a member of the SS. Therefore, if I supposedly committed those crimes, I ask for only one grace, that the full measure for my alleged crimes should be applied. Because if a doctor, a former member of the Harvard Post Graduate Medical teaching staff, has committed such crimes, then die he shall and die he must.

"I am not afraid of death," Ellenbogen continued, "but I am afraid of life with Cain's stigma on my forehead. I was described here as an SS helper, as a Gestapo helper. Therefore, judges, I ask you for one grace. Apply to me the highest penalty which is in your hands."

Ellenbogen resumed his place and Ilse Koch took the stand. "May it please the court," she said, "I had not intended to take the witness stand another time, but now that the court has found me guilty I think it is my duty to mention the following points. After I took the stand on the tenth of July, an article appeared in the periodical *Newsweek* that clearly establishes that my photo albums are in the possession of the U.S. military government. In these albums are pictures of my house from several different dates. I think it would be an easy thing to determine from these pictures what these lampshades were made out of. They were bound not with human skin but in dark leather.

"Now I must make a statement about parts of the article that refer to my private life, because the point of issue is not only myself but also my children. I don't know who this reporter received his information from. At any rate, he did not get it from me. It says there, among other things, that I had admitted—well, you can read it. It is not my way to use that type of language. These are the most vulgar lies that I ever have read about myself in any paper. I was a housewife and a mother. I had nothing to do with concentration camps. My husband never told me about it, and I never saw nor heard of any of these things that are being talked about here."

"The defense has nothing further to offer in the way of extenuating circumstances," Dr. Renner said. "We would like to thank the court for its patience and kind consideration during the course of this trial."

The court was closed at 11:40 A.M. on August 12, 1947.

42

The Sentences

As he awaited the court's determination concerning sentences, Denson would have considered that, with regard to verdicts in his trials, their confirmation by the army's review board was relatively certain. No matter what agenda had prompted the commutation of sentences that had begun recently, nothing could possibly reverse the findings of guilt against Hitler's henchmen. Sentences, however, were another matter. If some ulterior purpose were lurking behind the recent commutations, then his hard-earned death sentences might not stand. At nine o'clock the court came to order. Court president Kiel called each witness to stand before the tribunal.

"Hans Eisele, the court sentences you to death by hanging, at such time and place as higher authority may direct." Denson had secured a death sentence against Hans Eisele in the Dachau trial, but on review the sentence had been commuted to life imprisonment. Now he had again won a death sentence against The Butcher. Would the sentence stand this time?

"Edwin Katzen-Ellenbogen, the court sentences you to life imprisonment, commencing forthwith, at War Crimes Prison Number One, Landsberg, Germany, or such other places as may be designated by competent military authority." Katzen-Ellenbogen had insisted that the tribunal sentence him to death—and they had given him life. Denson would not let this one go without an argument.

"Ilse Koch, the court sentences you to life imprisonment, commencing forthwith, at War Crimes Prison Number One, Landsberg, Germany, or such other places as may be designated by competent military authority." That one was predictable.

"Hans Merbach, the court sentences you to death by hanging at such time and place as higher authority may direct." Merbach had argued that he had shown compassion toward prisoners on Buchenwald's final transport. Survivors of that transport testified that he had gone down the line of railroad cars and systematically shot dozens of wounded or dying inmates.

"Hermann Pister, the court sentences you to death by hanging at such time and place as higher authority may direct." The tribunal had agreed with Denson in his position on the camp commandant: whether or not Russia had signed the Geneva Convention, Russian prisoners of war were entitled to protection. The tribunal's sentence said that Pister, by virtue of his position in the camp while executions were going on, was guilty of violating the laws and usages of war.

Kiel completed his announcement of the sentences. From thirty-one accused, twenty-two were sentenced to death by hanging, five to life imprisonment, and the rest to fifteen to twenty years' hard labor. It was less than the prosecution might have hoped.

"The court at this time expresses its appreciation," Kiel said, "to the prosecution and defense counsel for their zeal and devotion to duty in the conduct of this trial. Is there anything further to be presented to the court?"

"May it please the court," Denson said, "I think that I would be remiss in my duties if I did not at this time thank the court on behalf of each and every member of the prosecution staff for the kind, attentive, and patient manner in which this court has heard this case. The prosecution has nothing further."

At 10:15 A.M. on August 14, 1947, the court adjourned. Denson approached members of the tribunal and asked them to explain why Katzen-Ellenbogen's life had been spared.

"He wanted to be hanged," they told him, "and we did not want to accede to his wishes."

"That old goat didn't want to be hanged any more than you or I do," Denson fumed. "He used his knowledge of psychology to get you to give him a life sentence." Maybe this would be corrected on review of the transcripts, he thought. Press and others seeking their usual copies of trial proceedings were told, however, that transcripts were not available. No explanation was given.

When the Nuremberg trials ended, chief prosecutor Robert Jackson returned to his post on the U.S. Supreme Court. When the Dachau trials ended, chief prosecutor William Denson went looking for a job. There was no payoff on completion of his work in Dachau; no offers to publish his memoirs, hardly even a fare-thee-well from JAG senior officers. On his application for federal employment, Denson indicated he would accept an appointment anywhere in the world, was willing to travel as much or as little as required, and would be content with the same annual salary he had been receiving for the past two years: ten thousand dollars. Leaving Germany after twenty-one months must have seemed, at best, anticlimactic, devoid even of lasting bonds that other battlefields created for other soldiers. JAGs who served at Dachau were no band of brothers. When they met in the years after repatriation, it was usually at reunions of liberation soldiers or former victims—other people's parties. No libraries were named after them, no plaques hung in their honor. No books analyzed their deeds, no movies honored their success in bringing Nazis to justice. Barely a mention of their work appeared in the press. They were ghosts of a massive legal enterprise that would have faded into complete oblivion had it not been for a scandal of monumental proportions that erupted a year later.

New York Times,
October 24, 1947

Chief Prosecutor Returns Home

MUNICH—At the main airport in Frankfurt on the Main on Sunday morning, former Lieut. Col. William D. Denson will take a plane for the United States to return to civilian life. Colonel Denson has been outstanding for his intensive work on the prosecution staff of the War Crimes Commission at Dachau. Frequently trying one major case during the daytime and working far into the night on the preparation of another, he had become over a period of two years a symbol of justice among the SS men and women administrators in Adolf Hitler's concentration camps. . . .

PART FIVE

Aftermath

—————

When I was a child, I spake as a child,
I understood as a child, I thought as a child.
But when I became a man, I put away childish things.
For now we see through a glass, darkly . . .

—I Corinthians 13:11–12

43

Homecoming, 1947

On receiving notice that their son was returning from Germany, Denson's parents promptly called the press. Within days of his arrival, Denson found himself in the offices of the *Birmingham News* being interviewed by staff writer Virginia Van Der Veer. Perhaps unaware of its irony, the writer titled her piece "War Prosecutor Tries to Forget."

"The young man had a mild face and a slight build," she wrote in the December 6 issue. "Amid the busy confusion of the city room, he was scarcely noticed. Old-timers in the office, experts at casting their visitors, might have taken him for a minister with a weekly church notice. But that soft, Alabama accent had sounded in a German courtroom only two months ago. . . . He is trying now to forget the details of those two years. He will never forget, however, the evidence that normal, educated human beings can be brutalized to the level of beasts in a few short months."

Returning to Birmingham no doubt stirred memories of the simpler life he had left behind. The topography of Alabama had not changed. The rivers he fished as a boy flowed just as swiftly, pike and bigmouth bass jumping just as high when hooked. But something irrevocable had come between him and normalcy. How does someone who has seen the stone quarry of Mauthausen revert to the patterns and complacencies of a peacetime world? How could he adjust to life without fighting another righteous battle? Birmingham was not for him, despite its warm nights and good fishing and the comfort of home-cooked meals.

The Cold War was on everyone's mind, its deep and persistent threat of nuclear war portending a future even worse than the recent past. A former classmate from Harvard Law School, Adrian Fisher, was now chief counsel for the Atomic Energy Commission and brought Denson in for an interview. What better place for the man who prosecuted henchmen of mass destruction than the agency monitoring mass destruction's latest weapons? In November 1947, Denson started working as co–chief legal counsel to the AEC, with highest government clearance. The post, however, provided only a modest income, and by Christmas he had accepted an invitation to move in with his former classmate and four other bachelor-lawyers. By pooling their resources they were able to rent the spacious west wing of the Robert Todd Lincoln house, a private residence that coincidentally had been the home of the former general counsel to the AEC, Herbert S. Marks. None of them knew what to do in a kitchen, and their careers left little time for niceties like laundry. So they hired a cook and house-cleaner, and for all practical purposes Denson might have felt himself in an upscale version of a West Point dormitory. They rose early, gulped a quick breakfast, and grabbed the streetcar heading down Pennsylvania Avenue to their respective offices. The tall Southerner was the house favorite, always a gentleman and generous to a fault.

He gradually emerged from his cocoon. His health slowly returned, and the excitement of reestablishing a career and social life filled his waking hours. But at night, when the flurry of his new job had abated and prayers were done, Denson sensed the Dachau aroma creeping back and with it the nightmares he had known during months of trials. He never sought professional help, never burdened his housemates with what kept him awake, preferring instead to counter images of the camps with memories of his time with Huschi. Where were the young German countess and her baby? Soon the time would come to find them now that his divorce was final, his affairs in order, and the traumas behind him.

The past, however, was about to catch up with him, and it would take another year before the tides of change calmed sufficiently for affairs of the heart to have their turn.

44

Justice Betrayed, 1948

There are philosophies that urge us to judge a person's life in its entirety and with compassion. Yet often a single act defines for all time, fairly or not, an individual's mark on the world. Gen. Lucius D. Clay's defining act said little of his noble life in its entirety and much about the dangers of politics.

By 1948, Clay had earned an outstanding reputation as head of European theater operations, conciliating the Germans and integrating them into a democratic state under American influence. By the time of the Buchenwald trial he was confronting a rapidly spreading crisis of confidence over the war crimes program. If unchecked, doubts about the trials' integrity would undermine his efforts at winning Germany's support against Soviet Russia. To deal with accusations of coercion and other transgressions, the army established five boards of review that would report to Clay and make recommendations for confirming, amending, or overturning verdicts and judgments in war crimes trials.

Pressured by Washington to reassure Germany of America's good intentions, the boards took a lenient stance in their reviews and recommended that Clay reduce sentences against many of the convicted Nazis. Overwhelmed by the number of cases awaiting review, Clay approved almost all of the boards' recommendations and reduced the number of death sentences from 426 to 298. Just how far the reversal of sentences went was demonstrated in the case of twenty-one leaders of Hitler's mobile killing squads *(Einsatzgruppen).* The American tribunal had sentenced fourteen of the twenty-one leaders to death for their involvement in the murder of approximately two million victims. Only four were executed.

Despite the seriousness of the charges against her, Clay also reduced Ilse Koch's sentence from life to four years on the grounds that there was insufficient credible evidence to sustain a life sentence.

"Of course it was incredible!" Denson exclaimed looking back on the debacle almost a half century later. "General Clay did not himself see those individuals who swore before Almighty God that they had not participated in such activities. Credibility is for the trial court, not the appellate or reviewing court. Clay fell into the same pitfall I fell into when I first heard these stories."

Intuiting that there would be strong negative reaction if these reductions were made public, Clay told the boards to keep their actions under wraps. Having successfully molded public opinion to favor trials, the government could not reasonably expect the public to reverse its opinion and condone lenient treatment for the guilty.

The secret did not remain secret for long. The first public notice of Koch's commutation came when the German edition of the army's newspaper *Stars and Stripes* revealed the story on September 15, three months after the fact. Hiding the reduction only exacerbated the offense in the public's mind—a tacit admission that war crimes trials were not about justice but about politics.

Once it leaked, news of the commutations—in particular of the sentence of Ilse Koch—made headlines nationwide. The *New York Post* called them an example of "perverse stupidities" that plagued the government's policies toward Germany, and the *Philadelphia Inquirer* called Koch's commutation "malodorous." "If Ilse Koch is not guilty," said ABC radio's Dorothy Fuldheim, "then neither was Himmler or Hitler." A *New York*

Times editorial on September 30 concluded, "If someone had deliberately planned to sabotage the United States' standing in Germany and in the world, he could not have picked a better subject with which to do it than the case of Ilse Koch. Some way, somehow, this stupid error should be corrected." Ray Henle on NBC radio warned with uncanny prescience, "Look for real fireworks over the reduction of sentence of the so-called Belle of Buchenwald."

Denson first read of the commutation on Saturday, September 18, 1948. His reaction was surprise, then shock, then anger that led him to launch an aggressive campaign in the press. His letter to editors drew praise and support nationwide and was reprinted in dozens of papers across the country.

"In my opinion," Denson wrote, "to cut Ilse Koch's sentence to four years is to make mockery of the administration of justice." The press agreed. Headlines continued to demand an explanation for why the army would let the Bitch of Buchenwald go free. The outcry led to an investigation by a Senate subcommittee chaired by Sen. Homer Ferguson of Michigan.

Schnectady Union-Star

"Buchenwald 'Housemother' Called Most Sadistic Person in History."

Washington, Sept. 27 (Overseas News Agency)—When Ilse Koch was sentenced to life imprisonment on August 14, 1947, I knew that justice had not been too stern with her. If I had been told that in a little more than a year the military government authorities in Germany would commute her sentence to four years, I simply would not have believed it.

I know Frau Ilse Koch well. I was chief prosecutor at her Dachau trial. I know the extent, the quantity and the quality of the evidence against this handsome, red-haired, blue-eyed woman. Indeed, there was so much evidence—almost everybody released from Buchenwald had something to say about Ilse Koch's habits—that I was forced to use restraint in presenting my prosecution before the tribunal. I presented only 10 witnesses when there were scores more anxious to testify against her. For the sake of brevity, I deliberately under-emphasized the overwhelming case against her.

I know much more about Ilse Koch than went into the trial proceedings, too. Investigations resulted in a full picture of this incredible woman, much of which could not be brought into the trial. A large part of her story cannot be told here either, because it is so unspeakably indecent.

Suffice it to say that Ilse Koch developed into a sadistic pervert of monumental proportions, unmatched in history. This was no woman in the usual sense that I gradually got to know, but a creature from some tortured other world. . . .

45

Senate Hearings Begin

Denson sat in room 424 of the Senate Office Building on Tuesday, September 28, 1948, waiting to give the subcommittee a polite piece of his mind. Around him sat former victims of Buchenwald and officers from the Dachau trials. At the head table, white-haired, bespectacled Homer Ferguson caucused with fellow committee members Sen. Herbert O'Conor and subcommittee chief counsel William Rogers. Looking around the room, Denson recognized Kenneth Royall. The army secretary had recently retreated from his defense of Koch's commutation and instead was now urging the army to determine whether new charges could be brought against her. Denson noted the presence of a number of former colleagues and senior officers: Emil Kiel, who had been president of the Buchenwald tribunal; Carl Whitney, Denson's counterpart on the Buchenwald defense team; and Clio "Mickey" Straight, the JAG officer who early on had encouraged Denson to "do his best," then, when priorities in Germany shifted from punishment to democratization, had changed direction. "Don't let the Buchenwald trial drag out," he had told Denson. After the trials ended, Denson had listed Straight as a reference on job applications. Now, however, Denson's statements in the press were responsible for Straight's presence at a Senate hearing that would oblige him to answer uncomfortable questions. The atmosphere between them may have been less than cordial.

Next to Straight sat Col. Edward Young. The two had been inseparable in Munich. Straight was Chief, Litigation Branch. Young was Chief, War Crimes Branch. Together they had charge of all matters pertaining to the Dachau trials, reporting to General Clay. It was not certain at that moment, prior to the hearing, whether they had encouraged Clay to approve Ilse Koch's commutation or whether they had something to do with the missing trial transcripts. Denson must have had his suspicions.

Senator O'Conor called the room to order. Royall and others who would speak first were sworn in. Ferguson began with preliminary questions concerning the setup of the war crimes courts in Germany, then Royall brought the discussion around to the possibility of reversing the commutation. He had headed up an investigation into wrongdoings in the war crimes program and acknowledged that there had been accusations of torture and beatings by American investigating officers—"the other side of the picture," as he called it. But he urged the subcommittee to not let that affect their decision in the Koch case. "The fact that one case where we may have made a mistake has aroused all of this prejudice and passion," he said referring to Malmédy, "is unfortunate." But that should not stop the subcommittee from giving Ilse Koch her due. Rogers turned to Colonel Young and asked him to explain just how the commutation had occurred.

"It was Colonel Straight," Young said, quickly distancing himself from responsibility. "It was his recommendation that the sentence and findings be approved, but that the sentence be reduced to imprisonment for four years, commencing the eighteenth of October 1945."

"What was the next step?"

"The whole record—naturally with nine thousand pages, they had to make a very succinct summation of the evidence—with his review went to the judge advocate of the theater, who makes a similar review. That was Col. James L. Harbaugh. His board goes over the record and goes into the question of credibility. As in any appellate procedure, they did not call witnesses. They merely acted on the record."

"Do they not anywhere along the line indicate their reasons why they so seriously disagreed with the original court?" Rogers asked.

"Not other than what is stated there."

"That is very singular, colonel," O'Conor said, "because there are instances cited where this woman observed men with tattoos and then they were never seen anymore, but the tattoo was later found in her possession."

"Yes, but whether the testimony is good testimony or not . . ." Young and Straight took the position that certain witnesses who testified against Ilse Koch seemed, at least from their review of the "succinct summation" of the trial record, unreliable.

"Is it not fundamental," Ferguson asked, "that those who hear and see the witnesses, they are the best judges of the facts?"

Denson may have taken heart hearing this question. The notion of bureaucrats who had never seen the defendants on the stand reversing sentences based on a review of paper documents—this was the travesty of justice he had been decrying in newspapers across the country.

"What occurs to the committee," Rogers added, "is that if any of these things is truth, how could you possibly reduce the sentence to four years?"

"Bearing in mind that I am not the reviewing officer," Young said, continuing to remove himself from blame, "they tried thirty people of common design, and you proportion sentences based on the degree of guilt and participation. Now, the record says this woman did beat somebody. I have not seen the record, but I think probably it will show that this was not a serious beating. I'm just saying they have to apportion."

"Except it is inherent in the sentence," Senator O'Conor corrected. "The very fact that they gave her a life sentence is tantamount to saying she is pretty guilty. Their actions speak louder than the words."

"Could the committee send us any records which would show the justification for this?" Rogers inquired.

"I will ask, but I'm almost convinced that there is no official record other than the review mentioned."

"That is very surprising," O'Conor repeated. "All of us who ever had any part in trials know full well how undependable memory is, how treacherous it is, and where you have undertaken such a serious thing as this—for your own protection you should have it in writing."

Rogers agreed. "Now, take New York City," he said. "We have thirty thousand cases a year in New York, and I have never seen a case where the evidence was not better evaluated than this. This review says nothing about the evidence. It is embarrassing to our occupation forces. They are being daily criticized, and the committee has been deluged with letters and telegrams about doing something. If there is a justification, for your own sake it should be made public."

The possibility of implication in a growing scandal elicited a response from Young that fell just short of an accusation. "You have these statements in the papers—it was Mr. Denson who gave them out. One of the points I noticed in his statement—as a layman and not in my official position—is that he said he had ten other witnesses he could have used. If a prosecutor says that, I would say he should have used them."

Denson did not need to be prompted twice and stood to answer Young's insinuations. If the army intended to make him their fall guy, it would not be without a fight. Ferguson had him sworn in.

"I think I can help a little bit," he began, "by telling you this. To prove a case against all, we had the problem of establishing that the operation in general was criminal. I began my case by putting on background witnesses, to give a picture of life in the camp as a whole, the horrible conditions that existed there. In order to shorten it, we tried to take witnesses who could testify against as many accused as we had."

Rogers volunteered some words of support, telling the subcommittee, "Mr. Denson tried a great number of cases, one hundred seventy-seven Germans in all. Dachau, Mauthausen, Flossenburg, then Buchenwald."

"You made one particularly significant statement in your letter," O'Conor said, "that I think might be of interest to the committee: 'These witnesses were but a small fraction of those who had personally suffered from her cruel and inhuman machinations. There were others, but to put them all on the stand would have merely prolonged the trial, and relatively speaking, overemphasized her misconduct.' So these ten were not the whole story?"

"Frankly, sir," Denson said, "everybody who came to Dachau as a witness in that case wanted to say something about Ilse Koch."

"I recall from the contents of your letter that it was from one of her own witnesses that you proved that human skin was used."

"That was Dr. Morgen, who had been sent to investigate the activities of Colonel Koch and his wife with respect to mistreatment of prisoners. Let me say, in all sincerity, I did not feel that this skin business was of so much importance. The gravamen of her action was in beating prisoners and causing them to be beaten so that they died. That was really the basis for that sentence, I am sure."

"In your letter," Rogers continued, "you say, 'In my opinion, to cut Ilse Koch's sentence to four years is to make a mockery of the administration of justice.' Do you feel that way now?"

"I do."

"Based on your knowledge of this case, would you say she was less culpable than the other defendants?"

"I think she was more culpable. This was gratuitous on her part. There was no reason in the world for her exercising the authority she exercised. I will say this: the people I talked to felt the only reason she was sentenced to life imprisonment instead of death was because she was pregnant. Decent German people are also shocked by the reduction of sentence. Four years will be up in the next year—and she will be free unless something is done."

———

The Federated Press sent a reporter, Alden Todd, to interview Denson at the Atomic Energy Commission. In an article that appeared nationwide on October 1, 1948, Todd wrote, "An honest and courageous man spoke up in Washington last week against a shameful act by the American army in Germany. . . . Denson is a friendly, warm sort of man who scarcely looks his 34 years except for a little gray around the ears. . . . I asked him whether he had yet seen any sound reason for overturning the findings of the court before which he acted as prosecutor. 'No,' he said emphatically, 'It is most unsound . . .' But, he said, he had got the matter off his chest with his letters to the newspapers and did not intend to make any more of it as a private citizen. As I left, I wondered whether this sincere young lawyer might not find his opinion in the *Koch* case distasteful to some of the professional loyalty probers around town. After all, he protested an act by some important military officials, which has an effect in the realm of foreign policy. In these days of so-called loyalty probes, men have been investigated for less than that."

The writer's concerns were not unfounded. Despite Denson's privileged position with the AEC, anticommunist hysteria was spreading across the country. Anyone espousing even vague antigovernment sentiments ran the risk of being added to Sen. Joseph McCarthy's blacklist. Denson had taken not only a stance against the U.S. Army's review of the Dachau trials, but a vociferous and very public one. "William Dowdell Denson has become now the Army's principal critic," declared the *Harvard Law School Record*.

On October 18, Denson's co-counsel at Buchenwald, Robert L. Kunzig, sent him a letter of support. "Assistant Chief Counsel of the Ferguson Committee was up here to interview me," he wrote, "and I gave him as full a story of my viewpoint as I could. I feel very deeply about this because I know, as you know, that we conducted this trial in as fair and as humane a way as would be possible anywhere. I will not permit fly-by-night crackpots to go unchallenged when they try to accuse us of misdeeds." Kunzig, who was now a Pennsylvania deputy attorney general, joined Denson on the public record that month by agreeing to an interview with the *Philadelphia Evening Bulletin*. The article quoted him as saying that American civilian investigators "leaned over backwards" in according fair treatment to the thirty-one defendants in the Buchenwald war crimes case. Their cause drew support from author William Shirer, who wrote, "Of Gen. Clay's sincerity there is no doubt. His judgment, however, is debatable, and the effect in Germany, indeed in Europe, has been deplorable—some think disastrous."

In his inimitable manner, Walter Winchell in the *New York Mirror* portrayed the Koch scandal with more earthy aplomb: "General Clay says the commutation of the Ilse Koch verdict stands. He means it crawls."

46

Senate Hearings Conclude

On Wednesday, December 8, 1948, the subcommittee held its closing session.

"Colonel Harbaugh," committee member Senator McClellan began, "is there no record whatsoever as to what considerations may have prompted a reduction of the sentence?"

"The reasons were in our minds," Harbaugh said. "Unfortunately, they weren't put down."

"Are you a lawyer?" Senator Ferguson asked bluntly.

"Yes, sir."

"Have you ever known appellate courts to do that?"

"No, sir. But these were different kinds of trials. After the trial was completed, the review was typed and sent to the office of the deputy judge advocate for war crimes. That was Colonel Straight, who was in immediate charge of the war crimes program."

"All right. He gets the record in typewriting. Then what?"

"He had what we call the post-trial section review it in the first instance. They take the record and tear it apart and write the review in draft—"

"Wait, now. They 'tear it apart'?" Ferguson was having a hard time believing this was the American legal system at work.

"I beg your pardon. They summarize the evidence, and that rough draft is submitted to the chief of the post-trial branch."

"These men who 'tear the record apart,'" Ferguson said, "do they pass on the credibility?"

"Yes, sir."

"But they have not seen a witness. They take the record cold, is that right?"

"After the record was typed," Harbaugh continued, choosing to side-step the question, "it was submitted to the deputy judge advocate for war crimes—that was Colonel Straight. He went over it with the men who wrote the review, then it was forwarded to my office. I referred it to the chief of the War Crimes Board of Review Section, who assigned it to a board of review. They wrote a report to me stating what their views were. Then I prepared my recommendations and forwarded that to the deputy chief of staff. It would go from him to the chief of staff and from there to General Clay."

"Now, I want to get an idea," McClellan replied, "of who first determined that the sentence should be commuted."

"The deputy judge advocate."

"Did he set forth the reasons in writing?"

"Not directly. No, sir. I would like to say that we had eight courts sitting at Dachau and four boards of review functioning all the time. There were a great many cases being handled. It was not like we sat down with one case a month. . . ."

"Did you ever read the entire record?" Ferguson interjected.

"No, sir. I read the summaries."

"You read the summaries. Did they point out anywhere why they did not believe the witnesses?"

"I do not believe that was in any of the written reviews. I mean, they did have petitions, which came in after the trial, concerning witnesses . . ."

"*After* the trial?" Ferguson said, incredulous. "So the review board had different evidence than the court had?"

"Yes, sir."

"And for that reason they disregarded certain testimony and that caused them to reduce the sentence? And you followed that procedure as a lawyer?"

"Yes, sir."

"Do you know of any procedure in America," Ferguson demanded emphatically, "in our administration of justice that allows the appellate court to consider evidence that was not before the trial? Is that in conformity with our ideas of justice?"

"But the trials were so different from any civilian court . . ."

"Were we not trying over there to do justice in accordance with American principles of justice? How long has it been since you practiced law, colonel?"

"I have been in the Judge Advocate General's Department since 1933."

"Are you a law graduate?"

"Yes, sir."

"What law school?"

"New York University—we were trying to finish the trials . . ."

"—but you have to do that in accordance with justice."

"We thought we were."

Straight came to Harbaugh's aid. "The point is," he said to the subcommittee, "that we want to do justice, but American municipal criminal law court rules are not applicable to these things at all."

"Was the prosecution given an opportunity to know what was being said?" O'Conor asked.

"The reviewers were impartial people. They were interested in justice . . ."

"But they did not have the detailed information that would be in the hands of the prosecutor, did they?" O'Conor said. "The prosecution had lived with this case over an extended period, prepared it thoroughly, had worked it up for presentation to the court, and resulted in a verdict of guilty all down the line. The board of review is coming down with no prior knowledge. Why would the prosecution not have been advised of this newly discovered evidence and given a chance to rebut?"

"In most instances," Harbaugh conjectured, "the prosecution was probably gone."

Ferguson looked at Harbaugh and said sternly, "He may be gone, but not forgotten. Show me in writing where you had the authority to do that. Show me some place that you had authority by virtue of a rule."

"I do not know that it was ever written down," Harbaugh said. "We regarded the court's verdict in very high manner but we considered everything in the interests of doing justice . . ."

"Well, you see I am troubled with the question of whether four years is justice if this person is guilty."

"In my review," Straight said, offering Harbaugh a way out, "I referred to insufficiency of evidence as to Ilse Koch's participation. I have substantial reason to believe that Colonel Harbaugh understood that statement as I intended it. It was my judgment that no other participation in the common design was proved."

"Then, colonel, you substituted your judgment for eight men who were the trial court," Ferguson summarized.

"I considered it my duty to do so in this case. Somebody had to be responsible for holding the line and having some uniformity in connection with the punishment imposed."

Chief Counsel Rogers intervened. "I am reading from Winthrop on military law and precedents: 'The court martial, by reason of the superior education and intelligence of its members, is particularly qualified to estimate the credibility of oral testimony. Where the evidence is conflicting, it will in general be wiser for the reviewing officer to defer, rather than disapprove, its conclusions.'"

"I do not agree with that statement," Straight said.

"Why," Rogers asked, "do you disagree with what appears to be the rules?"

Straight, true to form, answered baldly and with no apparent remorse, "I did it because from General Eisenhower on down that is what the theater commander wanted."

"The *President* wanted the appellate court to pass on credibility?" Ferguson demanded. The explosive possibility that sentence reductions had occurred for covert political purposes hung precariously between his question and Straight's answer.

"I suggest it was merely—they wanted it," Straight stammered, "and it was required, and it was done in all instances and therefore it was stronger than any written rules since it was done in every case. It was even stronger than a written rule that might be stuck back someplace."

Ferguson, perhaps not knowing quite how to respond to this revelation, suggested, "We had better recess until ten o'clock tomorrow morning."

———

The subcommittee reconvened on Thursday, December 9, 1948, at ten o'clock. No mention was made of Straight's admission. Instead, Ferguson went to the heart of the legal issue and asked Colonel Young, "Under our domestic law, can a court not grant a rehearing and change the sentence again?"

"We do not permit putting a defendant in double jeopardy," Young said.

"Not double jeopardy," O'Conor said, reinforcing Ferguson's proposal. "The guilt has been established. Only on the question as to length of sentence."

"I would say it would be against the American system of jurisprudence," Young replied. Then, sensing perhaps that the subcommittee was suggesting a way they might all emerge from under the weight of this fiasco, he added, "but I would also say that General Clay could certainly be ordered to exercise his discretion differently."

"Who could order him?" Ferguson asked.

"The President could order him."

"Colonel Harbaugh, do you think this could be appealed to the President?"

Harbaugh dismissed the idea. "The rules of military commissions are to the effect that the appointing authority is the final authority. It does not go any higher for review in any way."

Mickey Straight shook his head. He wanted out as badly as the others but also saw no merit in the subcommittee's recommendation. "Look at it from the practical point of view. You establish that practice and you will have a thousand petitions going to the President. What's more, it would be a violation of universally accepted standards of justice for the President of the United States to delegate authority to somebody and then jerk it back."

"What would be the objection," McClellan proposed, "to now establishing a precedent by letting General Clay reopen the case?"

"The only reason," Straight replied, "is that this one case has damaged the entire war crimes program in the eyes of the German people to such an extent that it is pitiful. People in Germany question whether we have persecuted Germans as badly as they persecuted us. I have to think of the other cases as well. We have thousands of petitions coming into my office every day at a time when we are trying to terminate the program."

"In other words, assuming that a mistake has been made in this instance," McClellan said, offering everyone the comfort of hearing "mistake" and not "bungled manipulation of law," "it would do far more harm in undertaking to go back and correct this mistake?"

Chief Counsel Rogers opened a book and said, "Take title five—can I read this? 'Number four: the authority to increase any sentence where a petition for review, which is considered frivolous, has been filed and the evidence warrants such an increase.'"

"That provision has never been exercised," Harbaugh commented.

"It is in there, though," Rogers said pointing to the page.

"That was an unfortunate thing to get in there," Straight replied, "and it was never exercised because we were afraid we would be right here at this table if we ever did it. It violates all universal conceptions of justice to do such a thing. We tried Japanese colonels and gave them death for doing just what you want General Clay to do. Under international law, he cannot do it."

Harbaugh nodded in agreement. "We are trying in Germany to preach the ideas of democracy. I can't imagine anything that is further afield from democracy than to have him reconsider and do the same thing the Nazis used to do and increase the punishment."

McClellan refused to accept that Ilse Koch would go free. "From what I know so far about this case, the woman should have her neck broken. But it has been done, and we're not dealing with this case alone. We're dealing with world opinion and with our own conscience. General Clay was wholly wrong in reducing this sentence, and I might criticize what has been done. But what I'm thinking about is, will another mistake make it better?"

The frustration of such an impasse was more than committee chairman Ferguson could bear quietly. "When you gentlemen reviewed this case, you violated one of the fundamental principles of justice in America," he said, "and that was to pass on the credibility of witnesses and determine from outside evidence that you could say that a certain witness lied."

Straight refused to let the comment go. He may have erred, but he was as much a patriot as these politicians on the subcommittee. "I would like to tell you something, since this is executive session," he said. "The war crimes program in Germany was under attack by a lot of sources—that we were too stiff in our sentences, that the procedure was not sufficiently careful, that there were professional criminals used as witnesses, and all sorts of things— with well-greased and organized propaganda machines. And I can tell you why I didn't say it, even in cases where there were witnesses well known as being perjurers and people who couldn't be relied upon. I didn't say it for the reason that these reviews are open to the public, and I didn't want to furnish enemies of the United States of America with further ammunition to attack the program. That's why I didn't put it in writing."

Rogers was not placated by the display of self-righteousness. "As a matter of fact," he asked point-blank, "you haven't reviewed the records, have you?"

"I have not, no, sir. But I want to state this: that in addition to being in charge of these cases, I was commander of the 7708 War Crimes Group, with something short of a thousand personnel, with motor maintenance shops and everything else, in addition to being in charge of the extradition program of war criminal suspects to other United Nations members. And you must visualize that I reviewed all these cases, and in retrospect they blend together a little."

Young finally stepped in to share responsibility. "We didn't have strict rules in these trials, and that is where we are being criticized by everyone. And that is the reason that in the next war crimes trials we are going to have that rule."

Committee Chief Counsel Rogers wanted a way out for all concerned. "Have you made any effort to find out if there was evidence of another crime for which she may be tried? In other words, without violating the rule of double jeopardy?"

"Any crimes she might have committed against Germans, in violation of German law, would be a matter for the German courts," Harbaugh said.

"What was said by the German people in the press and radio about the reduction of this sentence?" Ferguson asked.

"I understand it was sort of unfavorable," Harbaugh replied in classic understatement.

"That's pretty much true from America, too," Young added. "I get all of the mail, families who want revenge, Jewish societies writing on behalf of the people who were the most persecuted. It's easy to see why we get the other side."

"Suppose," Rogers posited, "the Germans try this woman and convict her. Do you think that would be harmful to our position because the Russians would exploit that?"

"They would exploit anything," Harbaugh scoffed. "But I don't know that the Germans have anything to try her on."

Denson, ever the gentleman, stood slowly and said with calm, "Class Two Category. According to German law, if you profited from being a follower, you fall into Class Two Category."

Immediately the pieces came together. "Dr. Morgen testified that her personal fortune increased from 121 to 80,000 marks," Rogers recalled. "If that could be established, Mr. Denson, do you think she might be tried under the German law?"

"Yes, sir."

"In the trial that you held, the question of what she did to Germans was not considered, was it? It had to be non-Germans. What I have in mind," Rogers said, "is if you are able to determine evidence that on her account Germans received atrocities, that would not violate the rule of double jeopardy. In other words, if the German courts could find a charge that didn't violate double jeopardy or *ex post facto* or any other rules as we know them, and all we did was to cooperate with them in getting witnesses and things like that . . ."

"I don't think anybody would object to that," Harbaugh interjected, feigned neutrality barely covering his enthusiasm over a possible egress from infamy.

"Is there any person here that wants to give his views, or any statement to the committee?" Ferguson asked to the gallery in attendance. A hand went up.

"All right, major. Will you come forward, please? Will you raise your right hand? Do you solemnly swear to tell the truth, the whole truth, and nothing but the truth, so help you God?"

"I do," said Maj. Carl E. Whitney.

"What was your connection with the Buchenwald case?"

"I was the chief defense counsel, appointed to defend the thirty-one defendants."

"Therefore you feel responsible for the defense of Ilse Koch?"

"Yes, sir. I am responsible. It is my version that she could have been acquitted. And Colonel Straight said that his reviewers were also of that opinion."

"Did you argue the same argument that these three men used, that she was not part of the common design?"

"That is the crucial point. We didn't argue it in a closing argument. We waived argument. And it is my contention that the prosecution never should have. He refused to sum up the case for the government, and now he is complaining, on appeal, that he didn't have a chance to present the government's side."

"Well, major," O'Conor said in Denson's defense, "on the other hand, he made a full presentation of all the facts in evidence—and the fact that he did a good job is borne out by the verdict. He succeeded in proving the case as it was charged. Now, I fail to see any evidence where he was derelict in his duty, because certainly what he set out to do, in fulfillment of his responsibility, he did."

"I don't quite agree," Whitney replied. "You see, if he had accomplished his mission, the sentence would never have been reduced."

"Mr. Denson, do you have anything to say?" Rogers asked.

"Sir," Denson said with characteristic restraint, "I could say a lot. I don't know if you want to hear it or not."

Young could not resist confronting the man who was, in large measure, responsible for bringing them before a Senate subcommittee. "May I ask a question? Would you have issued those letters to the press if the sentence had been reduced on review to twenty years instead of four years?"

Denson reflected, then replied, "I would say that twenty years, to my mind, for a woman of her age would be sufficient."

"Therefore, the method of review and the reasons for reduction of sentence are not disputed by you at all?"

Young could not have been further off base in his assessment of the young Southerner, thinking Denson would play ball, dismiss gross transgressions of justice with a knowing wink and a brotherly elbow in the ribs. Denson had studied some engineering in college. He knew the importance of flexibility. Without give, the steel pilings holding up the Empire State

Building would snap like twigs. He remembered that in his dealings with others. But even flexible pilings have their limits.

"The method I object to strenuously," he said without hesitation. "That is, where you adopt, in the last analysis, the method of trying to justify what has taken place by questioning the credibility of the witnesses and capriciously disregarding their testimony—that is a method for which I have nothing but contempt." If they were going to crucify him, let them do it for upholding the law, not for supporting its transgression.

Too late, Young realized he had underestimated the depth of Denson's outrage. "As to sentence," he said, "I just want that clear. As to sentence."

Ferguson intervened. "We will excuse the witnesses at this time. I do not want to say this definitely, but as far as I know, the case is closed."

The subcommittee saw no justification for the reduction of sentences. Ferguson's staff saw through the pretext of review procedures: the system was simply overloaded. Reviews were an expedient way of finishing up thousands of cases and placating a government more and more intent on letting the trials fade into history. In his report on December 27, 1948, Ferguson stated, "Every act committed by Ilse Koch as shown by the evidence was that of a volunteer. Such voluntary action, contrary to every decent human instinct, deserves utter contempt and denies mitigation. Aside from the reduction of sentence itself, the most serious error made by the military authorities was their failure to make a public announcement of the reduction. To mete out justice was important, but to do it so that our action made sense to the people of our own Nation and the rest of the world was also vitally important. In this case, involving a person of such widespread infamy, the action of the military authorities appeared to be an effort to suppress the facts. Nothing so quickly arouses the public to the belief of possible impropriety as concealment. Our concern in the case is based on our paramount interest in the democratic principles of justice. The error in the Koch case is an isolated blemish on the vigilance and certainty of this democratic justice. Its repetition must be prevented."

New York Times
December 9, 1948

Senators Bar Open Hearings on Koch Case

Berlin Crisis Seen as Factor in the Decision

WASHINGTON—Senate investigators closed late today their inquiry into the Ilse Koch case and simultaneously decided to hold no open hearings into the Army's clemency to the infamous "woman of Buchenwald."

This decision, it was learned, was founded at least in part on the fear of some members of the Senate investigations subcommittee that prolonged public testimony might give the Russians an opportunity for hostile propaganda. A factor also was an unwillingness to provide a forum for any possible public embarrassment just now to the United States commander in Germany, Gen. Lucius D. Clay, as he confronted the Russians across the crisis of Berlin.

The subcommittee chairman, Senator Homer Ferguson, Republican, of Michigan asserted that the whole question of military justice should be reviewed in the armed services. Once such a review had been completed, he added, Congress ought to proceed to a "fundamental alteration" of military justice, as it applied to military personnel themselves and as it might apply in any future case similar to that of Frau Koch.

Asked if this did not imply that he was "highly dissatisfied" with the Koch commutation, Mr. Ferguson said: "Let's say rather that there was room for improvement in that matter."

———

It was a hollow victory for Denson, a redress that came too late to make much difference in the scheme of things. His hard work had been undone, and the men whose orders he had carried out now painted him as a rebel. Almost by way of a consolation prize, two weeks after reading Ferguson's report, Denson received a letter from Paris. He had been awarded the Croix de Chevalier of the Legion of Honor for his work in prosecuting Nazi war criminals. At least the French were happy with what he had done.

Shortly after his election to the French Legion of Honor, Denson left the army and joined the air force. If the military ever called him to serve again, he joked, there would be fewer adversaries in the air than on the ground.

Denson loved the energy of courtroom debate, but Senate hearings and public controversy had left him raw and discouraged. With great regret, he vowed to never again set foot in a criminal court. His days of courtroom litigation had come to an end.

47

Huschi

Two years after his return from Germany, Denson still had not settled in. A big part of him had remained in Bavaria, strolling beneath the arches of a rococo church, sharing oranges and exchanging glances with a twenty-two-year-old blond girl who had saved her family from invading Russians and surrendered a village to the Americans. He finally tracked her down in Southampton, on the eastern shore of Long Island, in January 1949.

"Bill who?" she said into the phone.

"Denson. Remember?"

"Oh, Bill! I—I can't see you now . . ."

"You're not married, are you?"

"No, but there's someone coming tonight, and . . ."

"Oh, I won't stay long. I'll be there shortly."

Ignoring speed limits, he made the trip from Washington in ten hours. She gave him ten minutes, then made him leave. Years later, they calculated he traveled more than eleven thousand miles back and forth courting her. He proposed in June 1949.

"No, no," she told him, not wanting to trade the Hampton beaches for Washington politics. He just kept coming, not wanting to lose the most important case of his career. She grimaced at his lack of fashion sense, although he did wear sensible shoes and always carried a handkerchief. The day came, toward the end of all those miles, for Huschi to meet William Denson Senior. "I want to look at this one," he told his son. "Your first one was a mess." Denson Senior was staying at the Gramercy Park Hotel, swank digs in the late 1940s. They met in the dining room. The little Napoleon with tight lips looked her up and down and said, "Bill doesn't smoke, doesn't drink, and he goes to church twice on Sundays."

Huschi promptly lit a cigarette, ordered a scotch, told him she could care less about going to church, and asked if there was anything else he wanted to know about her. Napoleon's stolid expression melted and the two chatted like magpies. When the waiter presented the tab, Huschi watched Denson Sr. lay down a lonely dollar-bill tip.

"Leave more," she told him. "This is New York." That clinched it. The old man called his son.

"Take her, Bill. She'll run circles round you."

Death threats started shortly after their move to Washington. From the caller's demands it appeared that Katzen-Ellenbogen was using every connection he had to get released from Landsberg prison. A letter from Germany the following week supported Denson's suspicions.

> *E. K. Ellenbogen*
> *Landsberg/Lech, Hindenburgring 12*
> *Bavaria, Germany*

Mr. William Dowdell Denson Esq.
Washington, D.C.

> *March 12, 1950*

Dear Mr. Denson,

> *Being 68 years old and lying for weeks in bed with critical heart failure, I have lot of leisure to think matters over. Retrospectively I ponder over the Buchenwald trial in which we were adversaries. I am sure had I have you as my lawyer, I would not have been convicted although my own lawyer Capt. Lewis was a very able one, but he had not much chance with the court. You stole the show. I often*

objectively admired you and having had a vast experience as court expert with District Attorneys I must hand it to you that you were the ablest one. I much enjoyed our duel while I was on the witness stand and you must admit that I scored many points over you. I think we both enjoyed it. But you had a free show while I was in danger to lose my liberty.

You will wonder why I am writing to you. Is your conscience toward me clean? In your heart of hearts you knew me innocent, I am sure.

Mr. Denson, you have attained your point. You are now an attorney for the Atomic Energy Committee, which is a great career for a young man of your age. You are also as I read a member-in-law of the German aristocracy. Being so satiated the sense of justice and fair play probably return to you. Do you think after the sentence of Ilse Koch was reduced to 4 years, that I was justly convicted? If you want proves about my own curriculum you can get sufficient evidence from my friends, my family and my son-in-law, who is in US in the Army.

I expect with curiosity your answer and shall wonder whether you will answer.

Very truly yours,
E. K. Ellenbogen M.D. Ph.D.

P.S.

Here is extract from Capt. Lewis' letter of November 17, 1947: "I still have high hopes that these reviewing authorities can see your case in its true light, not overshadowed by the terrible crimes of the others. It is my firm conviction that you were convicted because of the general bad reputation of Buchenwald as a whole and not for any specific acts that you might have been charged with. You were caught up in the maelstrom. A calm analysis of the evidence would surely indicate that you were not and could not be a part of any common design. It is unfortunate that only now many persons are protesting the verdict."

New York Times
December 31, 1949

William D. Denson Marries Countess

AEC Counsel and Constance Von Francken-Sierstorpff Wed in Mountain Lakes

MOUNTAIN LAKES, N.J.—Countess Constance von Francken-Sierstorpff of Southampton, L.I., daughter of Princess Elizabeth Hohenlohe-Oehringen von Francken-Sierstorpff of Oehringen, Germany, and the late Count Hans Clemens von Francken-Sierstorpff, was married here this afternoon to William Dowdell Denson of Washington, son of Mr. and Mrs. William Augustus Denson of Birmingham.

Mrs. Denson attended the Universities of Munich and Geneva. Her previous marriage was terminated by divorce and she resumed the use of her maiden name.

Mr. Denson, an alumnus of the United States Military Academy and the Harvard University Law School, received a captain's commission in the army in 1942. He was an instructor at West Point until 1945, later joined the Third Army as a member of the staff of Gen. George S. Patton, Jr., and at the end of the war became chief prosecutor at war crimes trials in concentration camps in Germany.

After being placed on inactive duty as a lieutenant colonel he continued his duties as chief prosecutor until 1948, for which he received the French Legion of Honor. He and his former wife were divorced. The couple will reside in Washington, where the bridegroom is in charge of litigation for the Atomic Energy Commission.

Shortly after sending the letter, Katzen-Ellenbogen died of his ailments, and life for the Densons settled into an agreeable calm. By 1958 the family included fourteen-year-old Yvonne, son Billy, and daughter Olivia. The time had come to leave Washington. Denson moved his family to Long Island, built a career with a major New York law firm, then resigned to join a smaller firm closer to home. Small, after all that had happened in his life, was just fine.

Accusations that Ilse Koch had collected tattooed skins and ordered personal items manufactured from prisoners' bones were never proved beyond doubt. In 1949 a German court tried and convicted her of murders and brutal acts against German prisoners. Her attorney, Alfred Seidel, submitted many requests for pardon, including one that suggested she was the victim of lobbying efforts by American Jews. The petitions were rejected. Ilse Koch was sent to prison and forgotten. She appeared in headlines twice more after her incarceration. The first time was in 1963, when her son Uwe discovered his identity at age nineteen, began visiting her, and told his story to *The New York Times*. The second was on September 1, 1967, when Uwe arrived for a visit and learned that his mother had hanged herself the night before in her cell. She was buried in a *staatliche Beerdigung*, a civil function without clergy.

Epilogue

Fifty Years Later

June 5, 1997. The crowded Drew University auditorium erupted in applause. Two hundred graduating students rose to their feet as Denson approached the podium. Eighty-four years old, his slow pace hinted at the heart attack from which he had recently recovered. Morning ablutions and a simple breakfast were already an exhausting ordeal. No one could know he had little more than a year to live: poise covered the toll to his nervous system. The young lawyers took their seats and he began, his voice still modulated, his drawl still seductive. But the projection that had carried his words to the corners of the Dachau courtroom fifty years before was gone. People strained forward.

"I had it backwards," he said. "The highlight of my career happened not at the end when it's supposed to, but at the beginning." He told his story with candor. How his father's father had been a colonel in the Confederate Army. How he had been selected as chief prosecutor. How the Jews had been singled out for the hardest tasks, the most brutal beatings, given the least to eat. How prisoners in the camps "suffered in ways the English language can't describe." He raised his fist high and brought it down on the podium, echoing the blows of the punishment stick on raw backs. He told how, after all the commutations and reversals had been carried out, 97 of the 177 men he prosecuted had hanged. No one in the auditorium dared breathe.

The lecture was not his first. After waging his unsuccessful letter campaign against the commutation of Ilse Koch's sentence, he had put it all behind him. Fed up with the hypocrisy and concerned that speaking out against his JAG superiors had won him no friends in the army, he said not a word to anyone about the role he had played in bringing Hitler's henchmen to justice. And the mood of the nation supported his silence: in the 1950s and early '60s little attention was given to the Holocaust.

The Vietnam War changed that. Napalm, the My Lai massacre, and other aggressive acts prompted journalists and historians to reexamine America's wartime policies past and present. Trials of Nazi criminals played an important part in a growing awareness of the Holocaust. Victims, liberators, and those who took part in the trials moved from the shadows to the spotlight as witnesses to a critical time in human history. Denson never saw himself as a crusader and preferred anonymity, but he was among the last living witnesses to the pursuit of justice in the aftermath of "history's darkest hour." He was also the one most qualified to explain what had happened in the Dachau trials.

As the years passed, reasons to resurrect awareness of the Dachau trials surrounded him. Genocide raged around the globe. President Sadat was assassinated and attempts made on the lives of Pope John Paul II and President Reagan. The IRA began a campaign of violence in the UK. There was unrest and bloodshed in Sri Lanka, El Salvador, India, Afghanistan, Lebanon. Iraq unleashed massive amounts of chemical weapons in its war with Iran. The turning point came when Denson learned that the Hutus of Rwanda had slaughtered millions of their neighboring Tutsis. He was horrified that extermination on such a scale was happening again. If the world knew about the Dachau trials and the precedents established there, might that help to bring human rights violators to trial sooner and get them convicted? At the very least, the Dachau trials should not stay buried in government archives and newspaper morgues.

With encouragement from his law partners, he began accepting offers to speak at law school symposia, college classes, and community gatherings. He started compiling every newspaper article, every page of transcript, every photograph, letter, and document he could find relating to the trials. He purchased old magazines and exercised his prerogative as a former officer to secure copies of photographs that had been used as evidence. From his own personal effects he excavated letters that had arrived over the years since the war. He traveled to the National Archives in Washington, D.C., spent weeks sifting through crates of unmarked files. Each spool of microfilm found was a personal victory, one more piece of the puzzle safeguarded from loss. He transported the materials back to his law office on Long Island and worked late each night sorting, cataloging, noting references. Early each morning he drove the materials back home and stored them in his basement. Sorting through the cache, he discovered an important piece of that puzzle: the Buchenwald trial transcripts. According to testimony by Clio Straight in the subcommittee hearing, those transcripts had gone missing when the stenographers' office in Dachau was moved to a new location. Whatever the reason, here they were.

—————

Denson, Huschi, and their three children moved into a rambling old house on Long Island's south shore in 1958. They went camping, attended church, and did not speak of Dachau. He loved his wife with the passion of their youth and never stopped loving her. At home he was always fixing something or else playing with the kids or reading history books. He made his own rods and flies, went fishing and skeet shooting with buddies. He wore his West Point jacket and ring right up to the day he died and continued to carry his small pocketknife for emergency repairs. For a while he was mayor of their small town. The basement archive grew larger each year. The Drew University lecture was one of his last.

—————

An hour later he was done speaking. Hands went up. Denson pointed, and a young man in the back stood up.

"Mr. Denson, you got to observe Nazi war criminals up close. Did you come up with a personality sketch that explained how these people got that way—I guess I'm asking, do you think this could happen again?"

"Amen, yes," he said with a sober expression. "Some of you here were not even born yet when that horror occurred that we call the Holocaust.

But you are witnesses to what's happening today in Bosnia, what's happening in Rwanda. And as lawyers, you inherit the legacy of what was done at the Dachau trials. Happen again? When has it not happened? When have we succeeded in controlling our lower nature? I met the families of these butchers. The wife of one convicted officer approached me asking that I intercede to get her husband's sentence reduced. 'He is a good man,' she said, 'a good father from a family of Austrian nobility. That's why they made him *Obergruppenführer*.' You know, this man had thrown human beings still alive into the crematory fire. Many of the Nazis were indeed good family men with wives, children—as normal as you and me. And there's the tragedy, that the moral fiber of normal human beings can be destroyed, with only primitive desires remaining. These people thought that what they were doing was correct."

Denson looked silently out on the class. For several uncomfortable moments they endured the penetrating gaze of a man who vividly remembered the ruins of "primitive desires." The intensity of those memories permeated the room like heat from a lamp. Another hand went up.

"Mr. Denson, people know about Nuremberg. Why haven't we heard of the trials at Dachau?"

"Because afterward we wanted to forget, get on with our lives—not just we who were there, but the U.S. and German governments, and the world at large. But right now there are a lot of potential accused in Bosnia, and what we did at Dachau was not useless. One of the most important things that happened for me is the recognition that even people who are defeated have rights, and those rights are in treatises—nothing spur of the moment. These were efforts to put teeth into the written word. That I think we did.

"We can't conclude there will never be another Holocaust. There will be, as long as people do not agree to enforce human rights. But we can use the records of these cases to give the lie to those who say that there never was a Holocaust. Be alert. Always act with vigor to protect those whose rights are being trampled. That is your job, and that is my job.

"I take no pride in the fact that I prosecuted one hundred and seventy-seven people in these trials. I take no pride in the fact that a lot of them were hanged and others received severe terms of imprisonment. There is something, however, that does create a sense of pride in my heart. When a survivor comes up to me and says, 'We thank you for what you've done for us.'

"That I'm proud of."

Another speaker shared the podium with Denson in April 1991 at Drew University. His name was Capt. Victor Wegard.

"In Dachau, I was a member of war crimes team 6832, commanded by Col. Douglas T. Bates. Our team was appointed defense counsel at Dachau. We spoke to the prisoners and were repulsed listening to them lie to us. But Doctor Schilling and Commandant Weiss stated to us after the trial was over that we did make the prosecution prove its case. 'You gave us a fair trial,' they said, and I think they were complimenting the prosecution as well as the defense. They said they were ready to meet the justice that was given to them.

"Shortly after June 1941, when Germany invaded Russia, the Germans needed airstrips every one hundred miles or so. They took Jews from Kovel, Poland, and once they had dug their airfields the Germans massacred them. The SS killed about forty-four thousand laborers in that action. The civil engineer in charge of that project was Andreas Mueller from Bamberg. We apprehended him after being tipped off by Simon Wiesenthal, who was one of our investigators at the time. Simon was a great man. If you needed something, he could get it for you. We had quite a case against Mueller, including witnesses who were ready to testify they had seen him give the *coup de grâce* with his Luger. It was a pretty thorough case. We referred the case to Wiesbaden, and it was remanded for trial.

"Shortly thereafter, we got a phone call from Wiesbaden advising us to drop the case and release Andreas Mueller. We couldn't understand this. Colonel Bates wanted to know why and phoned there.

"'None of your business,'" they told him. 'Just do as you're told. Release him.'

"Bates and I hopped in a jeep and went to Wiesbaden where we confronted colonels Charlie Cheever and Clio Straight, who were the judge advocates of U.S. Army HQ in charge of the war crimes program. They showed us a cablegram signed Secretary of State Stettinius. It said, 'This man is to be released from confinement and further trial and returned to his home, to his position as a civil engineer.' In short, the Iron Curtain was now falling and the government needed him as a civil engineer to build up

Furstenferberg, which he did. We were ordered out of Germany for our protests. I left Germany in November 1946. Before we left, I turned that over to Simon Wiesenthal to see what he could do. Fifteen years later, in 1961, I received a letter from Simon.

"'I have some bad news for you,' he wrote. 'Andreas Mueller died in bed in Bamberg last week a very wealthy man.' "

Wegard looked out over the audience. "That's justice for you," he said and sat down.

———

On May 28, 1948, Gen. Lucius Clay, U.S. military commander in West Germany, wrote in a private memorandum, "As a result of delays in review . . . there are now in excess of five hundred [death sentences] awaiting execution. . . . I find it difficult to adjust my own mental processes to requiring what looks to be almost a mass execution of more than five hundred persons. I believe it also gives an appearance of cruelty to the United States, even though there is no question in my mind that the crimes committed fully justify the death sentence. Moreover, more than three years have elapsed since the crimes were committed."

Historian Richard Evans writes that by 1948, "the eagerness of the Western Allies to prosecute, condemn, and execute Nazi war criminals was diminishing. The new priorities of resisting Communism and fighting the Cold War were casting the crimes and criminals of the Third Reich into a new light."

In 1949, former Assistant Secretary of War John J. McCloy took over administration of the American Zone from Lucius Clay. As first American high commissioner for Germany, McCloy agreed with West Germany's chancellor Konrad Adenauer that keeping convicted war criminals behind bars conflicted with Germany's integration into the West, and by 1951, McCloy had released nearly half of the remaining thirteen hundred Germans in Allied war crimes prisons. The official reason for the pardons was the discovery of "mitigating evidence." German industrialists went back to their factories, and guards and officers from the camps returned to their families and homes. McCloy described the releases as an educational tool meant to promote the superior values of democratic society. More accurately, they were a convenient means for dismantling the war crimes program without too much public scrutiny.

But 50 percent was not good enough for the German government. Adenauer warned McCloy that no defense contributions would be forthcoming unless further pardons were granted. By this time German rearmament against Soviet Russia had become critical, and Secretary of State Dean Acheson announced he would adopt measures for "the liquidation . . . of this serious irritant to Allied-German relations." The population of Landsberg prison dwindled. Seven inmates were hanged on June 7, 1951, the final executions carried out in West Germany.

In 1958 the last of the Nazi prisoners were released.

Postscript

Newsday
December 17, 1998

'Hero to All' Remembered

Tribute Held for Nazi War Crimes Prosecutor Denson

By Heather Knight

Standing beneath a gold cross, Gerald Wolf sang Psalm 23 in Hebrew: "He leads me in paths of righteousness for his name's sake . . . Thou preparest a table before me in the presence of my enemies . . ."

It seemed a fitting tribute for his close friend and former law colleague, William Denson, who served as chief U.S. prosecutor in Nazi war crimes trials in Dachau, Germany, and who died Dec. 13 at 85 of a heart condition. A standing-room-only crowd at Trinity–St. John's Episcopal Church in Hewlett gathered yesterday to remember the Lawrence resident, who tried 177 Nazis for committing murder, torture, and other offenses. . . . The Rev. Earle W. Pratt, the church's rector, explained why certain lines of the hymn were so appropriate in commemorating Denson's life. "Oh beautiful for hero's proved," Pratt said. "Bill was a hero to all. He stood for justice for those who could no longer speak for themselves. 'Oh beautiful for patriot's dreams.' He loved his country and he believed in the values of America: truth, freedom, responsibility, honor and duty."

"He was a soldier of the old school," Pratt confided later. "There were times I wished I had his faith."

———

The Dachau trials are a cautionary tale: the freeing of Nazi murderers is a blemish on the history of American jurisprudence. It is not, however, a condemnation of military tribunals. While few people know about the Dachau trials, those working in international criminal law today cite decisions, such as those in the Mauthausen trial, as critical in prosecuting war criminals. If Denson's career proved anything, it was that tribunals can be an effective tool for prosecuting those who abuse human rights. Despite their shortcomings, the Dachau trials documented overwhelming proof of atrocities committed in the concentration camps. The trials established that those who take part in such atrocities—either directly or by voluntarily supporting such atrocities—will be held personally responsible. The trials also achieved guilty verdicts despite powerful arguments by the defendants and their attorneys to discredit the evidence. Denson's greatest contribution, apart from his 100 percent record of convictions, was having achieved those convictions according to due process and recognized international law.

His story reminds us, however, that due process, like all great creations, is a slow, laborious endeavor. More than a half century after the close of the Dachau trials, an international tribunal with universal jurisdiction has yet to be established, and many questions concerning international law remain unanswered. Can any government be both victor and judge? If executions stand in the way of uniting against a common enemy, should the law be sacrificed for some greater cause? How sacrosanct is justice?

Bill Denson never pretended to have all the answers. Bill Denson never pretended at anything he did. His life is a reminder that achieving universal human rights demands integrity, perseverance, and an ability to choose the righteous path over the expedient one—the only way a man like Bill Denson knows how to behave.

Acknowledgments

My thanks go to the many people who contributed to this book. Adrienne O'Brien insisted I meet Denson's remarkable life companion Huschi, and the book owes its genesis to Adrienne's prodding. Chuck Bilich, Lew Meltzer, and their associates at Meltzer-Lippe were first to honor Bill Denson's achievements. They encouraged me to take up the task of telling his story, and their affection for the chief prosecutor is literally mounted on the walls of their firm. During the initial stages of research, I was honored to work in the company of Boris Chartan and his staff at the Holocaust Memorial and Educational Center of Nassau County. Their commitment to educating young people about the Holocaust period is exemplary. Barbara Harrod retyped thousands of trial transcript pages and provided impeccable work and good humor during months of immersion in sober subject matter. Katie Vince showed remarkable investigative skill in locating family members of the defense more than a half century after the fact. Linda Kahn and Benjamin Dreyer offered important editorial insights. Important feedback on the liberation of camp Dachau came from Barbara Distel, Director of the Dachau Concentration Camp Memorial; Dee Eberhart, veteran, 242–1, 42nd infantry Rainbow Division; and from Suellen McDaniel, president, Rainbow Division Veterans Millennium Family chapter. I thank them, as well as Charlie Singer, Shiva Kumar, Bonnie Garelick, Iva Kuznitz, Everett Wiles, Jason Liberman, Marcia Posner, Parvati Markus, and Matt Sizlowitz for their contributions.

Special thanks to Paul and Joan Guth for their patience and unqualified cooperation in helping reconstitute details of the trials. Paul passed away on the day the draft of this book arrived at his home. He deserved a chance to say whether he is fairly represented or not. During our time together, Paul once said, "We may have crossed the line once or twice, but our interrogations were conducted properly." I for one believe him. My thanks to Huschi for allowing me unlimited access to her archive, to Eli Rosenbaum for his valuable suggestions for clarifying points of international law, to Lawrence Douglas for generously giving his time and expertise to review the manuscript, to Joanna Pulcini for having transformed agenting into an act of friendship, to Suzanne Oaks for championing the project from its inception, and to Kristine Puopolo at Broadway Books for shepherding the hardcover edition through its various stages of refinement. I also wish to thank Murray Weiss, my agent, and Jon Malysiak, my editor at Ankerwycke Books, for publishing this paperback edition so many years after the original hardcover. Last, but by no means least, I thank my family—Cara, Emmanuel, Adele, and especially Esther—for their constant love and support.

Author's Note

The Dachau trial transcripts posed an unusual editing challenge. Witnesses who took the stand represented more than a dozen European nations, and each spoke in his or her native language. The transcripts are not verbatim quotes from those original languages but transcribed translations, and sometimes transcribed translations of translations. Only some of the translators who served in the Dachau trials were professionals. Many were refugees who had escaped Europe in the 1930s with only a rudimentary knowledge of English. As a result, both prosecutors and defense lawyers often took exception to the way a witness's remarks had been translated. In some instances the tribunal asked the translator to try again. Occasionally, when patience wore out completely, a new translator was brought in. Reporters, whose job was to take down the translators' words, did their best to make sense of convoluted sentences, unfamiliar terms, and grammatical idiosyncrasies. Reading transcripts in their entirety provided me a privileged overview of how conversations flowed. Knowing that readers of this book would have only excerpts, I had to determine how closely to adhere to the literal wording of the transcripts.

My previous experience with Holocaust testimony (*Witness: Voices from the Holocaust*, Free Press, 2000) was guided by authorities in the field: Professors Lawrence Langer, Geoffrey Hartman, and Joanne Rudof, all affiliated with the Fortunoff Video Archive for Holocaust Testimony at Yale University. Their groundbreaking work of videotaping survivors and other witnesses to the Holocaust is distinguished in part by their unswerving respect for the literal language of testimony, and my first impulse was to follow that example again. However, the testimony I quoted in my previous book was taken from English-language videotapes and involved neither translators nor reporters. One could not assume that the awkwardly worded Dachau transcripts were the actual words of the witnesses, and clarity, rather than literal accuracy, seemed to me of greater value to readers. Consequently, while excerpts are verbatim whenever reasonable, in many instances dialogue has been shortened, redundancies deleted, and awkward grammar corrected.

Space has permitted me to include only a few of the hundreds of witnesses and defendants who took the stand at Dachau between November 1945 and August 1947. To determine which voices to include, I began by listing persons to whom Denson himself had referred in interviews, speeches, and articles. He had, in effect, personally preselected the individuals who would play a part in this summary study.

Narrowing the cast of characters to a reasonable number, however, left thousands of pages to be still further condensed. How to determine which episodes to include? The Dachau trial transcript runs nearly 4,000 pages long, Mauthausen more than 5,000 pages, and Buchenwald nearly 6,000 pages—15,000 pages covering nearly seven years of camp operations. Following Denson's strategy for establishing the criminality of the camps as a whole, I included defendants from various areas of camp administration. To these I added witnesses whose testimony addressed legal challenges that Denson had to overcome. A further criterion for determining whom to include was emotional appeal. The trials were not only about dates and statistics but about extreme tragedy. Witnesses who conveyed that human dimension were critical to re-creating a feeling for what happened during the Dachau trials.

The basement cache in Denson's home included handwritten notes, transcripts of interviews and speeches, and other first-person accounts of his thoughts and reactions to what happened at Dachau. These provided language with which to re-create dialogue and describe his state of mind at various junctions. None of his letters home have survived, but the archive includes an abundance of material on issues that commanded his interest and concern: articles on charges of coercion used to extract confessions, essays exploring the history and philosophy of war crimes law, reports analyzing the successes and failures of the war crimes program.

Denson had also accumulated hundreds of original photos. My physical descriptions of participants in the trials are drawn largely from these images. Photos, however, could not describe what it was like to be there, and I set about looking for people who were present, as a way of supplementing the documents in Huschi's basement. Among the material was a letter from Leo Goodman, the person responsible for assigning reporters and other staff to each day's proceedings. At the end of Denson's final trial in November 1947, Goodman distributed a list of names and addresses of the Dachau war crimes group, "with the hope that it will assist us all to keep in touch with one another from time to time, and perhaps serve to bring back memories of the days we spent together at Dachau." There were no zip codes in those days. An assistant researched the codes and mailed requests for help to all 132 names on the list. Twelve replies came back. Ten were marked "undeliverable." We received two written replies. One said the addressee had been a distant relative who died years ago. The other disclaimed any knowledge of the addressee. What happened to all the other letters remains a mystery.

We had better luck with contacts provided by Denson's widow, Huschi, who gave us the name of our most important source in researching this book: Paul Guth, Denson's second-in-command for the Dachau and Mauthausen trials. After returning from Germany in 1946, Guth completed his degree at Columbia and went on to a distinguished law career in New York. Paul exercised an uncanny recall of detail and provided critical insights into the workings of the Dachau and Mauthausen trials. Huschi also put us in touch with Barbara Ann Murphy, stenographer at the Buchenwald trial, who happened to also live on Long Island. "I'll tell you this," she said at our first meeting. "I was given Ilse Koch's photo album to bring to headquarters in Freising—you know, the one that was supposed to be made of human skin? Well, I held that album and it was covered in cloth, not skin."

The web provided important information. Requests for help posted on military sites brought us into contact with Douglas T. Bates III, son of the late chief defense counsel for the Dachau trial. "In this whole world," Bates told me, "I never thought I'd talk with someone who could understand what it was like for my dad to defend Nazis." The senior Bates followed a path of love for God, country, and due process that paralleled Denson's with uncanny precision. The web also helped us locate the children of the late Ernst Oeding, chief defense counsel for the Mauthausen trial; and Herb Maistelman, who was twenty-one when he served as a guard in the Dachau courtroom. Herb described how each day he would put on white gloves, line his helmet with a white liner, and stand at attention while the court was in session. "I was the only Jew in the whole staff," he recalled, "but walking through Dachau, seeing the remnants of what had happened—I think that's when I really became a Jew."

Recommendations from archivists at Yad Vashem in Israel and Holocaust museums in the U.S. were helpful in locating some of the few people still alive who took part in the trials. We spoke with Ben Ferencz, an important member of the Nuremberg team and the officer who hung the sign "War Crimes Division" over the Dachau courtroom door. A survivor of Dachau living in Israel remembered being escorted into a large room where he and two hundred other potential prosecution witnesses were assembled. "They brought the Germans in one by one," he explained by phone. "The Americans asked them to say their name and rank, then they were taken out. We were asked to raise our hand if we knew something about that person or had known him in the camp—and that's about all I can remember."

From the Judge Advocate website we were able to contact Dee Eberhart, a Rainbow veteran, who vetted the introductory section on the liberation of camp Dachau. Materials he provided also yielded our only contact with a prosecution witness from the trials: Arthur Haulot, whose description of the dehumanizing experience of life in camp Dachau left the court so silent Denson said "you could hear a pin drop."

Certain topics at issue in the trials, which might have been included in a longer work, are absent here. Details concerning the meager food provided to prisoners, the duties and authority of camp administrators, the nationality of victims, dates of alleged crimes, and other matters that absorbed much of the twenty-one months of trials have been excluded not to minimize their importance but as a matter of necessity. The work at hand was intended to communicate some of the power of the proceedings, not provide a comprehensive record.

Worthy of mention as well is the lack of clear identification in the trial transcripts of which counsel speaks at any particular time. Witnesses are clearly indicated, but I have often had to use my best judgment, based on context, to identify who is asking the questions.

The chronology of the transcripts has been respected in the Dachau and Mauthausen chapters. In the section on Buchenwald, dialogue has been organized according to subject and defendant. While this disrupts the chronology, it provides readers with a more coherent picture of personalities and issues.

Endnotes

Preface

page xii *By the end:* Telford Taylor, who replaced Robert Jackson, oversaw the prosecution of a greater number: 183 in twelve subsequent trials. Taylor's staff, however, conducted several of these subsequent trials while Denson personally prosecuted 177 Nazi accused.

Part One: War's End

page 1 *He that is slow to anger . . . :* Bible verses quoted throughout the book were selected from among those Denson memorized as a child. His leather-bound edition of the King James Version contains a handwritten list, with the following note from his father: "I hereby certify that William Dowdell Denson has committed to memory the preceding two hundred and fifteen passages."

page 3 *By mid-March 1945:* This chapter is based on reports by liberation soldiers in *Dachau 29 April 1945: The Rainbow Liberation Memoirs,* edited by Sam Dann, Texas Tech University Press, 1998, and supplemented with details from *The Day of the Americans* by Nerin E. Gun, Fleet Publishing, 1966. Arthur Haulot, former prisoner and founder of the Comite International de Dachau, was present at the camp's liberation. "You must remember," he cautioned on reviewing the manuscript for this book, "that this is one 'factual' account among several," alluding to his own remembrances of the liberation—and to an important principle that should guide those who attempt to understand the history of the camps: no one point of view can represent the varied and often contradictory experiences of those who were there.

page 5 *"Wash your hands . . .":* Marcus Smith, *The Harrowing of Hell: Dachau* (Albuquerque: University of New Mexico Press, 1972), p. 95.

page 9 *Patton fell ill: The Buchenwald Report,* trans. David A. Hackett (Boulder: Westview Press, 1999), p. 10.

page 9 *"See what these . . .": Remember,* cited in *Dimensions,* vol. 9, no. 1 (New York: Anti-Defamation League, 1995), p. 11.

page 10 *In the May 19, 1945, issue:* Robert H. Abzug, *Inside the Vicious Heart* (New York: Oxford University Press, 1985), p. 136.

page 10 *That same month:* Ibid., p. 137.

page 10 *After one day in Ohrdruf:* Ibid., p. 132.

page 10 *War crimes trials had been: Documents on American Foreign Relations,* 1942–43, V, pp. 177–78.

page 10 *FDR's announcement:* Telford Taylor, *Nuremberg and Vietnam: An American Tragedy* (Chicago: Quadrangle Books, 1970), p. 24.

page 11 *Just how these trials:* Bradley F. Smith, *The Road to Nuremberg* (New York: Basic Books, 1981), pp. 12–47.

page 12 *A dedicated soldier:* Telford Taylor, *The Anatomy of the Nuremberg Trials* (New York: Knopf, 1992), p. 270.

page 12 *He was adrift:* Maximillian Koessler, "American War Crimes Trials in Europe," *Georgetown Law Journal,* vol. 39, no. 1, November 1950, p. 21.

page 14 *"Best wishes for a pleasant . . .":* Memo from Col. Charles W. West to Denson dated March 6, 1945, Denson archive.

page 15 *While the description:* At the Touro Law Conference in 1995, Dachau defense counsel Victor Wegard described, "We knew the camps existed. We heard the name Dachau for the first time in July 1944, at Cumberland University in Lebanon, Tennessee, where 103 officers had been transferred from the European theater to form war crimes teams. We were taught how to investigate cases and be on the lookout for war crimes. Nobody had exact details, though. We didn't know the depth of the atrocities. We knew there were massacres, we heard on the radio about people fleeing—but we did not know how organized it turned out to be."

page 15 *Membership in the privileged world:* Gun, *Day of the Americans,* p. 280.

page 15 *Those opposed:* Frank Buscher, *The U.S. War Crimes Trial Program in Germany, 1946–55* (Westport, Connecticut: Greenwood Press, 1989), p. 16.

page 16 *Killing them without due process:* William J. Bosch, *Judgment on Nuremberg* (Chapel Hill: University of North Carolina Press, 1970), p. 9.

page 16 *There was only enough money:* Koessler, "American War Crimes Trials," p. 67.

page 17 *Jackson was a celebrity:* Bosch, *Judgment on Nuremberg,* p. 10.

page 17 *His orders were to evaluate the evidence:* Buscher, *The U.S. War Crimes Trial Program in Germany,* p. 19.

page 17 *The fourth charge:* For an excellent analysis of the war crimes charges, see Lawrence Douglas, *The Memory of Judgment: Making Law and History in the Trials of the Holocaust* (New Haven: Yale University Press, 2001), chapter 2.

page 17 *"Amazing grace!":* Meltzer Lippe partners interview, March 20, 2002.

page 17 *Dachau trials stenographer:* Interview with Barbara Ann Murphy, September 13, 2000.

page 20 *"I finally reached a point . . .":* Video interview with Denson, August 25, 1994, U.S Holocaust Memorial Museum (USHMM), Denson archive.

page 20 *Within days:* Solomon Surowitz interview, March 25, 2002.

page 22 *"Forget everything they taught you . . .":* Paul Guth interview, February 26, 2001.

page 23 *"Third Army wants the trial . . .":* Denson interview by Horace Hansen, June 1984, Denson archive.

page 24 *Whether or not the citizens:* Ibid., p. 38.

page 25 *The U-shaped courthouse:* Harold Marcuse, *Legacies of Dachau* (New York: Cambridge University Press, 2001), p. 8.

page 27 *A report from Camp Butler: U.S. v. Martin Gottfried Weiss et al.* (Washington, D.C.: National Archives Microfilm Publications), Microfilm Publication M1174, Roll 1, Pretrial Documents, RG 338 and RG 153.

page 27 *In July 1945:* Buscher, *The U.S. War Crimes Trial Program in Germany,* p. 13.

page 28 *Try these department heads:* Directive of Headquarters, USFET, para. 11, June 26, 1946, stated in part, "In such trial of additional participants in the mass atrocity, the prosecuting officer will furnish the court certified copies of the charge and particulars of the findings and the sentences pronounced in the parent case. . . . The court will presume . . . that those shown by competent evidence to have participated in the mass atrocity knew of the criminal nature thereof." (Cited in Koessler, "American War Crimes Trials," p. 33.)

page 28 *Nearly a million refugees:* Marcuse, *Legacies of Dachau,* p. 130.

page 28 *In these camps:* Abraham J. Peck, "The Displaced," *Dimensions,* vol. 9, no. 1, 1995 p. 11.

page 28 *"I am Ruppert Kohl . . .":* USHMM video interview. See also Miami Beach lecture, March 24, 1991, Denson archive.

page 29 *Guth began by reviewing:* This information comes from a manuscript (p. 14–3) in the Denson archive, apparently an unpublished book by Horace Hansen who served as prosecutor in subsequent Dachau trials.

page 29 *"The process of interrogation . . .":* Paul Guth interview, February 26, 2001.

page 31 *The Brits had already conducted:* Hansen interview, p. 98.

page 31 *"You're sitting on . . ."*: Paul Guth interview, March 15, 2000.

page 32 *Of the forty named: Law Reports of Trials of War Criminals, Selected and prepared by The United Nations War Crimes Commission*, vol. XI (London: United Nations War Crimes Commission, 1949), p. 7.

page 32 *When Guth informed them:* Paul Guth interview, July 26, 2000.

Part Two: Dachau

page 35 *Admission to the:* Hansen manuscript, p. 14–3.

page 36 *The five men responsible for:* The same American official would have the opportunity of acting as a prosecutor in one Dachau trial and as a defense counsel in another. See Koessler, "American War Crimes Trials," p. 30.

page 36 *"We were on opposite sides . . ."*: Paul Guth interview, July 26, 2000.

page 37 *Lentz turned to the defendants:* Excerpts from the Dachau trial transcripts have been edited from National Archives case files 12-226 and 000-52-2 *United States of America v. Martin Gottfried Weiss et al.*

page 38 *The Geneva Convention:* The Geneva Convention of July 27, 1909, article 4.

page 38 *The Hague Convention:* Cited in *Law Reports of Trials of War Criminals*, vol. XV (London: His Majesty's Stationery Office, 1949), p. 11.

page 38 *Denson had come across:* Conot in *Judgment at Nuremberg* attributes the idea of common design to Lt. Col. Murray C. Bernays of the War Department's Special Projects Branch.

page 39 *He rejected the Nuremberg:* Aryeh Neier, *War Crimes* (New York: Times Books, 1998), p. 17.

page 39 *He stood:* "40 Nazis Face Execution for Dachau Deaths," AP, November 15, 1945.

page 40 *A former inmate of Dachau:* From "The Nameless Road," a typed manuscript account of the Dachau trial by an anonymous former inmate, Denson archive.

page 42 *Franz Blaha was:* "Medical Science Run Amok," included in *Medical Science Abused: German Medical Science as Practised in Concentration Camps and in the so-called Protectorate, reported by Czechoslovak doctors* (Prague: Orbis, 1946), pp. 13–37.

page 44 *There was a whipping bench:* Marcuse, *Legacies of Dachau*, illus. 17.

page 49 *Many of the translators:* Joseph Halow, *Innocent at Dachau* (Newport Beach, California: Institute for Historical Review, 1992), p. 62.

page 49 *Journalist Rebecca West:* "Reporter at Large," *New Yorker*, September 7, 1946. Journalists assigned to daily attendance at Nuremburg soberly joked that they were "the last victims of Nazi persecution." *Charlotte Observer,* October 6, 1946.

page 52 *Years later:* USHMM video interview.

page 52 *Douglas Bates was waging:* Phone interview with Arthur Haulot, June 1, 2002.

page 53 *A handwritten diary: Dachau,* a sixty-eight-page report with photos and a foreword by William W. Quinn, Colonel, G.S.C., published by the U.S. Army shortly after the liberation of Dachau in April 1945.

page 59 *Denson followed a pattern:* USHMM video interview.

page 64 *Still, to avoid the stigma:* Hansen interview.

page 65 *He did so well:* Marcuse, *Legacies of Dachau,* p. 51.

page 67 *Defense argued that: Law Reports of Trials of War Criminals,* p. 8.

page 68 *To establish a common design:* For an in-depth analysis of common design see *Law Reports of Trials of War Criminals,* pp. 94–99.

page 75 *Guth's family connections:* Nudi was not related to a defense lawyer of the same name, Dr. Viktor von der Lippe, who was at that time serving in Nuremberg.

page 79 *Nothing was left standing:* The bombing of Dresden was a defining moment in the war. Its ostensible purpose was to destroy railway yards and thus slow Germany's movement east, but the scope of the bombing led many historians to suggest that its true purpose was to destroy German morale. In three waves of bombings, nearly 3,500 tons of explosives and phosphorus fell on what had been one of Europe's most beautiful cities. (*New York Times* article, January 25, 1995, by Alan Cowell.) It was Shrove Tuesday, a day when residents of the city dressed their children in carnival clothes for annual parties.

page 91 *Testifying later:* Bosch, *Judgment on Nuremberg,* p. 296.

page 93 *Later he was transferred: The Buchenwald Report,* p. 64.

page 93 *His point was:* Hansen interview.

page 93 *In 1955:* Marcuse, *Legacies of Dachau,* pp. 99–100.

page 95 *None of the defense lawyers: Law Reports of Trials of War Criminals,* p. 13.

page 101 *The defendants were:* Ibid., p. 14.

page 102 *If a soldier is drafted:* For a more detailed analysis of the plea of superior orders, see *Law Reports of Trials of War Criminals,* pp. 157–60.

page 111 *He knew the facts:* Paul Guth interview, May 31, 2000.

page 114 *"Every one of them . . .":* Paul Guth interview, February 26, 2001.

page 115 *Was he wrong:* "Clemency is a proper thing to be exercised under proper conditions," Denson said in the USHMM video interview, "but I didn't have the power to wield that authority."

page 115 *Among them was a woman:* Paul Guth interview, February 26, 2001.

page 117 *"Colonel," the judge said:* Phone interview with Douglas T. Bates III, September 11, 2001.

page 118 *Prisoners could put their heads:* G. M. Gilbert, *Nuremberg Diary* (New York: Da Capo Press, 1974), pp. 98–100.

Part Three: Mauthausen

page 123 *She positioned people:* Interview with Huschi Denson, May 26, 2002.

page 125 *"Half, maybe all . . .":* Paul Johnson, *A History of the American People* (New York: HarperCollins, 1997), p. 806.

page 125 *Ellery Stone:* Ibid.

page 125 *William Donovan:* Ibid.

page 125 *At the Moscow Conference:* Ibid., p. 807.

page 125 *"I am tired . . .":* Ibid.

page 125 *Shortly after, Winston Churchill:* Martin Gilbert, *A History of the Twentieth Century*, vol. 2 (New York: William Morrow, 1998), p. 738.

page 125 *Polls indicated:* Johnson, *A History of the American People*, p. 807.

page 125 *Privately, officials were working:* Bosch, *Judgement on Nuremberg*, p. 33.

page 126 *To put their task:* Ibid., p. 60.

page 138 *Their task was:* Abzug, *Inside the Vicious Heart*, p. 105.

page 129 *The SS called those:* Taylor, *The Anatomy of the Nuremberg Trials*, p. 300.

page 129 *In one instance:* Abzug, *Inside the Vicious Heart*, p. 106

page 129 *This camp was one:* Ibid., p. 105. See also Konnilyn G. Feig, *Hitler's Death Camps* (New York: Holmes & Meier, 1979), p. 116.

page 129 *"I am sickly . . .":* The Nizkor Project camps/mauthausen/shadow.death

page 131 *Despite his confidence:* Interview with Ernie Oeding, September 15, 2001.

page 134 *Gasps of horror:* Douglas, *The Memory of Judgment*, p. 26.

page 134 Reichsmarschall *Hermann Göring:* Taylor, *Nuremberg Diary*, p. 49.

page 138 *The following night:* Cited in www.mauthausen-memorial.gv.at/engl/ Geschichtel/05.03.Ziereis-Protokoll.html

page 138 *Among those who spoke:* Albert J. Kosiek, "Liberation of Mauthausen," in *Thunderbolt*, the 11th Armored Division Association, vol. 8, no. 7, May–June 1955.

page 142 *An elaborate analysis:* Koessler, "American War Crimes Trials," pp. 83–93.

page 142 *"No court will punish . . .":* For further explanation of duress as an exception to responsibility, see Neier, *War Crimes*, pp. 241–44.

page 142 *The issue was complex:* Koessler, "American War Crimes Trials," pp. 84–85.

page 151 *In 1941:* Hans Marsalek, *The History of Concentration Camp Maut-hausen*, p. 174. Quoted on website www.mauthausenmemorial.gv.at/engl/Geschichte/05.06.Krebsbach.html

page 159 *"I'll hang him . . .":* USHMM video interview.

page 167 *Near Mauthausen:* Cited on www.mauthausen-memorial.gv.at/engl/Geschichte/07.05

page 169 *Over time, some camps: The Buchenwald Report*, pp. 32–33.

page 173 *August Eigruber was found guilty:* Landsberg is famous as the prison where Hitler was imprisoned in 1924 for his failed Munich coup and where he wrote *Mein Kampf.*

page 173 *The captain stated:* USHMM video interview.

page 173 *"Eigruber was a Nazi . . .":* Miami Beach lecture, March 24, 1991, Denson archive.

page 174 *Exposure to the constant:* Hansen manuscript, p. 14–4.

page 174 *The city had been heavily bombed:* Munich Found Online 9/10/2001.

page 175 *"I must have seen . . .":* Paul Guth interview, March 9, 2000.

page 185 *The charge sheet:* Koessler, "American War Crimes Trials," p. 59.

page 201 *"I was perfectly willing . . .":* USHMM video interview.

page 208 *Hitler had promulgated:* Bosch, *Judgment on Nuremberg*, pp. 299–300.

page 208 *Maurice Lampe:* Taylor, *Anatomy of the Nuremberg Trials*, pp. 300–301.

page 215 *Denson had nothing but admiration:* "Military Justice," lecture by Denson delivered at Dachau on August 9, 1946, Denson archive.

page 220 *The miracle of the Wies:* Cathedral souvenir booklet, Denson archive.

page 222 *Then, halfway:* Hansen interview.

page 222 *"They said I looked . . .":* USHMM video interview. See also Shoah Foundation video interview, March 1996.

Part Four: Buchenwald

page 227 *The court conducted:* Taylor, *Judgment on Nuremberg*, p. 13.

page 228 *Should these nations:* Taylor, *Judgment on Nuremberg*, p. 19.

page 228 *Supreme Court Justice:* Alpheus Thomas Mason, *Harland Fiske Stone, Pillar of the Law* (New York: Viking, 1956), p. 716.

page 228 *"About this whole judgment . . .":* Chicago Tribune, November 13, 1945.

page 228 *Their attorney, Willis Everett Jr.:* Buscher, *The U.S. War Crimes Trial Program in Germany*, p. 38.

page 228 *By the time of Denson's opening:* Ibid., p. 38.

page 229 *The date was overly ambitious:* Deputy Theater Judge Advocate Col. C. B. Mickelwait attributed the army's rush to "diminishing interest of the public in general in this field." To expedite matters, he suggested that "the avowed purposes of Military government may best be served by a gradual shift in emphasis from punishment for past misdeeds to guidance along appropriate paths of future conduct." Busch, *The U.S. War Crimes Trial Program in Germany, 1946–1955*, p. 52.

page 230 *A popular belief:* Abzug, *Inside the Vicious Heart*, p. 46.

page 231 *As a result, the camp:* Hackett, *The Buchenwald Report*, p. 29.

page 231 *"Hundreds of dead naked . . .":* Margaret Bourke-White, *"Dear Fatherland, Rest Quietly": A Report on the Collapse of Hitler's Thousand Years* (New York, 1946), p. 73.

page 231 *"As a soldier . . .":* Irving Faust, "Journey into War," *Dimensions*, vol. 9, no. 1 (New York: Anti-Defamation League, 1995), p. 19.

page 231 *Goethe had once prophesied:* Taylor, *Nuremberg Diary*, p. 426.

page 232 *Prisoners there were locked:* Hackett, *The Buchenwald Report*, p. 340.

page 232 *In September 1937:* Ibid., pp. 201–202.

page 233 *"Sing German songs! . . .":* Ibid., p. 275.

page 234 *Ilse, her biographer:* Cited in Segev, *Soldiers of Evil*, p. 142.

page 235 *The SS were selfish:* Paul Guth interview, May 31, 2000.

page 235 *Nazi senior officials:* Segev, *Soldiers of Evil*, p. 26.

page 235 *In one of these letters:* Ibid., p. 33.

page 238 *For Christmas, 1939:* Hackett, *The Buchenwald Report*, p. 42.

page 238 *"Every day they would . . .":* Morris Hubert, quoted in "Time Too Painful to Remember," by Aril Goldman, published in *The New York Times*, November 10, 1988.

page 239 *"If the court please . . .":* Excerpts from Buchenwald trial transcripts come from National Archives case no. 000–50–9: Buchenwald.

page 241 *The film had been produced:* Hackett, *The Buchenwald Report*, p. 13.

page 242 *The prosecution had discovered:* Solomon Surowitz recalled seeing the original version of Kogon's report during preparation for trial (interview of March 25, 2002).

page 242 *The report had taken:* Hackett, *The Buchenwald Report*, p. 18.

page 242 *By the time he was thirty-five:* Ibid., p. 16.

page 244 *The report was originally:* Ibid., p. 19.

page 247 *It was one he had:* Speech in Miami, Florida, 1991, Denson archive.

page 249 *This holds particularly true: Deutsche Allgemeine Zeitung*, May 28, 1944, cited in Taylor, *Nuremberg and Vietnam: An American Tragedy* p. 48.

page 252 *"Now, counsel for the defense . . .":* Article 2 of the Geneva Convention of 1929 forbids measures of reprisal being taken against prisoners of war.

page 253 *"My shirt collar . . .":* USHMM video interview.

page 261 *Jehovah's Witnesses: Hearings for the Investigations Subcommittee of the Committee on Expenditures in the Executive Departments, part 5, September 28; December 8 and 9, 1948* (Washington, D.C.: U.S. Government Printing Office, 1949), p. 1047.

page 267 *From Morgen's perspective:* Ulricht Herbert, *National Socialist Extermination Policies* (Frankfurt: Berghahn Books, 2000), p. 328.

page 269 *Surowitz, however, doubted the reliability:* Surowitz interview, March 25, 2002.

page 269 *"There was a difference . . .":* Surowitz interview, March 25, 2002.

page 270 *"And therefore when I say . . .":* Hearings for the Investigations Subcommittee, p. 1042.

page 272 *"She only stood there . . ."* Ibid., pp. 1058–61.

page 273 *His emotions surfacing:* Speech 1-A (no date), Denson archive.

page 274 *She was to his mind:* USHMM video interview.

page 275 *Years later: Hearings for the Investigations Subcommittee,* p. 1027.

page 287 *The Little Camp:* Miloslav Matousek, "Buchenwald Through a Doctor's Eyes," included in *Medical Science Abused: German Medical Science as Practised in Concentration Camps and in the so-called Protectorate, reported by Czechoslovak doctors* (Prague: Orbis, 1946), p. 52.

page 291 *Edwin Marie:* Miami Beach lecture, March 24, 1991, Denson archive.

page 311 *Press and others:* Taylor, *Judgment on Nuremberg,* p. 181.

Part Five: Aftermath

page 318 *Having successfully molded:* Taylor, *Judgment on Nuremberg,* p. 116.

page 318 *Once it leaked:* "The Army, on the whole, has seemed to be somewhat reticent to make a full and adequate disclosure of the record and other important facts. The press, however, took the initiative. In its entirety, the story had several sensational aspects, all of which made good copy." *Harvard Law School Record,* December 1, 1948, p. 3.

page 318 *The* New York Post: Department of the Army, Public Information Division, Analysis Branch, *The Ilse Koch Case: Digest of Editorial Comment, Radio Comment, and Press Opinion,* 19 September–18 October 1948, Denson archive.

page 318 *"If Ilse Koch . . .":* Ibid.

page 319 *Ray Henle on NBC radio:* Ibid.

page 322 *"Don't let the Buchenwald trial . . .":* Speech 1-A (no date), Denson archive.

page 322 *He had headed up:* "Unwarranted allegations of a highly vitriolic nature were published under the heading *American Atrocities in Germany* in *The Progressive* (February 1949). They appeared under the by-line of Judge Edward L. Van Roden (PA) who subsequently disclaimed his authorship and the correctness of part of the contents. The article had meanwhile been given a great amount of publicity, especially by the activities of the National Council for the Prevention of War . . ." Koessler, "American War Crimes Trials," vol. 39, no. 1, November 1950, footnote p. 26.

page 326 *"William Dowdell Denson . . .":* Harvard Law School Record, December 8, 1948, p. 1.

page 326 *In his inimitable manner:* Department of the Army, Public Information Division, Analysis Branch, *The Ilse Koch Case: Digest of Editorial Comment, Radio Comment, and Press Opinion,* 19 September–18 October 1948, Denson archive.

page 336 *The subcommittee: Conduct of Ilse Koch War Crimes Trial, Interim Report of the Investigations Subcommittee of the Committee on Expenditures in the Executive Departments* (Washington, D.C.: U.S. Government Printing Office, 1948), pp. 22–24.

page 336 *"Every act committed . . .": Conduct of Ilse Koch War Crimes Trial, Interim Report No. 1775, Part 3* (Washington, D.C.: U.S. Government Printing Office, 1948), pp. 403–407.

page 350 *"Moreover, more than . . .":* Quoted in Gilbert, *A History of the Twentieth Century,* p. 808.

page 350 *The new priorities:* Ibid.

Index